A Cultural History of Dress and Fashion
General Editor: Susan Vincent

Volume 1
A Cultural History of Dress and Fashion in Antiquity
Edited by Mary Harlow

Volume 2
A Cultural History of Dress and Fashion in the Medieval Age
Edited by Sarah-Grace Heller

Volume 3
A Cultural History of Dress and Fashion in the Renaissance
Edited by Elizabeth Currie

Volume 4
A Cultural History of Dress and Fashion in the Age of Enlightenment
Edited by Peter McNeil

Volume 5
A Cultural History of Dress and Fashion in the Age of Empire
Edited by Denise Amy Baxter

Volume 6
A Cultural History of Dress and Fashion in the Modern Age
Edited by Alexandra Palmer

A CULTURAL HISTORY OF DRESS AND FASHION

VOLUME 5

A CULTURAL HISTORY OF DRESS AND FASHION

IN THE AGE OF EMPIRE

Edited by Denise Amy Baxter

Bloomsbury Academic
An imprint of Bloomsbury Publishing Plc

B L O O M S B U R Y
LONDON · OXFORD · NEW YORK · NEW DELHI · SYDNEY

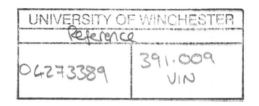
Bloomsbury Academic

An imprint of Bloomsbury Publishing Plc

50 Bedford Square   1385 Broadway
London   New York
WC1B 3DP   NY 10018
UK   USA

www.bloomsbury.com

BLOOMSBURY and the Diana logo are trademarks of Bloomsbury Publishing Plc

First published 2017

© Bloomsbury Publishing 2017

Denise Amy Baxter has asserted her right under the Copyright, Designs and Patents Act, 1988, to be identified as Editor of this work.

British Library Cataloguing-in-Publication Data
A catalogue record for this book is available from the British Library.

ISBN: HB: 978-0-8578-5684-5
        HB set: 978-1-4725-5749-0

Library of Congress Cataloging-in-Publication Data
A catalog record for this book is available from the Library of Congress.

Cover design: Sharon Mah
Cover image: Maximilian o Max Kurzweil (1867–1916), Lady in Yellow, 1889 (DEA/Getty Images)

Typeset by RefineCatch Limited, Bungay, Suffolk
Printed and bound in Great Britain

CONTENTS

LIST OF ILLUSTRATIONS

CHAPTER 4

CHAPTER 5

CHAPTER 6

CHAPTER 7

CHAPTER 8

CHAPTER 9

Introduction

DENISE AMY BAXTER

In claiming to present a cultural history of fashion in the age of Empire, this volume is positioned within specific discourses, such as those of the nineteenth-century colonial context, burgeoning forms of modernity, and the historiography of studies of fashion and dress, to name just a few. This brief essay will introduce and situate the volume's contributions.

As a cultural history of fashion, the chapters do not present an enunciation of period styles of Western fashionable dress from Empire style to Romanticism to the reign of the bustle. Nor does it explicitly focus on changing lines or cuts or fashionable profiles, even while bustles and corsets are each given their due. Neither is its focus trained exclusively on the makers of dress, either designers or fabricators, even though this is the era during which we witness the advent of both mass production and *haute couture* and the founding of the Chambre Syndicale de la Couture Parisienne in France. While specific classes of and individual wearers of dress and followers of fashion are treated within these chapters, their focus is not entirely upon consumers either. Indeed, garments themselves are not the volume's exclusive purview.

Equally important are representations of dress in such visual realms as advertisements, fashion plates (Figure 0.1), and fine art, as well as textual representations in literature and the popular press alike. In claiming to present a cultural history of fashion, therefore, these essays aspire to think through both representations and modes of dress of the long nineteenth century with a mind to approaches informed by visual and material culture studies, by which garments—realized and represented—are granted primacy as means by which cultural history of the period might be understood. Furthermore, within the century, fashion is particularly relevant for understanding burgeoning modernity.

Within an art historical context, the problem of representative modernity has long been understood as the problem of representing the monumentality of contemporary life without reverting to previous historical—or history painting—precedents. How is it possible, therefore, to be significant and meaningful, but of one's own time? The key element is fashion. Etymologically speaking, there is an inherent connection in the French language between the terms *mode* and *modernité*. While the English language term modernity had been in use since at least the seventeenth century according to the *Oxford English Dictionary*, in French it was a nineteenth-century neologism.[1] The links between *mode* and *modernité* are evident in Charles Baudelaire's definition of the term in *The Painter of Modern Life*, where he explains that, "By 'modernity' I mean the ephemeral, the fugitive, the contingent."[2] The modern is also, for Baudelaire, in its essence, the artificial. In *Éloge du maquillage*, or *Praise of Cosmetics*, Baudelaire praises "the lofty spiritual significance of the toilet" and "the majesty of artificial forms," and sees woman as the pinnacle of these qualities:[3]

Woman is quite within her rights, indeed she is even accomplishing a kind of duty, when she devotes herself to appearing magical and supernatural; she has to astonish and charm us; as an idol, she is obliged to adorn herself in order to be adored. Thus she has to lay all the arts under contribution for the means of lifting herself above Nature, the better to conquer hearts and rivet attention. It matters but little that the artifice and trickery are known to all, so long as their success is assured and their effect always irresistible.[4]

FIGURE 0.1: Promenade dresses from *Ackermann's Repository of Arts*, vol. 5, no. 30, June 1, 1811, pl. 36. Rijksmuseum, Amsterdam.

In other words, the modern she woman self-consciously self-presents and it is for her creativity and artificiality in such that is to be extolled. It is through fashion, therefore, that modern selves were most readily capable of being fashioned, within a cultural context that inaugurated the widespread belief in the self as at least equally represented and crafted as essential. Taking Baudelaire in this sense as our guide and at his word, we are asked to reconsider works such as the fashionable depictions of Achille Devéria.

Although both Achille and his brother Eugène Devéria exhibited history paintings in the annual Parisian Salon. Eugène was best known for this official career while Achille's renown was based upon his lithographic production. Achille Devéria's emphasis on social mores and the particularities of fashion—both contemporary and historical—are evident in his print series *Les Heures du Jour* (c. 1829), a suite of eighteen colored lithographs of an elegant Parisienne (Figure 0.2), and the 125 prints of *Les Costume Historiques* (1831–45). The very focus of *Les Heures du Jour* is fashion and fashionable comportment, causing Charles Baudelaire to describe the series as expressing both the "ethics and aesthetics of the time."[5]

FIGURE 0.2: Achille Devéria, *Four o'clock in the evening* from the *Hours of the Day* series, lithograph, c. 1829. Photo: DEA Picture Library/Getty Images.

Arguably the aspects of Devéria's work that most appealed to Baudelaire was its particularity, artificiality, and transitory nature, in other words, its very fashionability— the extremity of the sleeves, the color of the textile's stripes, the echo of these in the specificity of the blooms in the hair, which appear to have originated from the vase on the table, and are in the process of being reproduced by her hand. The *Parisienne* of *Four o'clock in the evening* is patently a self-creation, a momentary vision, pleasing in her construction, sufficiently artificial to be nearly immediately out of fashion, or *démodé*. It is the useless and fugitive rather than the immutable—the qualities most lauded in the putatively moral and eternal pictorial genres of history painting—that for Baudelaire are both the most beautiful and the most modern of their time.

A useful case in point might be that of the crinoline, here considered not as a mere stopping point on a timeline of the history of dress, but instead as a site at which Baudelaire's understanding of the modern and Karl Marx's conceptualization of the commodity are made manifest. Crinolines have their origins in other forms of undergarments, such as petticoats and paniers, created to extend skirts away from the body and to augment their volume. Progressing from layers of fabric, the crinoline cage, introduced mid-century by Auguste Person, offered a technological solution to the desire for volume.

The progression of form and scale of these structures and the developing technology to facilitate them have been fascinating to historians of dress.[6] Figures 0.3a and 0.3b demonstrate both the metal cage proper, and also the cotton covering of the cage that would form an intermediary barrier between the steel and fine textiles. At least equally striking, however, are the concurrent and pervasively self-conscious associations between the rapid extremity of this style and the social, political, and economic situations of the time.[7] Walter Benjamin appeared interested in this aspect of nineteenth-century fashion, the crinoline in particular, and its association with the perceived excess and amorality of the French Second Empire. Within the magisterial compendium of the *Arcades Project* he collected analyses such as those of F. Th. Vischer from Stuttgart in 1879 who argued that, "We took the crinoline to be the symbol of the Second Empire in France—of its overblown lies, its hollow and purse-bound impudence."[8] The crinoline, therefore, allowed women to don an armature of patent artificiality—and beauty—but this construct became conceptually directly linked to the market, and beautiful women to prostitutes.

The pervasive nature of this association is evident in Honoré Daumier's lithograph of two women—in expansive crinolines—entering a carriage (Figure 0.4). The visual joke at play was one that echoed the lived experiences of fashionable women of the era. How does one enter circumscribed spaces such as the carriage while wearing this fashionable silhouette? Or, perhaps, the difficulties of being a woman in public, or the humor of the attempt, is also a root of the joke. Yet, without the close association between fashionable attire with the denizens of the demi-monde, the wordplay about the women's skirts not being demi-jupes would be incomprehensible. Instead, the linkage reiterates that which is already understood. Fashionable women are equally available for purchase as fashionable skirts, neither of which come in half measures. Or, as Walter Benjamin had noted, within the era of Napoleon III, "the paragon of fashion is the *grande dame* who plays the cocotte."[9] The realm of the Emperor came to be associated culturally with that of the *ancien régime*.[10] With the revival of rococo styles in the arts, including the crinoline as a reinterpretation and augmentation of the panier, came the increasing association of the regime itself with what was then perceived of as the illegitimacy of that previous era, such that even the *grande dame* could be seen in her fashionability as nothing more than a whore. In his inaugural definition of the commodity, Karl Marx explained that the

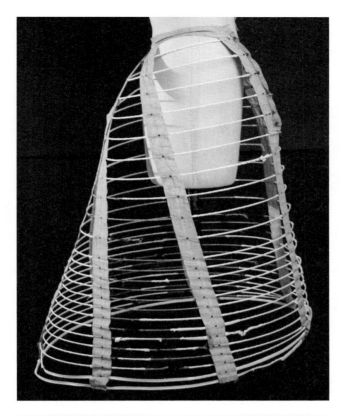

FIGURE 0.3 (top): American cage crinoline, 1862, steel and cotton. The Metropolitan Museum of Art, New York; (bottom): British cage crinoline, c. 1862, metal and cotton. The Metropolitan Museum of Art, New York.

FIGURE 0.4: *Des dames d'un demi-monde, mais n'ayant pas de demi-jupes*, from *Actualités*, Honoré Daumier, published in *Le Charivari*, May 11, 1855. Lithograph. The Metropolitan Museum of Art, New York.

"commodity appears, at first sight an extremely obvious, trivial thing. But its analysis brings out that it is a very strange thing, abounding in metaphysical subtleties and theological niceties."[11] It is clear that the crinoline contained within it significantly more than its use, material, and labor values.

Yet the empire of the crinoline extended well beyond the borders of Second Empire France, as the American and British-made examples of crinoline cages as shown demonstrate. The era itself—the long nineteenth-century—is defined within the volume's title as the age of Empire. Within recent historiography, the term "age of Empire" is most closely associated with Eric Hobsbawm's highly influential book, *The Age of Empire, 1875–1914*, which followed his volumes on *The Age of Revolution, 1789–1848* and *The Age of Capital, 1848–1875*.[12] In this manner, Hobsbawn differentiates between the imperial domination of global capitalism and more explicitly political Empire, yet the imbrications between these are unavoidable within the realm of cultural history. In conceptualizing this volume's scope of a cultural history of fashion within the age of Empire, the authors focus on Western modes while recognizing, as Anne McClintock has pointed out, that "imperialism is not something that happened elsewhere—a disagreeable fact of history external to Western identity. Rather, imperialism and the invention of race were fundamental aspects of Western industrial modernity."[13] In thinking through the cultural history of fashion within the inherently imperial context of the nineteenth century, therefore, the contributors to this volume are working through burgeoning conceptions of "new imperial history," wherein the transnational circulation of goods has not only economic significance, but also provides a means by which imperial power might be enabled or contested, even if not self-consciously so.[14]

The nine authors of this volume have therefore looked at the cultural history of fashion in the age of Empire through different lenses. In exploring Textiles (1), Philip Sykas introduces the reader to novel color and print production, but also elucidates changes in production of textiles. He notes that this is the period of time both for a transformation from hand-craft to machine production and for an imperially-based change in trading and production patterns. The pursuit of novelty—in pattern, color, and weave alike—is interpreted by Sykas within the context of imperial and class ambitions. In Production and Distribution (2), Susan Hiner focuses primarily on the Parisian context. Recognizing, as Marx did, that the fetishism of the commodity that arose during this nascent period of mass-production and consumerism fostered alienation between producers, the fruits of their labor, and consumers, Hiner endeavors to chart the cultural history of the "little hands" of the fashion industry, seamstresses and salesgirls alike. Denise Amy Baxter similarly frames her essay on Belief (4) in terms of both religious and ceremonial clothing, but also in relation to issues of propriety and the perceived relationships between dress and morality and finery and "fallen" women.

In focusing on The Body (3) and Gender and Sexuality (5) both Annette Becker and Ariel Beaujot focus on the relationships between bodies and the dress that concealed, revealed, and shaped them in various ways. Mapping what she refers to as the "extreme volatility of fashion and society alike" during our period, Becker considers a selection of garment types, including leg o' mutton sleeves, the cuirass bodice, and pantaloons, or Bloomer dress. With these, she investigates the tensions between fashionable and reform dress, presenting parallels between dress that controls or exaggerates the body's form and social stability in contrast with concomitant social and physical liberation. Beaujot expands Becker's focus from the body's forms to a more explicit focus on gender and sexuality, grounded in the theoretical approaches of psychoanalytic theory. Following upon the arguments of Judith Butler regarding the constructed and performative nature of both gender and sexuality, Beaujot focuses primarily on the masculine suit and feminine corset in order to acknowledge both gender norms and nineteenth-century cases in which heterosexual normativity was also challenged through dress.

In Status (6), Vivienne Richmond argues for the usefulness of taking England as a representative case study as the greatest imperial power of the era and the center of industrialization. Training her attention on the working classes rather than sartorial elites, Richmond explicates English uses of "dress as a means of social separation," whether that be in the particular textiles associated with the poor, clothes charity, or the necessity of explicitly differentiating between the middle classes and servants with the advent of increased availability of fashionably styled clothes at relatively inexpensive costs made possible by burgeoning mass production. For Richmond, by century's end, clothing was no longer capable of being the same stable marker of class that it had hitherto been.

In Ethnicity (7), Sarah Cheang investigates the means by which the dressed body was made to express ethnicity and ethnic difference during the age of Empire and its developing "scientific" racial theories. Cheang does not provide, as many nineteenth-century publications did, a compendium of types of ethnic dress.[15] She instead points to cases of negotiations of the signification of dress in the shifting cultural construction of ethnicity within the contexts of western imperialism and the history of slavery and its abolition. Cheang offers a perspicacious analysis of cases demonstrating how the coding of race and ethnicity was frequently negotiated through dress, for example, as an aspect of subjugation, as in slave dress, or self-definition, as in the attire of black dandies.

Justine De Young and Heidi Brevik-Zender tackle fashion's visual (8) and textual (9) representations. De Young focuses on France, as the fashion capital of Europe, and explores various mediated experiences of viewing dress, ranging from fashion prints, caricatures, and advertisements to paintings, photography, and ultimately film. Brevik-Zender analyzes self-consciously modern literary depictions in which dress and clothing are not only used to reflect character, but are presented as having a significant relationship to social and economic stability. Rather than focusing exclusively on French or British examples, although Jane Austen's *Northanger Abbey*, Honoré de Balzac's *Père Goriot*, and Émile Zola's *The Ladies' Paradise* (*Au Bonheur des dames*) receive their due, Brevik-Zender also explores the representational significance of dress in Theodore Dreiser's *Sister Carrie*, the 1848 Chinese *Courtesans and Opium* (*Fengyue meng*), and Argentinian author Juana Manuela Gorriti's *The Oasis in Life* (*Oasis en la vida*).

CHAPTER ONE

Textiles

PHILIP SYKAS

Textile fabrics are conceived by the manufacturer in terms of their material composition and processes of production, but perceived by the consumer firstly in terms of appearance and handle. Both are deeply implicated in the economic and cultural issues behind the wearing of cloth: cost, quality, meaning. We must look from these several perspectives to understand the drivers behind the introduction of fabrics to the market, and the collective response to them in the form of fashion. A major preoccupation during our time frame was novelty. On the supply side, novelty gave a competitive edge, stimulated fashion change and accelerated the cycle of consumption. On the demand side, novelty provided pleasure, a way to get noticed, and new social signifiers. But novelty can act in contradictory ways: as an instrument for sustaining a fashion elite by facilitating costly style changes, and as an agent for breaking down fashion barriers by making elite modes more affordable. It can drive fashion both by promoting new looks, and later by acting to make those looks outmoded. During the long nineteenth century, the desire for novelty was supported by the widely accepted philosophical view of progress: that *new* also implied improved or more advanced, hence that novelty was a reflection of modernity.

This chapter examines textiles for dress from 1800 to 1920, a period that completed the changeover from hand-craft to machine production, and through Europe's imperial ambitions, saw the reversal of East/West trading patterns. To chart all the fashionable fabric introductions and modifications during such a tumultuous period would require a lengthy dictionary. Rather than attempt a comprehensive survey, it is proposed to select a mere score of examples that either characterize a fashion period, or engage with the theme of Empire. The analyses presented will serve to introduce methods and sources for studying fabrics that can be applied to other cases. They will also allow us to probe the notion of novelty alongside other cultural drivers for fashion materials. A wider aim is to address the gap highlighted by curator Lesley Miller: that "fashion historians have tended to concentrate on the cut and style of dress without giving due consideration to its material components."[1]

PLAINS: ACTUAL AND SYMBOLIC MODERNITY

In plain weave, fabrics reach their greatest balance: "The artlessness of plain-weave cloth arises from a fundamental agreement between structure and appearance."[2] Unpatterned fabrics gain attention through subtle characteristics: reflectiveness, opacity, texture, and qualities of handle such as stiffness or suppleness. They are suited to understatement, to conveying ideas of purity and solidity, as well as for setting up a counter-play to supposed *vulgarity* in taste. Still, the plainest fabrics offered scope for fashion distinction. When Jane Austen commissioned her sister to purchase two dress lengths of brown cambric muslin for herself and their mother in 1801, she specified, "Buy two brown ones, if you please [. . .] but the kind of brown is left to your own choice, and I had rather they were different, as it will be always something to say, to dispute about which is the prettiest."[3]

Plains form a necessary foil to patterned fabrics, avoiding the brashness of pattern on pattern. While plains dominate fashion, the attention of historians has focused on patterned fabrics. This tendency is redressed here by highlighting instances where plains have demonstrated something new. Such was the case at the start of our period when the Swedish traveler Eric Svedenstierna, visiting England in 1803, wrote of the "dazzling whiteness" given to cotton goods by artificial bleaching.[4] Whiteness, being generally available for the first time, became such a prominent feature of fashion in the first decades of the nineteenth century that women were chided for resembling so many ghosts. Plains can also symbolize the new as with *gros de Suez*, the ribbed silk taken up after 1869 associating its straight channels with the technological feat of the new canal.[5] While connection with the canal was an afterthought, and the ribs were actually concerned with achieving a smoothness of form to suit the new fashion silhouette, both shared a sense of modernity.

CALICO AND NANKEEN: THE NATURALIZATION OF COTTON

European cotton fabrics rose to prominence in the 1780s, after the development of machine spinning led to the ability to imitate and undercut cottons imported from India. Philipp Andreas Nemnich, who visited Manchester in 1799, summarized current developments in cottons.[6] Mechanical spinning had given rise to three yarn types spun on different machines: water twist which was the strongest and reserved for warps (only available then as fine as 50 hanks per pound); mule yarn not so strongly twisted (from 40 to 200 hanks per pound and above); and jenny spun yarn, weak and suitable only for weft (spun in the coarser counts). These types were linked to procurement from different global sources of cotton fiber because each demanded certain qualities: water twist used cottons of middle degree from the West Indies and Brazil, while jenny yarns made use of the lower sorts from the Levant. The mule spun yarns required cotton of higher quality the finer the yarn that was desired, entailing the expensive Georgia and Bourbon types for yarns finer than 70 hanks per pound.

Combinations of cotton yarn spun on different machines created distinct fabrics. For calicos, water twist was used for the warp and jenny spun yarn for the weft (Figure 1.1). Nemnich distinguished three grades: common yard-wide (actually twenty-seven inches), superfine yard-wide (a better grade costing two pence a yard more), and ell-wide (actually 36 inches) of the same quality as the superfines.[7] For nankeens, he gives precise details: "Twist is used for the weft as well as the warp. The weft must be at least two numbers higher than the warp: for example, if the warp is No. 32, the weft is No. 34. All nankeens are dyed in the yarn [. . .] The ordinary [. . .] colour (buff or chamois) of nankeens does not fade easily because the colour is prepared from so-called iron liquor [. . .] iron oxide dissolved in acid."[8] Nankeens imitated the natural yellow cotton goods imported from China, and associated with Nankin (Nanjing).[9]

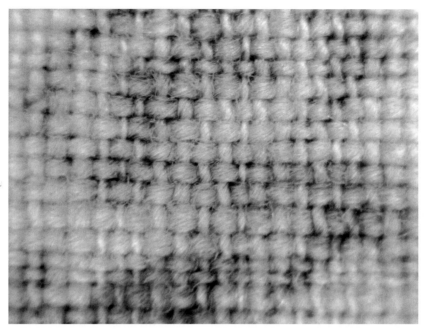

FIGURE 1.1: Photomicrograph (65× magnification) of the reverse of a block-printed calico gown, 1780s. This shows the typical calico construction of smooth warps, twisted on the water frame in the Z direction; and spongier wefts spun on the jenny in the S direction. Photo: Philip Sykas. © Royal Ontario Museum.

Thus, the mechanized spinning technologies gave rise to new cottons near the start of our period, although these fabrics were based on pre-existing Eastern types. Pride was taken in the modernity reflected by the technological achievement, placing cottons at the forefront of fashion. A contemporary commentator extols the new machines as "undoubtedly, the most wonderful productions of the human art [. . .] They enable the manufacturer to produce a better article than can be made by the hand, in consequence of the uniformity and certainty of their operations . . ."[10] Valorizing uniformity of surface points to a developing aesthetic of machine-made goods, which carried connotations of integrity, being uncorrupted by handling. Importantly, by the first decade of the nineteenth century, machine production allowed cotton to seem naturalized, to be viewed as a domestic product rather than an exotic luxury. And freed from its orientalizing associations, cotton was able to be worn next to the skin without giving rise to moral fears.

LAPPET-WEAVE MUSLINS: FROM NOVELTY TO EXPORT

Muslin in general has been treated by Sonia Ashmore, so it is proposed here to focus on a specialized production: lappet-weave patterned muslin.[11] Lappet weaving employed a special patterning device to control the movement of extra warps (known as whip threads) held by needles spaced across the width of the loom in a frame, making them zig-zag to form small figures resembling those of the jamdani muslins of Dacca. Commercialization of lappet muslins probably occurred in Scotland not long before 1800; in 1794, the Scottish Commissioners for Manufactures and Improvements advertised a premium for "Muslin, in imitation of the India Jamdannies, with regard to both the quality of the cloth and neatness of the pattern . . . the yarn to be spun in Britain."[12] The grooved pattern wheel that controlled the movement of the lappet frame later became known as the Scotch wheel. In lappet muslins, the pattern warp traveled from side-to-side in the figures but vertically between separate figures; the linking threads could then be cropped away. Since the device that traced the grooves in the pattern wheel allowed minor variations so that succeeding repeats of a motif had slight differences, the cropped lappet weave resembled hand-embroidery.[13]

By 1799, Gilchrist and Co. of Edinburgh advertised a range including ". . . Lappet Muslins, of the most elegant patterns ever exhibited in this country." Lappet-patterned muslins rose in consumption; George Hill, a London draper, advertised "200 dresses of coloured and white lappet muslins from 10s. to 21s. the full round dress" along with other British and Indian cottons in 1802. The British product competed with the Indian import in the second decade of the nineteenth century; in 1811, Foster and Co. of London advertised "39 Jamdannies, with every description of curious Articles from India, which are now much cheaper than ever." But by 1820, not only had lappet muslins passed their peak in European fashion, they had begun to be exported to India.

A shipment book holding counterpart samples of lappet muslins that sailed for Bombay in May 1822 gives an idea of the appearance of such fabrics in the early nineteenth century (Figure 1.2).[14] It is difficult to know whether fashion interest in lappet muslins arose because of the ingenuity of the invention, or from the cheaper replication of an expensive hand-patterned Eastern original. However, their advertisement as lappets, rather than as jamdanis, signals that their novelty as home-produced goods was part of their appeal.

Unusually, lappet muslins are a case of machine production that does not produce uniformity, and this may have been to their detriment in Western fashion. Lappet-weave muslins found a market in South America by the mid-nineteenth century, and later they were introduced to the Arab market where they found favor for the men's headscarf known as keddiyeh. This fashion aftermath represents a typical pathway for European fabrics during our period, that of pursuing sales in one or more of the expanding foreign markets supported by European imperialism.

VALENTIA, GAMBROON, DELAINE, AND ALPACA: MIXING TRADITIONS

Isabella Ducrot sees in the warp and weft of weaving a marriage of masculine and feminine elements, an idea expressed as far back as Plato's *Laws* in which the firmness of the warp is seen as male and the adaptability of the weft as female.[15] Master weaver Peter Collingwood retained the impression of animated roles for the woven elements, but perceptively feminized the warp as pregnant with possibilities for various offspring.[16] The concept of mixture fabrics arises from this basic nature of weaving as an interchange of contrasting elements. A mixture fabric uses pure yarns of one fiber type (or different yarns plied together) so as to retain the properties of each fiber, as opposed to blended fibers that result in a more uniform response. One early line of development in mixture fabrics was stimulated by Islamic culture where men were proscribed from wearing pure silk fabrics. This gave rise, for example, to mashru, a satin-weave mixture of cotton and silk

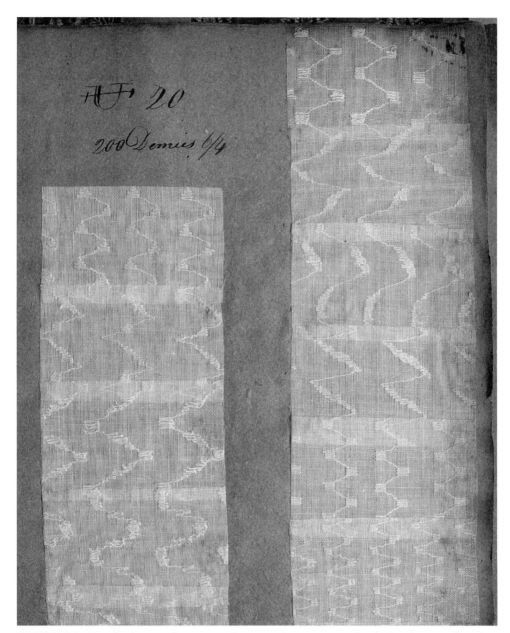

FIGURE 1.2: Detail of a page from a warehouseman's counterpart book showing samples of lappet muslins exported to Bombay in May 1822. Image: Coats plc.

that maximizes the visual effect of silk on the surface where long silk warp floats occur, but places the cotton next to the skin, where the silk only appears as single binding points.[17] In Britain, bombazine, a mixture of silk and worsted with matte appearance, was used for mourning dress, and this cultural association may have delayed experimentation with mixture fabrics until stimulated by the rise of cotton in fashion.

Britain's damp climate was inimical to the prominence of cotton fashions during the first decades of our period, and would naturally have spawned thoughts of mixing wool with cotton to lend body and warmth to fabrics. The development of lightweight mixture fabrics of cotton along with silk or worsted wool received much attention from British manufacturers from the 1810s to the 1840s. Valencias were an early example; silk-striped valencias for waistcoats are noted by *Ackermann's Repository* in 1809,[18] and were advertised for waistcoatings by a merchant tailor traveling from London to the worsted weaving center, Norwich, in 1813.[19] The order book of the wool printer Henry Cooke of White Conduit Fields details a rising demand for printed valencias from 1821.[20] Cooke's valencias were probably produced in Yorkshire given his numerous contacts in that county.

His samples show white cotton warp and cream worsted weft mixtures, occasionally highlighted with narrow silk stripes (Figure 1.3); the fabrics play with the contrast between matte and bright luster aided by a texture of thick and thin warps.

Another worsted mixture cloth, gambroon, appears to have been initiated by the London draper George Fox. Employing mohair in its composition, Fox claimed it as a "patent" rain resistant cloth as early as 1812.[21] In 1823, Fox advertised, "To prevent imposition by any description of persons whatever offering or selling worsted Valencias

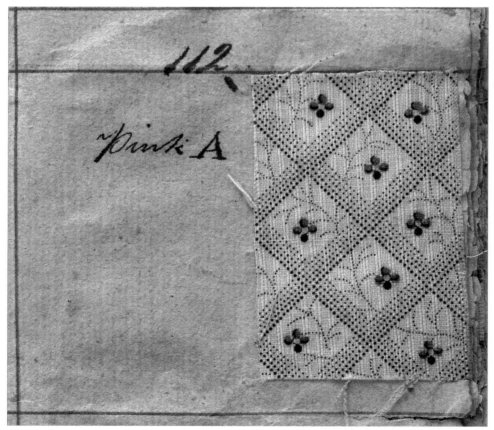

FIGURE 1.3: Detail of a printed valencia from Henry Cooke's order book of 1821 showing cotton warp and worsted weft. G.P & J. Baker Archives.

for the real Mohair Gambroons, they are stamped on the back—'Fox's Patent Gambroons' . . ."[22] The *Gentleman's Magazine of Fashions* for June 1828 described a "Riding Frock Coat [. . .] made of superfine patent gambroon" worn with a "waistcoat of light fawn chequered Valencia,"[23] while in September 1831, it featured a "Shooting Dress [. . .] of twilled gambroon" with matching waistcoat.[24] Such references indicate that gambroon enjoyed favor for masculine outdoor wear, especially for the summer season. However, the fabric was not considered suitable for indoors. In the 1830s, an artist wishing to travel light purchased "a knapsack [and] a suit of gambroon" for his journey up the Rhine but notes his discomfiture at wearing the suit in a hotel, something he would not even have considered doing in London.[25]

Fox's persistent marketing earned the fabric a sneering reference in *The New Monthly Magazine* where it was associated with other much-touted wonders: "'patent percussion guns,' [. . .] 'pedometers for the waistcoat jacket,' [. . .] 'gambroon shooting-jackets of an entirely new cut,' and 'waterproof hats on a new principle' . . ."[26] This suggests a fall in status. Fox continued to market mohair gambroons emphasizing their utilitarian qualities: "dust and dirt will not adhere to them; they do not spot or cockle with the wet and will turn more rain than cloth."[27] A blatant appeal to functional qualities may have been acceptable to men under the banner of new technical invention, but fashion normally shuns practicality. Since the fabric filled a genuine need for lightweight outdoor wear, it became more widely manufactured from 1834. In fact, John James described it as entering the market at this date, constructed from a warp of "separate threads of cotton and worsted twisted together" and a cotton weft. Possibly, its "re-launch" emphasized the pleasing, subdued coloration, rather than utility.[28]

The gambroons registered by Ibotson & John Walker, Buckley Brothers, and Frederick Harrison under the 1839 Design Copyright Act show variations of plying together white cotton and brown worsted (Figure 1.4).[29] A trials book from the Swaisland archive holds printed gambroons dated 1838 to 1839; these are trouserings plate-printed with indeterminate mottled patterns, emphasizing the importance of the speckled coloration.[30] Despite such attractions, the fashion exit of gambroons is signaled by their offer as a low-priced export cloth for southern Europe and South America. Their banishment was complete by 1854 when a journalist touring a Manchester warehouse claimed to have heard for the first time of waistcoatings called valentias and gambroons.[31]

The premier British mixture fabric of the mid-nineteenth century was the delaine. This term is not simply a shortened name for the French *mousseline de laine* that was introduced around 1830, but rather an adaptation of the French luxury wool product to a lower-priced mixture of cotton warp and worsted weft. This version combined the cotton technology of Lancashire and the worsted expertise of Yorkshire to imitate the softness and drape of the French original. The challenge to dyeing posed by the combination of vegetable and animal fibers was solved by the 1840s with steam-fixed colors. Dyes were applied by hand-block printing to achieve the depth of shade desired in this decade of rich coloring, with the attendant labor cost of hand work. John Mercer's development of chlorination of wool around 1842 improved receptivity to dyes enabling the machine printing of delaines, bringing them within reach of a much wider public.[32] Nevertheless, machine printing entailed patterns with smaller repeat units and simpler motifs (Figure 1.5a).

The fashionable patterns of the mid-1840s set by the Paris elite were large and bold, accompanied by a revival of hand-blocked rainbow grounds (Figure 1.5b). These appear calculated to assert the primacy of the hand-processed luxury cloth over its roller-printed

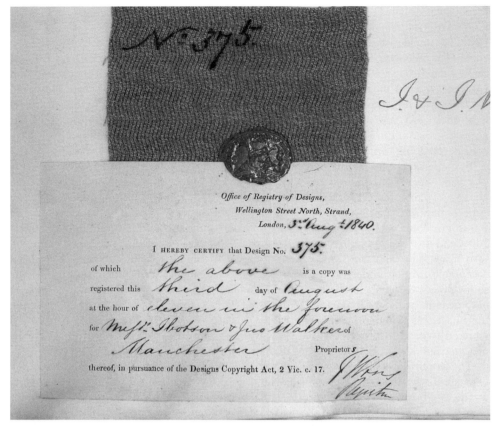

FIGURE 1.4: Gambroon registered by Ibotson & Walker in 1840, showing variegated color produced by plying together cotton and worsted yarns in alternate wefts. The National Archives BT42/2.

imitation. Thus, for a short time, the elite sacrificed their usual claim to understatement in dress to maintain fashion supremacy when faced with the leveling effect of new technology.

In 1836, the textile entrepreneur Titus Salt took a chance on some bales of animal hair lying in a Liverpool warehouse. Charles Dickens transformed the incident into legend, portraying the Yorkshireman as a figure of ingenuity able to see beyond the "dirty bales of frowsy South American stuff" to a new fabric enterprise.[33] Salt was not the first in England to use alpaca, but probably the first to develop it as a cloth in its own right.[34] Many trials were necessary before the alpaca could be worked successfully on wool machinery, and the initial results were rather coarse and unappealing. It was in combination with other fibers that alpaca first found favor, and its qualities of luster and lightness coupled with durability and moth-resistance added value. Worked with silk warps, it formed a substitute for pure silk, and with cotton, a mixture adapted to multiple uses: "ladies dresses and children's frocks of light summer make [. . .] waistcoating as cool as any cotton, yet rich and lustrous as the best silk patterns."[35] Commercially introduced around 1841, the reputation of alpaca grew in the 1850s and 1860s. A ladies' magazine boasted of the

FIGURE 1.5a: Page from a pattern book showing machine-printed delaines, 1846, possibly from Broad Oak print works. Roller-printed delaines were made possible by Mercer's wool chlorination process. Author's collection.

FIGURE 1.5b: Fashion plate reflecting French styles for large-scale block printed delaines. *La Belle Assemblée*, July 1845. Downing Collection at Manchester Metropolitan University.

reversal of the usual direction of fashion emulation: a "French lady coming to England always takes back with her so many yards of the coveted alpaca cut into dress lengths."[36]

Popularity led to adulteration of genuine alpaca with over-large proportions of long-staple wool by unscrupulous manufacturers; such imitation alpacas puckered with rain-wetting, thus lacking the suitability for walking dresses that endeared the fabric to British consumers.[37] Insisting on undyed shades ensured against adulteration, purity which was then reconstrued as refinement: "it must be always black, grey, white or buff, any other colours are not according to good taste."[38] Thus alpaca iterates several aspects noted with other materials: the "naturalization" of a foreign material through enterprise and technology, a passion for smoothness, and a desire for lightness of weight. But we also see the linking of pure fiber cloth with concepts of refinement, steering the trend away from mixture fabrics by the 1860s.

CHECKED AND STRIPED SILKS: THE OTHER HALF

The jacquard attachment for weaving, commercially introduced around 1804 in France, was to transform weaving from craft to industry during our period. Adoption was gradual; as Natalie Rothstein has shown, in England the jacquard was not significantly taken up until the 1830s.[39] The influence of the jacquard mechanism on design of figured fabrics has been treated in several books on silk.[40] Therefore, we will trace here the more overlooked checked and striped silks. Dresses in these lesser silks have not been preserved in the quantities of the more elaborate jacquards, but survival of the pattern archive of the Lancashire firm Hilton and Son enables the mapping of significant design features across a twenty-five-year period from the late 1840s to early 1870s.

The most distinctive introductions can be cited. Shaded warps are first seen in 1851; finely barred grounds with wefts alternating in groups of four black and four color were introduced in 1853 and phased out after 1855. The seasons from 1857 to 1858 saw a vogue for simple square checks, followed in 1858 to 1859 by broad cross-wise banded effects. The years 1859 to 1860 witnessed a return to finely-barred grounds, but this time with alternations of two wefts each. In 1861, a spaced bar effect with bright yellow highlights beneath the bars commenced. Fashions for 1863 returned to softer effects and smoother textures, and 1864 saw the introduction of the gros texture, a fine corded effect. In 1866, broad stripes came into fashion, especially paired and triplet stripes, while the late 1860s brought calendered glacé silks to the forefront. Such changes reveal that checked and striped silks, far from being staple goods, had recognizable fashions often lasting no more than two or three seasons.

In Britain, these simpler silks were a Lancashire speciality, with Spitalfields undertaking most of the complex silk patterns. It cannot be chance that after the Anglo-French free trade agreement of 1860, when the English silk industry was put in jeopardy, that Victoria and Albert were photographed with the Queen wearing a chequered flounce silk and the Prince sporting a checked waistcoat with predominant warp stripes, both types woven in Lancashire (Figure 1.6a and 1.6b).

The royal couple expressed solidarity with the home industry at a time of difficulty by avoiding wearing anything of French influence. The silk industry had often been supported by elite patronage, but this is a rare instance of patronizing a lesser mode. The association of French fabrics with extravagance and frivolity in comparison with the sobriety of

FIGURE 1.6a: Queen Victoria and Prince Albert wearing Lancashire silks. *Carte-de-visite* photograph by John J.E. Mayall, February 1861. © National Portrait Gallery, London.

FIGURE 1.6b: Detail of a painted flounce design and corresponding woven silk of autumn 1860. Charles Hilton pattern books. The Museum of Wigan Life, Wigan Council.

national taste was a paradigm later invoked in Britain and other countries to curb consumer preference at a time when Paris dominated women's fashions.

BLUE PRINTS AND PURPLE PRINTS: FOSSILIZATION OF FASHION

Although the print trade largely depended on seasonally-changing patterns, the cheapest prints for the working classes were a staple commodity. An "Old Draper" recalled retailing in the early nineteenth century when "The common people and servant girls generally wore [. . .] navy-blue prints, with a small white or yellow spot . . ."[41] A step above was the wash-fast, madder-dyed article which was introduced as day wear for the middle classes. Thomas Hoyle and Sons produced a madder purple "superior in brilliancy, fastness and utility for domestic wear" that became the by-word for this style in England.[42]

A Hoyle pattern incorporating touches of red shown in the *Journal of Design* as "a slight departure from the ordinary style of the Mayfield Works" evidences an attempt to retain a sense of fashion change for purple prints (Figure 1.7).[43] But calico printer Edmund Potter linked purple prints with "The sober careful classes of society [who] cling to an inoffensive taste, which will not look obsolete and extravagant after the lapse of such a time as would render a garment comparatively tasteless and unfashionable in a higher class."[44] By the middle of the century, purple prints had dropped in status, superseding indigo blue prints for servants' dress, with similar but less practical light pink and pale blue styles the choice for middle class day wear. In the 1880s, even servants began to eschew the purple print. A writer favoring modernization in servants' behavior, begins her support by evoking empathy: "How should we like [to return to] the old-fashioned purple print gowns of bygone days . . ."[45] In the 1890s, purple prints became a signifier of the elderly and "grandmother's days." Nevertheless, this trajectory is a British one; in America, purple prints had a longer run in fashion. Joan Severa cites "the neat & varied designs of Hoyle's prints" recommended for second mourning in *Godey's Lady's Book*, March 1861.[46] And on the Continent indigo resist prints remained in use, entering into folk dress revival. Missionaries brought the style to South Africa by the mid-nineteenth century where indigo prints were known as shweshwe, and are still used for skirts, aprons, and head wraps.

PRINTED SHIRTINGS: CONCEALING MASCULINE FRIVOLITY

A caricature of 1846 in the *Allgemeine Theaterzeitung* shows men relaxing at a bathing place in shirts printed with loud motifs; below, washerwomen hang the figured shirts on a line, while the caption asks, "Why shouldn't shirts also have their fashions?"[47] By gaining the attention of the caricaturist, it would appear that such shirts were a novelty. A history of Alsatian textile printing based on original documents states that Dollfus-Meig and Frères Koechlin began printing *chemises à sujets* in 1847, indicating that such shirtings had moved into mainstream fashion.[48] The mode seems to have transferred from prior waistcoat styles, with waistcoats becoming increasingly sober, and the motifs moving a layer inward.

Sporting and animal motifs, many sourced from works by Henry Thomas Alken or Edwin Henry Landseer, were frequently chosen as themes (Figure 1.8). It was as if the

Selected Patterns for Dress.

CALICO, PRINTED BY THOMAS HOYLE AND SONS.

This graceful design, with its tiny red dots, is a slight departure from the ordinary style of the Mayfield works. We are apt to associate the Hoyle purple with the humbler class of wearers, but the present pattern is such a successful union of quiet grace and liveliness, that it might, we think, be worn by all or any who are not too grand to use a calico print. A ribbon of bright light blue, amber, or cherry colour, at the wearer's neck, would be an harmonious combination.

FIGURE 1.7: Purple print by Thomas Hoyle & Sons, from the *Journal of Design and Manufactures*, 2 (Nov.), 1849, p. 108. Author's collection.

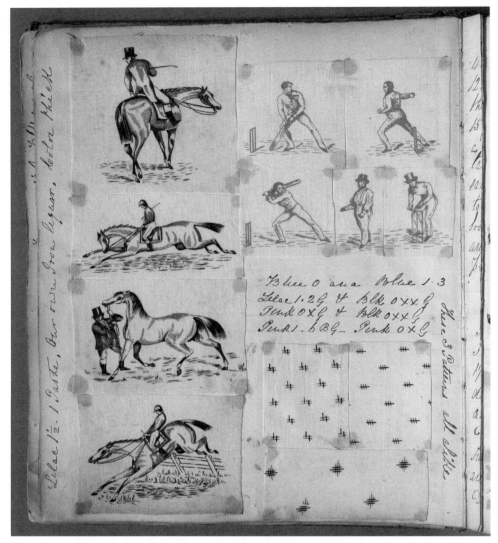

FIGURE 1.8: Page from a colorist's notebook showing printed shirtings with sporting motifs. Charles Swaisland, Crayford, 1850s. Downing Collection at Manchester Metropolitan University.

leisure interests that men wished to express had to be hidden, only to be revealed on relaxed occasions when shirtsleeves could be shown: an embodiment of Flügel's concept of the "Great Masculine Renunciation."[49]

During the 1870s, the motifs chosen for shirtings were reoriented from sports to humor, and at the start of the next decade, the genre seems to have transferred from menswear to the dress of women and children with increasingly playful motifs. At the same time, figurative printed motifs began to be used as linings for men's clothing, concealing this aspect of men's expression one layer deeper.

FIGURE 1.9: Lining print featuring the actress Lillie Langtry, by James Hardcastle & Co. From Antonio Sansone, *The Printing of Cotton Fabrics* (Manchester: Abel Heywood & Son, 1887), pl. 1. Author's collection.

Perhaps only among close associates would a man reveal the lining of his necktie with an image of a popular actress or politician (Figure 1.9). We can trace in this progression an attitude toward materials used for outward and inward dress. In Western culture, truth is an inner quality; that which is hidden from view represents the inner self. For centuries, this was symbolized by pure white linen worn next to the skin, but during the third quarter of the nineteenth century a change occurred. Not only was cotton exchanged for linen, but undergarments began to be shaped to the body, and embellishments added. Men's printed shirtings can be seen as the first decorated undergarments: possibly a concealed rebellion against "renunciation."

MOIRÉ ANTIQUE: RETURN TO NATURE

The finishing technique of moiré or watering originated long before our period. Samuel Pepys "bought some greene watered Moyre for a morning wastcoate" in 1660.[50] In the mid-nineteenth century, new techniques coupled with the crinoline fashion stimulated a revival of the fabric. Moiré requires as its basis a weft-ribbed fabric. In the moiré antique process, the fabric is folded in half selvage-to-selvage so that the ribs lie nearly parallel, but due to slight variations in the weave, the ribs cross in places. The deviation of the ribs is normally heightened by running the hand or wooden forms over the folded fabric. When the prepared fabric is afterward pressed under heavy weight, this causes localized displacement and flattening at the intersections of the ribs. On opening the fold, the crushed portions of the ribs reflect light, showing as bright wavering lines or filets on a dark ground; and the pattern is symmetrical on opposite halves of the cloth. Thus moiré antique is a material-and-process-based ornament. James Trilling saw this class of ornament as the distinctive idiom of modernist design; so ironically, moiré antique may be viewed as the most modern fabric of our period.[51]

Thomas Seamer, a Cheapside mercer, showed moiré antique in the British silks section of the Great Exhibition, and by 1853, it was advertised for both dresses and waistcoats. Newspaper advertisements suggest the fashion for moiré antique reached its height between 1858 and 1866 when the fabric could be displayed to advantage on the wide crinoline frame. The British seem to have led the trend, possibly because of technical advances in calendering. A report of 1861 claims it was once "a manufacture which was almost exclusively English, and brought by them to great perfection" but that Lyon silk finishers had since advanced the technique so as to be competitive in both beauty and price.[52]

Its stiffness, weight, and great expense made moiré antique appropriate for special occasions, equal to velvets and the heavier satins. Like these, it held an air of gravity and symbolized wealth. In white, it became the bridal wear of aspiration. In a novel of 1859, "the bride, being a widow [. . .] could [not] adopt the *regulation* costume of a white moiré antique gown and a lace veil."[53] Likewise in 1862, we read of a wedding toast given to the bride's maids, hoping that "before long pink tarlatanes might be exchanged for white moire antique and myrtle wreaths bud into orange blossoms. . ."[54] Moiré antique was a fabric to wear for a portrait, whether painted or photographic; Florence Nightingale chose moiré antique for a photograph of 1854.[55] The central crease that demonstrates the symmetry of the true *à l'antique* type is visible in the picture, and its broad filets indicate a moiré of the highest caliber. Unlike mechanized production, the ethereal forms of moiré arise between the touch of the craftsman and the imperfections of the fabric, only partially controlled. Moiré seems to reflect the spiritual side of mid-century Victorian society; at a time of awakening anxieties about the destructiveness of industrial growth and renewed interest in nature.

FROM CRAPE TO CRÊPE: CHANGING SURFACE VALUES

Silk crapes were a speciality of Bologna, widely recorded in use since the sixteenth century for mourning accessories and by religious orders. From the seventeenth century, crapes were imitated in France, and the production came to England with the Huguenot refugees. The Bolognese product remained the most admired, and efforts to gain the secrets of the industry were still being foiled in the eighteenth century.[56] The story of crape in our period begins with the industrialization of the product. The Courtauld family began crape weaving in 1827, using power looms from 1832.[57] Courtaulds began at an opportune moment as the use of mourning crape was to escalate as middle-class women took up mourning dress, mourning periods grew longer, and mourning wear became based on fashionable clothing styles (which entailed increasing amounts of trimming), while in addition, mourning crape had the advantage of immunity from changing colors. Courtaulds' success was based on a finishing process that mechanically imitated the crimp of traditional crape. This was achieved by an embossing process followed by releasing the natural crimp arising from the over-twisted weft yarns.[58] However, in the 1880s the use of mourning crape began to decline, and lost royal patronage after the death of Queen Victoria; overseas and Empire markets were relied upon to boost sales until the 1930s.

Fortunately, Courtaulds was able to apply its knowledge of spinning and weaving for crape to production of *crêpe de chine*. Crêpe weave silks had been available as Chinese imports, sometimes used for shawls or bonnet trimmings, but the fashion for *crêpe de chine* dresses appears to have begun in 1870, probably alongside the growing European fascination with the Japonesque. *The Milliner* for June of that year reported: "Costumes of poult de soie and crepe de Chine are in vogue in London [. . .] true elegance seeks the quiet effects produced by different tissues of the same colour."[59] By December, it was claimed, "Crepe de Chine is the *ne plus ultra* material for evening wear, but it requires a very well filled purse to afford the luxury . . ."[60] *The Queen* reported in May 1872, "A good many dresses of *crêpe de Chine* are seen at evening parties, apricot, pale and bright green, coral colour, and salmon colour, but it is seldom that the entire dress is composed of *crêpe de Chine*, which is rather too soft and clinging when used alone. It generally combined with silk or tulle, and less often with satin."[61]

Courtaulds began production of *crêpe de chine* in 1896 when soft draping fabrics had become more widely adopted. In the move from crape to crêpe, we see the valorization of a matte surface quality over the desire for sheen.[62] The dullness once associated with mourning was remodeled as an aesthetic taste (Figure 1.10). Glossiness was later to become associated with flashiness and pretension.

FIGURE 1.10: Mary Constance Wyndham (Lady Elcho) wearing a dress probably of silk crêpe and satin, in a setting of Japanese objects. Watercolor by Edward John Poynter, exhibited 1886. Private Collection.

KHAKI DRILL: THE NEW INVISIBILITY

G.W. Armitage ascribes the origins of khaki drill to a conversation in India between an English army colonel and a Swiss traveler, John Leemann. The colonel observed that a fabric was required for the troops that would not shrink, show dust, or fade. Leemann put the problem to the chemist, Frederick Albert Gatty, whose subsequent experiments led to an extremely fast dye based on iron oxide that was patented in 1884. The men found E. Spinner & Co. willing to take on their project to produce the dye, hence "the brand of Leemann & Gatty Fast Khaki Dye began."[63] Armitage's own firm, Armitage & Rigby, having declined the dyeing, nevertheless offered to weave the cloth, and the first pieces of khaki drill ever made were woven at their Rodney Street Mill in Warrington. The original khaki dye was not fast to acid, which prompted further investigation leading to an after-treatment in silicate of soda, patented in 1897. This elevated khaki to "a degree of fastness, hitherto unattainable by any natural or artificial true dyestuff . . ."[64]

In that year, khaki was issued to all British regiments being posted abroad, and it had its first major trial in the Boer War. The First World War brought a great escalation in production of khaki drill which was to embed it in collective memory. Jane Tynan has shown how khaki came to embody the new approaches to warfare, with the concepts of camouflage and functionality replacing the old idea of fearsome spectacle.[65] Khaki became a metonym for the soldier, widely adopted in everyday language and literature, and came to represent new ideas about the citizen soldier. Regretting the passing of scarlet and brass, a wartime journalist saw "the now familiar khaki suggest[ive of] cold duty, drills, drab routine and the prosaic side of war, shorn of its romance."[66] With its visual leveling, and evocation of earth, khaki drill served to make our memories of the Great War those of the experience of the common soldier.

GABARDINE: CROSSING THE GENDER DIVIDE

Thomas Burberry patented gabardine in 1888, described as a layered construction: an outer shell of twilled or plain linen, and lining of waterproofed cloth.[67] The crucial innovation, not clear from the patent, seems to have been that of using Egyptian cotton treated for water resistance in the yarn before weaving.[68] Not until a further patent of 1897, along with Frederick Daniel Unwin, did Burberry specify a weave structure called drabbet: a twilled cloth usually made from unbleached linen. The patented improvement in "manufacture of drabbet cloth for gabardine fabrics" implies that from that time, gabardine referred to the combination of weave and waterproofing.[69] The patent states that gabardine is made from pure linen, or a linen and cotton mixture, and depicts the combination twill weave used to produce the characteristic closely-packed steep twill of gabardine: alternate wefts weave 4/2 twill and 3/3 twill. Adding to the complexity, the twill is sometimes broken, and some shots are repeated. Later constructions retain the steep combination twill, but regularize the weave.

From the start, the lightness of gabardine—on top of being windproof, waterproof, and thorn-proof—made it a fabric suited to sportswear for both sexes. Already in 1889, *The Cornishman* noted a father who encouraged his daughters to accompany him to shoot in winter: "Instead of a lounge in an armchair and a trashy novel this *pater familias* says, in effect:– Put up cloth knickerbocker breeches (ladies') strong boots, tidy leathern gaiters, a skirt of Burberry's gabardine, and a jacket [. . .] and shoot and grow hardy . . ."[70] Cunnington signals the revolutionary importance of sports clothing for women: "an attire designed ad hoc in which the [. . .] effect on the male was scarcely considered."[71] While the Cornish father was not concerned with the allure of the material, the article emphasized that the health benefit would fit the girls for their roles as mothers-to-be, thus neutralizing any potential radicalism.

But outdoor activity for women was a growing aspect of leisure, and by the early 1900s, Burberry's took advantage of the opportunity for marketing gabardine to ladies: "Now that they spend so much time in the open-air, and claim full share of what were once considered solely male prerogatives, far more attention is given to attire as a means for [. . .] affording the fullest opportunity for the exercise of physical energy and skill" (Figure 1.11).[72] The company offered gabardine in five weights: "Tropical, Airylight,

FIGURE 1.11: Burberry's advertised gabardine for the widest range of women's sporting activity, depicting women in an active role. Image courtesy of Manchester Art Gallery.

Summer, Autumn and Winter" advising that "The first three, being lighter, are those usually required by women."[73] Hence, we have the same material worn by men and women, but gendered through the factor of lightness of weight. The rise of Burberry's gabardine to an iconic fabric of the twentieth century may relate in part to this ability to cross gender by combining technical inventiveness with marketing skill.

SHIRTINGS AND DRESSES: THE DISCIPLINE OF STRIPES

In the early nineteenth century, striped dress materials were rendered more widely available by improvements in engraved cylinder printing. In woven stripes, the setting is determined by the color sequence of the warps and cannot be changed without remounting the loom. Roller printing allowed striped fabrics to be made and varied with ease for the first time. A pattern book of 1806 to 1808, from the prominent Manchester engravers Joseph Lockett & Son, shows that stripes were in steady demand.[74] Known as bengals, striped rollers were charged by the number of lines per inch—which could be up to fifty. During his years in Manchester, the enterprising German businessman Nathan Rothschild purchased heavily in roller-printed stripes and checks to be sold on the Hamburg market.[75] Thus, it could be said that such cottons laid the foundation for a banking empire of the nineteenth century.

Stripe and check designers formed a rank of their own, with entire careers spent in the discipline of fine discrimination among abstract linear forms. There are two main aspects to designing stripes: the proportion of the stripes, which determines the coverage of the ground, and their coloring. Conventions for coverage probably developed alongside the gendering of cloth during the latter half of our period. By the early 1900s, white-ground men's shirtings were based on 15 to 25 percent color: 15 percent for medium-weight materials, 20 percent for Oxfords, and more for zephyrs. Men's shirtings had above all to be clean-looking, with emphasis on whiteness. Women's dress goods required upwards of 25 percent color, aiming at distinctiveness, delicacy of coloring, and a light appearance.[76] The goal in both cases was one of visual balance in which neither stripe nor ground strikes the eye first. While obeying the rules, stripes could still vary in character from subdued to sharply-defined giving a range of possibilities to suit the personality of the wearer. While conformity to dress codes was observed in the large, the desire for personal expression could be afforded by the small.

FLANNELETTE: VOLATILE FASHIONS

The light cotton dress materials that were worn throughout our period were extraordinarily perilous in Western homes where fires were used for heating during the winter months. Untreated cotton is highly flammable, igniting from a single spark and propagating flame unless extinguished or suffocated. The risks were well known in the eighteenth century when cotton was mainly confined to accessories such as sleeve ruffles or aprons, but became much greater when whole garments were composed of cotton, and were further heightened by the introduction of the cage crinoline.[77] Unsupervised children were especially vulnerable. "Another death from burning" is frequently reported in newspapers through the mid-nineteenth century alongside warnings: "As the winter is coming on—a season in which a week scarcely occurs that we have not the melancholy task of recording the deaths of two or three children from fire [. . .] we would strongly urge upon parents, among the labouring classes especially, to clothe their children in woollen dresses . . ."[78] Chemical rinses were recommended to give flame retardant properties, with alum and borax probably the most effective, but these chemicals dusted off in wear, and had to be renewed with each wash.

The flammability problem rose to a head again in the 1890s with the proliferation of flannelette nightwear (Figure 1.12). Flannelette is a raised cotton calico, and the fine, downy nap is especially susceptible to flame which flashes over the surface. The loosely-woven and cheaper varieties bought by the working classes were even more easily ignited. It wasn't until 1912 that a commercially-viable fireproofing treatment able to withstand washing was discovered (Perkin's stannic oxide process), and supplies of non-inflammable flannelette were available from Whipp Brothers & Tod of Manchester.[79] In 1913, the Fabrics (Misdescription) Act began to provide the British consumer with protection from unscrupulous merchants selling fugitive fire-proofed flannelettes as permanent. So we find in the final years of our period a transition to the contemporary attitude toward fabric safety—one of legislation and regulation.

RUBBER AND WHALEBONE: MOULDED BY UNSUSTAINABILITY

The long nineteenth century saw the expansion or transformation of several manufactures employing non-textile materials: straw for millinery, jet for jewelry, and steel for corsetry. One of the few truly new introductions was rubber: a material sourced from imperial plantations. Nancy Rexford has outlined the introduction of rubber for waterproof garments, shoes, and elastic webbing; and the rainwear industry has been treated by Sarah Levitt.[80] But it is worth drawing attention to rubber as an early instance of a material not expected to last the lifespan of the garment. A trademark stamp of 1885 used on rubber goring for shoes by a Boston firm included "a date mark of the month it was made, stamped on the white back of the goring [. . .] included because it was advertised to wear eighteen months after it was made . . ."[81] This seems to signal a significant change in attitude; clothes were no longer something expected to outlive the wearer.

Another change of outlook is signified by the alarm about the threat to animals hunted in the name of fashion. Robin Doughty has thoroughly covered the topic of feather fashions and the rise of bird protection societies.[82] Curiously, whales did not arouse similar feelings. Although whales were sought mainly for their oil and spermaceti, whalebone for fashion use was more than a mere by-product, and provided the reason for fishing particular species. The right whale (*Balena mysticetus*) found near Greenland yielded whalebone of the finest quality, black and highly elastic.[83] By the mid-1850s, overfishing meant that whalebone was in short supply just when it was wanted for cage crinoline manufacture, leading to prices nearly doubling.[84] In 1866, it was recognized that "for more than two centuries [. . .] ceaseless warfare, carried on chiefly by the English, Dutch, and Danish whalers [. . .] brought the species to the verge of extinction."[85] Low stocks led whalers to pursue the common rorqual (*Balenoptera musculus*) in the southern oceans although its whalebone was of inferior quality, of slate-color variegated with yellow or brown. Crinoline makers made use of this lesser quality by braiding strips together into lengthy bands; the black braiding thread hiding the color variation. Unlike the hunting of birds, the destructiveness of whale fishing did not enter public consciousness. The song bird was part of childhood lessons in virtue, but whales were remote from daily life.

FIGURE 1.12: Dacca Mills flannelette, from Rylands & Sons Ltd. Manchester price list 1923, p. 40. Manchester Metropolitan University Library.

The Romantic era viewed nature as a gift of Providence for the use of humankind. Priscilla Wakefield (1800: 4–7) explains: "We may admire the goodness of Providence, who leaves not the most obscure corner of the globe without its peculiar riches . . ." further expounding, "Providence has wisely endued mankind with as great a variety of inclinations and pursuits, as there is diversity in their persons; some shew a very early inclination for a sea-life that no danger can deter [. . .] which appears to be implanted for the purpose of providing the means of an intercourse between the inhabitants of distant countries, by which each party may reap advantage by interchanging the superfluous produce of distant climes. . ."[86] Wakefield thus justifies at once the exploitation of natural resources and imperial trade.[87]

CONCLUSIONS

We began by positing novelty as a major driver of change for fashion materials during the long nineteenth century. Certainly, manufacturers producing patterned goods felt the relentless drive for novelty: "Every calico-printer must have the means of producing a constant succession of new patterns [. . .] although millions of patterns have preceded those of any particular year, yet the patterns each year must be stamped with the characteristic of novelty, or they will not sell."[88] Novelties by definition have a brief life span and novel fabrics can only survive if they are refreshed by new variations. Checked silks were updated by seasonal changes over a lengthy period, but novel designs were not sufficient to sustain the fashionability of purple prints. As novelty wore off in the home market, goods often found new markets in the Empire. Such was the case with purple prints, and the indigo prints that preceded them; and we have also seen this strategy employed with lappet muslins, gambroons and mourning crapes.

Dress materials served to embody values of the age. In the new calicos, nankeens, and mixture fabrics, we find not only the embracing of machine production, but the ability of machines to transform and even domesticate a foreign staple. Here, the new represented a modernity which believed in progress, and in the commercial underpinnings of imperial power. Mechanical production and finishing processes brought a new uniformity to the surface of cloth, a flawlessness unknown previously, and the increasing uniformity of surface was endowed with ideologies of virtue. This could act counter to mixture fabrics; for a time pure, undyed alpaca was the ultimate in refinement—its flawless, smooth surface projecting sobriety and understated wealth.

The materials of fashionable dress can be dangerous, in different ways, to those who procure them, those who make them, and those who wear them. The adoption of cotton dresses in an era of open fires and candlelight may seem a preposterous choice, but the risks undertaken for such fashions serve to underline the depth of the underlying values that support them. As the century progressed, there appears to have been a shift in belief: that safety was not simply a personal matter, but it was the collective responsibility of manufacturers to solve dilemmas within their domain. As to the animals whose lives were endangered by fashion, there was an awakening consciousness brought about by the excesses in feather fashions toward the end of our period that represented a shift from belief in a providential nature to a nature that must be cared for.

The oscillation between class distinction and leveling through fabrics provided a creative tension throughout our period. Delaines saw a move to loud hand-blocked patterns in the mid-1840s to counter the new machine printed versions. Practicalities were welcomed by fashion when new, but later shunned. With khaki drill, a textile finally marks a shift in class values, finding nobility in the common soldier, who partakes of the color of the earth, and was sadly often returned to it.

The gendering of textiles has been observed throughout our period. Printed shirtings formed a case where designs were re-gendered to exert a continued demand. In stripes we saw a rigid gender code that ascribed color and delicacy to women, and cleanly appearance to men. The creation of gabardine not only allowed women to enjoy outdoor leisure pursuits once limited to men, but saw lightness of weight as the final delimiter of the gender divide.

Finally, the anxieties of the age show the tensions between extravagance and sobriety played out in an ambivalence toward bright and matte lusters seen in mixture fabrics and crêpes. Anxiety about modernity was also found in the espousal of the natural patterning of moiré antique. Isabella Ducrot compares the interacting forces present in woven cloth to the rhythmic alteration of breathing, "systoles and diastoles, contractions and distensions," a metaphor for life itself.[89] Textiles embody the aspirations and struggles of people during the long nineteenth century, marking imperial ambitions, a belief in progress, class and gender distinctions, and a drive for change fed by new anxieties as well as novelty.

CHAPTER TWO

Production and Distribution

SUSAN HINER

In the twilight of a Paris evening, the colonne Vendôme rises in the background, and twinkling shops close for the night as groups of smartly-dressed women stroll along the rue de la Paix, some released from their day's work at the Maison Paquin, one of the premier fashion houses of the Belle Époque, and others perhaps patrons of that same shop. Jean Béraud, known for his lively Paris street scenes, captures the bustle of quitting time for the seamstresses of Paris's elite *couturiers* at the turn of the twentieth century, when approximately 90,000 women worked in the French fashion industry, many in couture *ateliers* on this very street (Figure 2.1).[1] To the right, "Paquin" appears in gold letters over the storefront *atelier* and showroom of Jeanne Paquin, a celebrated female designer in a domain largely dominated by men. The word "modes" appears on both sides of the back corner building just beneath the illuminated window in the distant left of the painting, which depicts the rue de la Paix as one of Paris's most illustrious fashion streets, where one could find the House of Worth at number 7, along with Doucet, Cartier, and other luxury houses.

As fashion workers and shoppers flood the streets, some in the company of men, some arm-in-arm with other women, almost all toting a handbag—emblematic of the new buying power and public visibility of women—the viewer is struck by the sheer number of female workers and strollers, and by the varied representation of class their dress suggests. Some women trail boas and frothy veils; others wear simple black ties on their shirtwaists, lace shawls, or elaborately embellished hats replete with silk ribbons, bows, and lace; others still wear classic straw hats with a single black ribbon. All these women, regardless of social rank, are accessorized and visibly engaged in the cultural practice of fashion.

Shoppers are nearly indistinguishable from seamstresses because the producers of fashion were also its consumers. Béraud's scene depicts the industry at work precisely when mass production was meeting *haute couture* and women were entering the needle trades in droves, finding paid employment for what had long been considered a gendered domestic duty. "As women entered the paid labor market in increasingly large numbers by the late nineteenth century," writes Nancy Green, "an industrious lower-middle class of female employees and shopkeepers all had both a little more disposable income and more clothing needs to spend it on."[2] Béraud's painting captures the time and place where producer meets consumer and fashionability has been democratized as prêt-à-porter, ironically on the very doorstep of one of *haute couture*'s most elite establishments.

The seamstresses of Paris were not always so visible, however, and the so-called "clothing revolution" of the nineteenth century was not a straightforward process. From the French Revolution to the Great War, fashion and its meanings, modes of production,

FIGURE 2.1: *La rue de la Paix*, Jean Béraud, 1907. Photo by Fine Art Images/Heritage Images/ Getty Images.

and methods of distribution would be radically transformed by modernity and its accompanying shifts in class and gender into a structure that resembles the fashion system of today.

What do we mean when we talk about the production and distribution of fashion? Production is both making and doing, as Susan Kaiser reminds us; fashion production encompasses garment workers who engage in the physical construction and creation of clothing as well as the consumers who engage in the "cultural practice" of fashion.[3] Distribution is equally multifaceted and can be conceived as both material and representational, ranging from activities associated with the transport and delivery of goods to buyers to the representational practices of marketing, fashion writing, advertising, display, and branding.[4] Production and distribution are thus interdependent processes inseparable from consumption itself.

Fashion is a cultural and social process—verbal, visual, and imaginary—as much as a material artifact. Its social function was perhaps most significant during the social upheavals of the nineteenth century. As Clare Crowston puts it, referring to fashion's capacity to empower people across class even as early as the seventeenth century, it "was an urban, particularly Parisian form of cultural capital, in which the *grisette* [fashion worker] could be 'richer' than a provincial noblewoman."[5] This observation points to what some have called the nineteenth-century revolutions in fashion. Just as gender binaries reflected and reproduced by fashion became ever more deeply entrenched, class distinctions grew more fluid, leading to both cultural anxieties and remarkable innovations and transformations. The production and distribution of fashion are as much about the networks of promotion and circulation—the fashion press, behavioral guides, and other marketing tools—as they are about the "real" spaces of garment making and retailing, the objects produced and sold, and the people who create and buy them.

Paris was the indisputable hub of these interdependent activities. Regina Blaszczyk describes the scope of the nineteenth-century "Parisian fashion-industrial complex" as encompassing "dressmakers, textile mills, dyers, and countless firms in ancillary businesses—the shoemakers, milliners, corset makers, stocking knitters, jewelers, parasol shops, beaders, ribbon makers, feather dyers, and more."[6] Not only the design and manufacture of fashion, but also the authors of its engines of marketing and dissemination—the fashion press and accompanying images and patterns for home sewing—were primarily located in Paris. Furthermore, Paris fashions circulated widely throughout Europe and the Americas through the networks of the fashion press, along with plates and descriptions originating in French publications like *Le Journal des Dames et des Modes*, *Modes de Paris*, and *La Mode illustrée* appropriated by journals such as *Godey's Lady's Book* and *Harper's* in the United States and *La Belle Assemblée* and *The Queen* in Britain.[7] Paris was the center of a vast distribution network of both goods and their representations.

This chapter thus focuses primarily on Paris, the "capital of the nineteenth century," in Walter Benjamin's famous formulation, and epicenter of the fashion industry—indeed, the "international capital of style," as Valerie Steele has asserted.[8] From the workrooms or *ateliers* behind the *modiste*'s and dressmaker's seductive storefronts to the specialty artisans, from the bustling halls of the great department stores of the mid-nineteenth century to the quiet studies of solitary fashion chroniclers, nineteenth-century Paris was indeed the crucible of fashion design, production, marketing, and distribution.

While the geographical focus of this chapter is logically Paris, its organizing themes are class and gender, for the production of fashion and its distribution to consumers were controlled and orchestrated through gendered and classed systems—social, spatial, and sexual. The face of nineteenth-century fashion, incarnate in the great *couturiers*, such as Charles Frederick Worth, who is credited with inventing *haute couture* in 1858, appeared as only the most visible (male) players in a veritable army of (mostly female) fashion workers.[9]

Gender and class were increasingly important categories in both the creation and consumption of nineteenth-century fashion: women fashion workers progressively had more autonomy over the dressing of female clients and entered the workforce visibly by the century's end, as we saw in Béraud's painting. Further, fashions themselves diverged dramatically along gender lines. At the level of class, nineteenth-century garment workers and petit-bourgeois shop workers could acquire fashion knowledge and learn to navigate shifting codes of distinction, even as they produced fashion. The slipperiness of social status was all the more potent as more people learned the signs of distinction and its codes. Similarly, the arbiters of taste, the legions of (primarily female) nineteenth-century fashion writers made legible those codes for an ever widening readership, and the artists who illustrated changing fashions each week provided guidance and models for copying. As the century progressed, social mobility and the democratization of fashion went hand-in-hand.[10]

This chapter considers essential figures, like tailors and seamstresses, core fabricators of the fundamentals of fashion; I will also discuss figures who emerged or came into their own in the nineteenth century—in particular *modistes* and *calicots*, both newcomers to the social landscape of modernity. Straddling production and consumption, these figures were at the heart of the fashion system, and the evolution of their roles over the century mirrored the structural transformations of the fashion industry wrought by modernity. *Couturiers* with their critical role in imagining and implementing *haute couture* are also key figures—

nineteenth-century reinterpretations of the figureheads of the paternalistic medieval guilds system. Finally, the Belle Epoque *midinettes*, those fashion-conscious Parisian garment workers and salesgirls whose nickname arose because they left the workshop or counter for lunch at noon (*midi*), illustrate the transformation of women's work in the nineteenth century and, in turn, hint at the disruptions in labor practices the twentieth century would bring. Together, these figures show the gendering and classing of fashion production and distribution throughout the century and offer a view into its social organization.

The changing spaces of fashion production and distribution are also important. From the *atelier* to the *grand magasin*, modes of production and consumption shifted dramatically over the course of the century and with the rise of modernity. The *magasins de nouveautés*, or fancy goods stores of the 1820s, 1830s, and 1840s, eventually developed into the vast emporiums of the second half of the century—department stores that revolutionized shopping and led to innovations we take for granted today, such as fixed pricing, standardized sizing, mail order, and home delivery.[11] Many of these practices were in fact already in place in the *magasins de nouveautés* during the first part of the century.[12] New technologies such as the sewing machine would also shape production and consumption and the expanding spaces needed to distribute fashion. Advertising increased with printing technology in the mid-nineteenth century, and fashion journals offered not only descriptive illustrations of changing trends but also product placement and endorsements of certain fashion houses.[13]

Nineteenth-century fashion became a paradoxical site of social contention enacted through the mechanisms of production and distribution: fashion as *haute couture* struggled to perpetuate elite class distinction, while fashion as democratic prêt-à-porter enabled social mobility. This chapter considers both poles of fashion production and distribution: first, the principal figures engaged in fashion production, from the lowly seamstress to the *couturier*, with particular attention to the ways in which these figures were understood and reproduced in visual and print culture; and second, the spaces of fashion distribution, focusing on the evolution of the department store and how the rise of the fashion press both foreshadows and replicates it.

FASHION PRODUCERS

In France, as elsewhere in Europe, since the Middle Ages, laws had governed the cutting of cloth and the design of garments for both women and men. This was a long-standing legal arrangement, residual from the medieval guild system, which rigidly organized labor along gender lines.[14] Men held exclusive rights to clothing design and the cutting of cloth—master tailors considered skilled enough to handle virgin fabrics and sharp tools, and intellectually equipped to envision abstract design; they oversaw daughters and wives, as well as hired seamstresses, many of whom worked from home, in the less important and less well-paid work of garment construction. As Waddell explains: "Being able to cut deftly, precisely and with verve is a great part of the tailor's art and why of course they were called tailors, from *tailler*, the French for 'to cut.'"[15] The tailors' guild thus exercised great power in the fashion industry from well before 1675, when Louis XIV finally legitimized the seamstresses' guild.[16] Until then, women had worked largely clandestinely and were subject to fines and seizure of fabric if they were caught infringing on the tailors' legal territory. This long-standing association with clandestine work, as well as the penury in which many seamstresses lived, no doubt contributed to the persistent association of seamstresses with prostitution. Louis XIV's edict granted them certain rights, but it would be decades before women dressmakers enjoyed the success and exclusivity of their male counterparts.

Sewing was the domain of seamstresses (*couturières*), whose seamless construction nearly rendered their existence figuratively invisible, but literally as well, since they typically worked out of public view in an *atelier* or at home. The refreshing and embellishment of garments, on the other hand, was the domain of *modistes*, who, in some cases, owned highly visible, successful shops. *Couturières* and *modistes* thus occupied different spaces in the social hierarchy of the garment industry; *modistes* had more influence and achieved greater recognition in the late eighteenth and early nineteenth centuries.

The cultural imagination, however, saw both seamstresses and *modistes* as women of loose morals. Their workshops were often depicted as licentious spaces permitting gender and class mixing, as in the Monnier print of 1826 (Figure 2.2). Here the seamstresses are dressed in the style of the period, roughly sketched in the background but clearly engaged in watching the antics of the two men roughhousing in the foreground. The top-hatted gentleman at the left

Henry Monnier   Lith. de Senefelder.

Attelier de Couture.
Gown maker's work-Room.

FIGURE 2.2: *Atelier de Couture* (*Gown maker's Work-room*), Henry Monnier, 1826.

is engaged in a conversation—or a transaction—with the *maîtresse*, identifiable from her more sober dress and hairstyle. The girl in pink to the far right, the youngest and most demure, seems engrossed in her sewing. Might she be the object of a transaction? A visible parallel between the structure of the *atelier* and that of the brothel emerges; this image suggests the repeated links between the two spaces throughout the century.

Seamstresses and female dressmakers largely took over the design and construction of clothing for women, while men's tailoring remained the purview of tailors and was heavily influenced by English style from the end of the eighteenth century. Standardization in clothing, the first step toward mechanization, began with menswear. As Green details, this occurred first in the 1820s in the United States when tailors "began using their slack time to make up garments ahead of time" for sailors, and in the 1830s and 1840s in France as workshops opened to produce military uniforms.[17] The growing influence of bourgeois values after the French Revolution helped propel the black suit to prominence, and the era of the so-called "great masculine renunciation" would endure even to this day.[18] Ready-made clothing for women appeared much later, beginning with outerwear in the 1870s; and by the end of the century, ready-made was standard in women's clothing.

Certain dressmakers, like certain tailors, became celebrities in the early nineteenth century: Rose Bertin, originally the *modiste* to Marie-Antoinette, became her dressmaker and continued to dress the aristocracy after the French Revolution. Louis Hippolyte Leroy was dressmaker to Josephine Bonaparte and Napoleon's court; and Victorine and Palmire, dressmakers to the aristocracy of the July Monarchy (1830–48), were frequently cited in the fashion press, which distinguished them from the many anonymous dressmakers of the era.[19] Dressmakers, like *modistes*, earned their reputations through apprenticeships— Victorine had worked for Leroy and would become the teacher-*maîtresse* to Palmire and others.[20] There was thus an almost genealogical structure that transmitted artisanal craftsmanship and expertise.[21] Through skill, a young apprentice could work her way up the hierarchy of the *atelier*: from *trottin* (delivery girl) to one of the anonymous *petites mains* (literally, little hands), low-level workers responsible for the grinding work of sewing, finally achieving the higher rank of *seconde*, or even *première* (head seamstress).

Early forms of fashion advertising included the dressing of a *poupée de la mode,* or a *pandore*—an outfitted fashion doll, sometimes life-sized, which would be sent to various aristocratic clients across Europe, who could then order versions of the fashions seen on the traveling doll. With the explosion of the fashion press, however, these *ambassadrices de la mode* became obsolete, and the names of celebrity dressmakers and tailors appeared in fashion magazines, where colored plates illustrated their fashions, with descriptions and addresses for avid consumers. They could also find publicity through literary outlets, such as the novels of Balzac, whose hero Lucien de Rubempré was dressed by the celebrity tailor Staub, Balzac's own tailor![22] Likewise, although Worth eclipsed other dressmakers of the Second Empire in France, and indeed in Europe and the United States, Perrot reminds us that "great couturières like Mmes Roger, Laferière, . . . Mlle Félicie and Laure still retained their prestige, as did milliners Mmes Virot, Rebout, and Braudès."[23] In a culture of growing bourgeois wealth and social mobility, visible displays of status were increasingly vital to establishing one's social position—a fashionable tailor or dressmaker could thus guarantee social ascendancy, as novels such as Balzac's *Le Père Goriot* (1835) or Zola's *La Curée* (1871) detail.

In spite of, or perhaps because of, the odd social power they wielded, tailors were often ridiculed in the popular press, as in Daumier's 1835 caricature (Figure 2.3). This tailor, whose name Daumier speculates as "Wahaterkermann" or "Pikprunman," is possibly a

FIGURE 2.3: "Le Tailleur," Types Français, Honoré Daumier, 1835. © The Trustees of the British Museum.

spoof of the two most famous tailors of the period—Staub and Humann—whose popularity helped inspire Louis Huart's 1841 *Physiologie du Tailleur*, as much a mocking critique of the aspiring consumer class as of those who dress them. A bundle of fabric clutched in one arm, the tailor's other, outsized hand suggests the shears indispensable to his trade. The caption reveals that while this tailor can cut his own clothes in the latest fashion, he lacks the taste and distinction of the bourgeois, since his hat and boots do not equal the splendor of his suit.[24]

A variation on the paternalistic guild structure reemerged with the great fashion houses of the mid-nineteenth century, for the gendered stratification of the nineteenth-century *couturier*'s workshop in many ways reproduced the earlier guild system. In the latter half of the nineteenth century, male designers, or *couturiers*, dominated high fashion, displacing the female dressmaker from the pinnacle of the industry's hierarchy and employing vast numbers of seamstresses and other workers. Worth was reported to have employed 1,200 such workers by 1871.[25] Along with the many sales clerks, male and female, who, as illustrated in Zola's *Au Bonheur des Dames* of 1883, worked on commission and struggled to get ahead in a hierarchical work force, department stores also "employed hundreds of seamstresses" who "received none of the benefits of the employees, such as free lodging or medical care."[26] Before turning to the rise of *haute couture*, the fashion designer, and the spaces of modernity that characterize fashion in the nineteenth century, let us look first at two types of fashion workers who were cultural and social products and agents of the early nineteenth century—cousins of the seamstresses and tailors we have been discussing.

MODISTES AND CALICOTS

Because they were close to fashion—that magical process and object through which identities could be reinvented—fashion workers and sales people aroused cultural anxiety in groups who saw a stable hierarchy as the desired social structure. As is apparent in Daumier's tailor caricature, the fashion worker both *is* a social climber and *enables* social climbing for the rising petit bourgeois. Rendered both seductive and repugnant—a paradox evoking old associations with the evils of fashion and its links to luxury and venality—figures of fashion workers, in both visual and print culture, take on a variety of signifying forms in the nineteenth century.

The *modiste* emerges at the end of the eighteenth century, when the long-restricted seamstresses' guild had finally gained enough ground against the male tailors' guild to have a measure of autonomy.[27] Because of this rise in status and expansion of the seamstresses' scope of work, other fashion workers began to appear and stake their territory, in particular the *marchandes de modes*, female fashion merchants, forerunners to the *modistes*, "who emerged from the shadows of the mercers' guild in mid-century and soon overshadowed the seamstresses in commercial status and prestige."[28] The *marchandes de modes* decorated the seamstresses' product by artfully arranging laces, cloth, and other accessories to create a stylish package. In 1776, however, the *marchandes* were accorded corporation status in France and were allowed to "make dresses, rather than just trim them," a new right that allowed these stylists and dress embellishers to rise in status and visibility and enabled them to dictate fashion trends.[29] The empowering of the individual stylist—Worth and, later, Chanel were known as "the dictators" of fashion—who created looks for famous (aristocratic) clients, shifted decisions about fabrics, silhouette, accessories, etc., to the designer/stylist and away from the client, thus changing the relationship model and paving the way, eventually, for the emergence of the *couturier* in the later nineteenth century.

Despite the celebrity of a Rose Bertin, much mystery still surrounds the genealogy of the *marchande de modes*, and this explains to a certain extent the continued confusion over the figure's evolution to *modiste* and its narrowing to milliner in the nineteenth century. Jennifer Jones writes: "the confusion over the origins of the *marchandes de modes* is telling. These women, who became the principal fashion merchants of their day, had risen, so to speak, from within the cracks in the corporate system."[30] This murkiness—regarding her origins, status, and activities—contributes to the more generalized instability surrounding the *modiste* of the late nineteenth century, which created an imaginative space ripe for mythologizing.[31]

From the beginning, then, the *modiste* inhabited a shadowy space, occupying a unique position like her ancestress, the *marchande de modes*. Tied in part to bygone practices of Old Regime extravagance, *modistes* were also progressive, their work combining old and new, thus literally allowing them to incarnate the paradoxical mechanism of fashion, which both refers to the past and introduces novelty. The *modistes* also formed connective tissue between consumers and producers, following fashion as well as introducing trends, as illustrated in the fashionable attire and coquettish poses of *modistes* at work trimming bonnets and closing a sale in this 1820s popular print (Figure 2.4).

Staples of the *modiste*'s trade proliferate in this print—the sign, or *enseigne*, which names the owner, Flore; the stacks of hatboxes, or *cartons*, suggesting the pleasures of luxury consumption; the wall of heavily ornamented bonnets behind the two seated *modistes* embellishing headwear with feathers, flowers, ribbons, etc., and the traditional black worker's apron worn by two of them. The object suggestively grasped between the knees of the *modiste* busy at work in the lower right corner is a *marotte*, or *tête* (head),

FIGURE 2.4: *La Marchande de Modes*, J.J. Chalon, 1822.

used in the fashioning of hats. Bald and rouged, this *marotte*'s strange gaze slyly replicates that of the top-hatted gentleman, who scrutinizes through his eyepiece not the elaborate bonnet his female companion seems to covet, but rather, the pretty *modiste* displaying her wares. Indeed, this scene stages a complex network of gazes that expresses the fundamental eroticism associated with consumption. Shopping and sexuality were already part of the visual lexicon of fashion, and *modistes* in particular were subject to conflation with prostitutes, due in part to their visibility as workers or saleswomen, and in the streets.

As Figure 2.4 illustrates, their *ateliers* doubled as shops for commerce, making workspace and marketplace interchangeable. The *modiste* was thus poised on the threshold of multiple identities, spaces, and functions, and this liminality only increased the potential to mythologize her. Roche develops further the particular task of the *modiste*, who, more than any other fashion worker, was responsible for creating the concept of fashion as a complex dance between old and new, "the triumph of artifice."[32] It was also, quite evidently, the art of salesmanship, as this caricature from the 1830s amply illustrates (Figure 2.5).

Bouchot's *marchande de modes* wears her wares—scarves, cacophonous fabrics, mismatched gloves, hat, bag, etc.—and from each item dangles a price tag. This female fashion merchant, while incarnating the abundance of consumable ready-to-wear goods available for purchase, is the opposite of elegant. Indeed, she figures commodification itself, a cultural slippage that became a key feature of nineteenth-century representations of *modistes* and other female fashion workers.

The figure of the *modiste* throughout the century is fraught with moral ambiguity: she seems to have distilled both cultural fears about the promiscuity of working women and fascination with her magical powers of aesthetic creation. She also repeatedly appears using the tools of her trade—hatpins, head forms, hats, and hat boxes—to comically contest the role that social and gender hierarchy had designated for her. By the end of the nineteenth century, the *modiste* was a trope of impressionist painting, indicating prostitution and the plight of the female worker.[33] Female fashion workers laboring, toiling in the *ateliers* of Paris couture at the turn of the twentieth century and into its first few decades can trace their lineage to the *modistes* of the end of the eighteenth and nineteenth centuries—figures consistently cast as poised on the threshold between innocence and experience, eligibility and spinsterhood, marriage and work.

If the *modiste* was constructed as a hyper-sexualized fashion worker, skilled at both fashion production and sales, whose emergence and mythology mark the transition from the visible, legible rigidity of Old Regime fashion institutions to the greater fluidity of modernity, another figure, the *calicot*, is her caricatured male counterpart. A salesman of fashion goods at the bottom of the commercial class who emerged in the first quarter of the nineteenth century in France, the *calicot* has an illustrious literary and iconographic history, through which the mythology of the salesman as a (failed) seducer of women became irrevocably tied to social climbing and fashion. While the *modiste* was at the top of the social hierarchy of female garment workers, the *calicot* was a poor relation of the tailor.

Calicots were drapers' assistants, working in dry goods and fabric shops and engaging in commerce, not clothing construction. Drapers sold notions and fabric by the yard to clients who would then take their uncut fabric to a dressmaker or tailor whom they would consult about designing and constructing the garment. This multilayered process changed dramatically with the rise of the designer and the concomitant rise of the department store, both of which effectively cut out the middleman.

Much like the *modiste*, who was mythologized as a loose woman in order to compensate for her potential to rise socially (via fashion) in the new society of

FIGURE 2.5: *La Marchande de Modes*, Frédéric Bouchot, 1815–50. Courtesy of The Lewis Walpole Library, Yale University.

nineteenth-century France, the *calicot* also illustrates French nineteenth-century class anxiety, imbricated as it was with both male (commercial) mobility and female (consumer) desire. Even in the eighteenth century, when they were still making clothes for women, tailors had a reputation for being effeminate. This was a kind of cultural repression or coping mechanism that allowed men to accept another man's eyes and hands on the bodies of their wives, mistresses, or daughters. "A special intimacy, a diffuse eroticism fluttered about these shops because the tailor could see and touch the bodies of his customers."[34]

Visual culture surrounding the *calicot* takes this feminization to an extreme. Consistently portrayed as foppish, with curled hair, fetishized moustache, and a form-fitting coat, he wears exaggerated spurs to suggest a (false) association with the heroes of Napoleon's *Grande Armée* and is frequently ridiculed for both his attempts to seduce ladies and his inadequacy to that task (Figure 2.6).

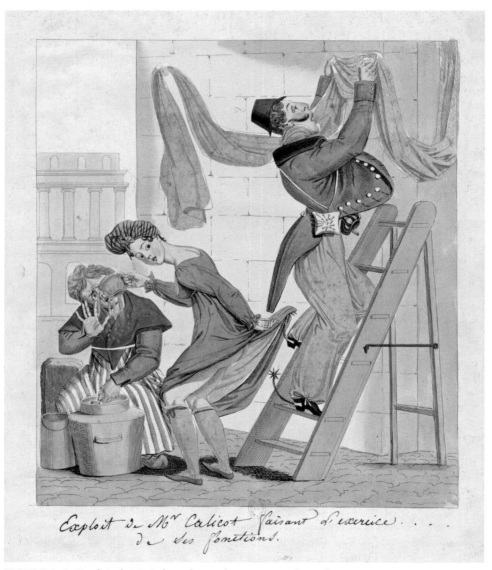

FIGURE 2.6: *Exploit de M. Calicot faisant l'exercice . . . de ses fonctions*, 1826–30. Bibliothèque nationale de France.

The awkward "exercise of his functions" referred to by the caption was called "*la montre*," the draping of fabric outside a shop to show off goods that could be acquired within, common practice before the advent of sidewalks, when goods became displayed at eye level in shop windows. Hardly the knowing seducer here, the *calicot* catches his hyperbolic spurs on the serving girl's hem, lifting her skirt to reveal her naked bottom and punning on "*la montre*"—the display. Despite his obliviousness, the *calicot*, combining pretensions of military prowess with effeminacy, is exposed as dangerous to the virtue of young ladies (even working-class ones) and consequently productive of chaos.[35] With his cavalier yawn and feigned association with the cavalry, the *calicot* is revealed as a fraud.

The *calicot,* so named for the cloth he sold in abundance in the first quarter of the nineteenth century from the counters of drapers' shops, had direct access to female clients; he dressed fashionably to encourage sales and was viewed as a vain, foppish figure. Widely caricatured on the vaudeville stage and in print, the *calicot* would eventually evolve into the department-store sales clerk, also sometimes called a *calicot*, as much for the nature of his work as for his reputation for smarmy seduction of female clients. The *calicot* should be read on a continuum with the *modiste*, who also supposedly traded in erotics. Like the *modiste,* the *calicot* was conflated in the popular imagination with the rising commercial class and unchecked sexuality, as exemplified in Émile Zola's character Octave Mouret, primary protagonist in two of his most famous novels, *Pot-Bouille* and *Au Bonheur des Dames,* of the 1880s, which detail the commercial transition mid-century from boutiques and fancy-goods stores to department stores. Zola's fictional portrayal of the founding and expansion of the Bon Marché remains a most useful illustration of this historical transition.[36]

THE INVENTION OF *HAUTE COUTURE*

Charles Frederick Worth is the name most frequently associated with the rise of the fashion designer and the world of *haute couture*, although, as noted earlier, celebrity dressmakers and tailors certainly existed before him, and other talented designers (men and women) would emerge alongside him in the second half of the nineteenth century. Worth remains the most influential and well-known *couturier*, likely as a consequence of his associations with the court of France's Second Empire, which opened the doors of other European courts, his English origins that gave access to the Anglophone world, and his resultant appeal to wealthy American "Grand Tourists." While he is understood as the father of *haute couture*, Worth was also responsible for many innovations in the fashion industry; and, although *haute couture* is by definition an elite enterprise focused on the creation of fashion as individual distinction and exclusivity, many of Worth's changes parallel those associated with mass culture and the department store.

Worth began, essentially, as a Parisian *calicot*, having immigrated to Paris from his native England in 1845. He worked as a sales clerk at Gagelin-Opigez et Cie, a *magasin de nouveautés*, or dry goods store. Gagelin specialized in shawls and wraps; here Worth met his future wife and muse, Marie Vernet, who was working as a *demoiselle de magasin*, or house mannequin—modeling coats, shawls, and the like for clients.[37] These kinds of outerwear garments, as pictured in the fashion plate from 1859 in Figure 2.7, showing the name "Gagelin" on the dress box in the foreground, were the first to be mass-produced for women as they required a less exacting fit and were thus available at stores, where alterations could occur. Worth's rise began at Gagelin, where in the early 1850s he initiated and became the head of a dressmaking department within the store, a "radical

FIGURE 2.7: Fashion plate: "*Suzanne, Gonzalve, Marguarita, Fonti, Zilda*," *Journal des Demoiselles*, May 1859. © Victoria and Albert Museum, London.

innovation," according to Anne Hollander, since ready-made women's clothing was not the practice yet and would not become institutionalized until the end of the nineteenth century.[38] In 1857–8 he started his own business partnership with a Swedish tailor, Otto Bobergh, in the rue de la Paix. With the contacts he had established at Gagelin with French textile manufacturers, plus his own strong reputation for expertise with fabric, color, and design, Worth created a new business model: he "provided his customers with everything—the conception, the fabrics, the details, the execution."[39]

Like Rose Bertin before him, Worth was more than a tailor; he was an image-maker who promoted his own individual taste and creativity to establish himself as premier tastemaker of the third quarter of the nineteenth century. His big break came when the Princess Pauline de Metternich, wife of a Viennese diplomat and a quirky Parisian socialite, became his client and introduced him to the Empress Eugénie, who engaged Worth the next day. Princess Pauline and Empress Eugénie subsequently brought to him the courts of Europe and, later, the wives of wealthy American industrialists, eager to establish their own standing among the European aristocracy.

Worth's designs were influenced by his passion for historic costume and his intimate knowledge of fabric. They capitalized on newly available fabrics such as ethereal, gauzy tulle and patterned silks commissioned from the Lyon silk factories that could be draped in waves and flounces over the wide expanse of the crinoline. His designs aptly expressed the values of Louis-Napoleon's Second Empire, with its agenda of recreating the grand, luxurious spectacle of earlier monarchies.[40] The glittering court was decked out in excess, and Worth's opulent designs flowed over the massive crinolines of the 1850s and 1860s, representing the wealth and delicacy of the ladies who wore them and the magnificence

FIGURE 2.8: Illustration after *The Empress Eugenie Surrounded by Her Ladies in Waiting*,
Franz-Xaver Winterhalter, 1855. Photo by Buyenlarge/Getty Images.

of the Empire in which they flourished. Although Franz-Xaver Winterhalter's 1855
painting *The Empress Eugenie Surrounded by Her Ladies in Waiting* (Figure 2.8) was
created before Worth's shop opened in 1858, it is a glorious representation of the style
and aesthetic that would make Worth famous. Both artists served and benefited from the
same illustrious clientele.

Ironically, under yards of diaphanous tulle and pastel silk, velvety ribbons, and spidery
lace—materials that incarnate fragility, reflecting in the garments the idealized elements
of nineteenth-century femininity, such as white, silken skin, flowing lines, and delicacy—
hidden beneath was the steel cage that kept it all afloat. Technology, involving "whalebone,
cane, and inflatable india rubber tubes," was developed, but the cage crinoline "made of
fabric-covered steel springs" would provide "light-weight support for the voluminous
skirts of the mid-century."[41] Widely caricatured, the crinoline's imposing size made a
showpiece of the woman who wore it even as it bolstered the textile industries in Lyon
and elsewhere, and employed crinoline makers in factories. The caricature from 1859 at
the height of the crinoline craze (*la crinolonomanie*) depicting the interior of an omnibus
illustrates the exaggerated size of the hoop skirt and hints at the erotic potential of the
swaying movement of the skirt, which could reveal a dainty foot or ankle; this image, of
course, also exposes the mechanism behind the effect, as the "cage" peeps out from under
the flounces of two ladies' skirts (Figure 2.9).

The women seem oblivious to the excessive volume of their dresses, and the placid
look on the face of the lady in the center belies the difficulty she must have in sitting on a
public transport bench in such a getup.[42] The story the picture doesn't tell is that of the

FIGURE 2.9: *Paris Grotesque*, 1859. © Musée Carnavalet/Roger-Viollet/TopFoto.

many deaths reported of women whose huge, gauzy skirts caught fire when they inadvertently came too close to a candle or fire; unable to gauge their own girth, the women would go up in flames, the fire fed by the "air under the cage of the crinoline."[43]

Worth is credited with changing the feminine silhouette in the 1860s and 1870s, first through his reshaping of the crinoline as the bell, and then through his invention of the bustle (Figure 2.10). Perhaps more significant, however, was his grasp of the business of fashion and his capitalization on its cyclical nature. This, along with his talent for securing wealthy, trend-setting clients cultivated through his international reputation and relationships with the aristocracy, made Worth the most renowned of *couturiers*.

Under the direction of his two sons, the House of Worth would endure into the twentieth century, buoyed not only by Worth senior's reputation for creativity and his associations with the wealthy classes of Europe and America, but also by the business-savvy diffusion of his models. These were samples designed by Worth (or later, his son Jean-Philippe) and constructed by his staff, worn in the showroom to model the garment. These samples were then purchased by *modistes* and dressmakers who reproduced them in their own *ateliers* and shops. Worth's designs were also diffused through fashion plates, many created by Antoine Sandoz and commissioned by Worth himself to be distributed globally by the fashion press, and patterns, which could be easily reproduced and sold. Pattern pieces were interchangeable, thus allowing dressmakers to mix and match different elements of Worth creations to create new designs.

PUBLISHED WEEKLY.
VOL. XXV. — NUMBER 15.

Copyright, 1892, by HARPER & BROTHERS. *All Rights Reserved.*

NEW YORK, SATURDAY, APRIL 9, 1892.

TEN CENTS A COPY.
WITH A SUPPLEMENT.

DUST CLOAKS FROM WORTH.—[SEE PAGE 286.]

FIGURE 2.10: *Harper's Bazaar*, A. Sandoz, 1892, vol. 25, no. 15. Photo: Steven Taylor, private collection.

Patterns (*patrons*) had long been available for home sewing through many of the popular fashion magazines, and the history of sewing patterns is thus deeply enmeshed with that of the fashion press. Kevin Seligman contends that it was likely in the burgeoning French fashion press at the end of the eighteenth century that "patterns were first presented and offered for purchase through mail order."[44] Many nineteenth-century fashion journals, including the *Journal des Demoiselles*, launched in 1833, offered instruction on moral behavior as well as fashionability to young ladies, providing patterns to accompany their fashion plates. Thus, the reader could approximate a look that was popular on the streets of Paris by using the scaled drawings and working with her local draper to purchase fabric or with her *modiste*, if she were not skilled enough to make the dress at home. Worth thus capitalized on a phenomenon that was already in place—instead of resisting the dissemination and reproduction of his designs, he embraced it.

Worth actively engaged in the industrialization of fashion, even as he strove to cultivate his rarefied identity as an artist—the creator of unique dresses for unique clients. From live models in the showroom, the modeling of new collections, early fashion shows, on-premises tailoring, mass-producing garment parts—like sleeves and bodices that could be mixed and matched—the creation and distribution of patterns and models, Worth's enterprise was already linked to ready-to-wear and more generally to the industrialization of fashion, in spite of his associations with *haute couture*, the opposite of ready-to-wear. As Perrot has pointed out, it was the burgeoning ready-to-wear industry in the domain of dressmaking that initially inspired Worth's modern advances, such as "buying directly from the manufacturer, selling the cloth, and making several models of a garment."[45] Worth's innovations reveal the work of the *couturier* as structurally similar to that of the department store, which did not appear suddenly in the mid-1850s but evolved, rather, from the specialty shops of the first decades of the century.

FASHION SPACES

Early shopping venues like the "passages," or arcades, made famous by Walter Benjamin's magisterial account of nineteenth-century Paris, had already begun to shift consumer practices away from the "closed world of courtly consumption" toward a model that would capitalize on spectacle and mobility, what Rosalind Williams, channeling Benjamin, has called the "dream world of mass consumption."[46]

"The arcades were centres of the luxury-goods trade," housing the *magasins de nouveautés*, which emerged during the Bourbon Restoration (1814–30) and flourished during the July Monarchy (1830–48), largely due to the expansion of the textile industry and more products, allowing shops to stock goods "on the premises."[47] Another early consumer space was the Temple Market, created officially in 1802 to give the wandering fripperers of Paris a static location (and presumably, to get them off the streets); it contributed, albeit at the bottommost rung, to the "distribution of bourgeois clothing"[48] (Figure 2.11).

Vendors here offered used clothing, a form of ready-to-wear, to working-class consumers; and while Temple Market survived into the twentieth century, the new ready-to-wear clothing industry, fostered and rehabilitated by the department store, led ultimately to its disappearance.[49] Other second-hand markets also existed well before the mid-nineteenth century, and some used clothing dealers "also stocked unwanted samples from tailors and dressmakers."[50] Already in the late eighteenth century, *modistes*, who were more like highly skilled stylists and dressmakers than simply hat makers, pieced together entire outfits from the separates they sold—"petticoats, trimmings, ribbons, frills, flounces, and bodices."[51]

827 — LES MARCHES DE PARIS. Marché du Temple Une Marchande à la toilette. ND. Phot.

FIGURE 2.11: Temple Market, n.d. Photo: Steven Taylor, private collection.

Many innovations attributed to the department stores of the mid-century were already in practice at these shops, which evolved from the drapers' and mercers' establishments as these merchants diversified by adding ready-made goods, mounted elaborate displays to draw clients through their doors, and posted fixed, visible prices on merchandise. One such dry goods store, *La Belle Jardinière*, established in 1824 near the Temple Market, introduced an early form of mass production by rationalizing the cutting process through the "simultaneous cutting of several thicknesses of cloth"; here also, one could already find fixed prices—a major innovation attributed to the department stores.[52]

The greatest, yet simplest, innovation of the department store was the elimination of middlemen, thus bringing "products and buyers" together under one vast roof.[53] Through a series of shifts in commercial practices made possible by a new emphasis on scale, speed, and spectacle, the department store created both impulse shopping and shopping as leisure, and new legions of shoppers were brought into the fold. Returns were accepted, credit was available, and alterations were done on the premises; sales clerks were incentivized through commissions; seasonal promotions and regular sales began; prices were visibly marked; members of any class could enter the store and have immediate access to goods; purchases were available for home delivery; and mail order was now possible. The advertising poster for the Grands Magasins de la Paix in Figure 2.12 illustrates clearly the enlarged scale, also showing how the concept of "nouveautés" carries over to the *grand magasin*, as the word appears several times in large black lettering all around the perimeter of the large building.

Carriages bearing the store's name pass in the street, on their way to deliver goods around the city, while other vehicles, possibly taxis, line up outside to deposit or pick up shoppers: mobility and circulation pervade the scene. Crowds line the sidewalks, making their way into the store or looking into the enormous glass display windows, some of

FIGURE 2.12: *Grands Magasins de la Paix*, Jules Chéret, 1875. Bibliothèque nationale de France.

which contain models the same size as the spectators. The massive scale of the building is emphasized by the contrast of the monumental structure with the tiny figures milling about, and the scale of goods is amply illustrated by a textual representation of merchandise. Over the vast windows, words can be deciphered indicating the wide variety of goods inside: laces and silks, scarves and ties, suits, fabric, embroidery, cotton goods and linens, and marriage baskets. The building continues beyond the picture plane and has sides the viewer cannot see, so we may imagine the infinite continuation of this textualization, which of course replicates the abundance of goods within.

Democratization—of both goods and access—resulted from a series of structural shifts not the least of which was, paradoxically, the opening of urban space through "Haussmannization." While Haussmann's transformations of Parisian streets and buildings produced gentrification on the one hand, in some respects, it also accomplished the opposite, as it invited more low-income people into the shopping centers of the metropolis and thus enabled greater access to social ascendancy. With the steam engine, bringing visitors and goods to urban areas, and the omnibuses, transporting people en masse around the city, shopping could expand beyond the confines of a single small neighborhood. Department stores could market their goods to a wide range of social classes and offer fashion at discounts; they could also purchase merchandise from factories outside of Paris, buying in bulk and selling with rapid turnover. The Parisian department store, and others in its wake, was thus a development of scale: the space itself was much grander than any previous stores, its architecture constructed to invite spectacle and circulation. With the widening of streets and sidewalks in Haussmann's Paris, the *vitrine* became a vital publicity tool, alongside advertisements on billboards and in catalogs, newspapers, and fashion journals. The scale of space facilitated scale of volume—both in terms of merchandise and customers: vast quantities of merchandise could be displayed, crowds of shoppers could be accommodated, and because of the volume of both, costs could be kept low. But to truly exploit the large-scale business model of the *grand magasin*, which required legions of customers to sustain turnover, regular publicity and advertising beyond the site became essential.

FASHION'S VIRTUAL MARKETPLACE

The illustrated fashion press expanded exponentially especially in the second half of the nineteenth century and indeed functioned as almost a virtual department store—a venue for display, advertisement, and forms of virtual consumption that would lead to its bricks-and-mortar counterpart. Here was where taste was dictated and disseminated by the fashion writers, many of whom were anonymous or pseudonymous, often assuming sobriquets to increase their prestige and intimacy with readers. As key tastemakers, these *chroniqueuses de mode* were responsible for training women in consumption practices, initiating them into the mysteries of French *élégance*, which was world renowned, and establishing the reputations of fashion houses, *couturiers*, and shops alike. They were, in a very real sense, marketing and distributing fashion to a wide audience and were thus instrumental to the creation of the fashion system.

Jeanne-Jacqueline Fouqueau de Pussy, or J.J., as she signed her column, was for the first twenty years of its existence the editor-in-chief and fashion correspondent for the popular *Journal des Demoiselles* (1833–96).[54] J.J. wrote a regular correspondence column in which she posed as a fashionable, respectable, bourgeois Parisian *demoiselle* who enlightened her provincial readers as to the latest trends and shops in the capital, thus circulating throughout France and beyond the standards of bourgeois good taste and the addresses where one might procure it. With each installment a pattern was included, so the provincial reader could fabricate the dress herself. Likewise, Emmeline Raymond, editor-in-chief and fashion writer for the wildly popular and internationally distributed *La Mode illustrée: Journal de la famille* (1860–1937), promoted specific houses, shops, and designers in her "description de toilettes" column. Her descriptive paragraphs accompanied richly colored plates, such as the one pictured in Figure 2.13, which indicated the shops that produced the fashions.

Raymond's description of the outfits created by Mesdemoiselles Rabouin at 67 rue Neuve des Petits Champs, offers a detailed linguistic version of the image, identified by the *couturières'* shop and address. The wide dissemination of the magazine explains the need to offer details of fabric, shapes, underskirts, and embellishments: those readers who did not inhabit Paris or could not afford the services of the demoiselles Rabouin could take such descriptions to their local seamstress, who could then approximate the dress according to the description. Like so many other fashion correspondents of the nineteenth century, Raymond successfully marketed fashion to a bourgeois public eager to attain the cultural capital associated with elegance while maintaining a moral, domestic framework. The *chroniqueuses* were indeed savvy creators of consumers as well as arbiters of fashion.

FIGURE 2.13: *La Mode illustrée*, 1865, Sunday, August 13, 1865, issue number 33, on an unnumbered page between 260 and 261. Archives & Special Collections Library, Vassar College.

CONCLUSION

The Belle Époque and early twentieth century saw a tremendous rise in ready-to-wear and an enormous influx of women workers into the fashion *ateliers* of Paris. Like Worth before her, Coco Chanel would assume the mantle of fashion's "dictator," ironically, however, through her pioneering of styles diametrically opposed to his, most notably in her rejection of the corset and adoption of jersey fabric and menswear.[55] In a now familiar pattern, Chanel began as a *modiste* and rose to the top of the fashion industry not once but twice in the course of her long career, emerging as the definitive face of twentieth-century *élégance*.

The revolutions of nineteenth-century fashion production and distribution—the invention of the sewing machine, the entry of women into the workforce, the boom in prêt-à-porter, crucial advances in modern transport, the creation of the department store, and the spread of information and products through a variety of media throughout the globe—radically transformed the elite world of *haute couture* that had evolved in the mid-nineteenth century from the aristocratic courts of earlier centuries. The democratization of fashion would be fully realized in the twentieth century, bringing with it greater access and lower costs but perpetuating many of the injustices experienced by the *petites mains* of an earlier era. Today's democratized fashion industry, mass-producing clothing for voracious consumers, has its antecedents in the nineteenth century. The distance between consumer and producer and the alienating anonymity that Marx named commodity fetishism at the height of nineteenth-century European and American empire-building endures today in the sweatshops of Bangladesh and China.[56] Now, as then, it is a challenging task to map the cultural history of the voiceless "little hands" of the fashion industry.

CHAPTER THREE

The Body

ANNETTE BECKER

A carefully dressed woman is indeed a being "fearfully and wonderfully made." Consider the labor she has performed, the time spent and the material—its quantity, variety, and shape—that is centred upon her. Reflect how many bones clasp her waist; the multitudes of pins that flash and hold and defend her; the innumerable hooks and eyes that look out, catch hold, and join to give strength, shape, and comeliness to hosts of nameless things . . .[1]

When George Ellington published *The Women of New York* in 1869, he wrote with concern for the immoral city's manipulation and reconstruction of the minds and bodies of its women. Their clothing subsumes their bodies, the bones and eyes of the garments becoming surrogates of their own body parts. Further "artifice and deception decorate their person."[2] Rather than flesh, cotton and horsehair form their bust lines, and sleeves padded with wool consume their arms. These fashionable ladies were not of nature but instead delicately and attractively constructed traps for sin and depravity. This "full and truthful account of how a woman is made up" both demonstrates and exaggerates the treatment of the fashionable, or fashioned, female body in the nineteenth century.[3]

Many fashion theorists draw connections between clothing, the body, and the values and beliefs of the social groups that fashion them. Joanne Entwistle asserts that the body is the product of a specific time and place, and in being so reflects the ideals and cultural norms of that environment.[4] In *Seeing Through Clothes*, Anne Hollander pushes bodies to the forefront of history, putting them forth as intrinsically shaped, much like styles in art,[5] and arguing that even unclothed, fashionable bodies reflect the dress of their times. Though these historical bodies no longer exist, through extant literary, visual, and material evidence we develop a more fleshed out understanding of the embodied experience of nineteenth-century fashion.

As a product of its cultural context, nineteenth-century Western fashion presents the body as a nexus for competing discourses of artifice and nature. This tension was particularly poignant for women, who were held as pillars of propriety through their behavior and dress. Their highly structured clothing was often worn in extremes, forcing the body into controlled and artificial forms. Restraint of the natural body was at times viewed an external signifier of morality, a triumph over the undeveloped, unruly, and uncivilized. Others viewed this manipulation as fleeting and transitory beauty, the fashionable form an indicator of contemporary society. As author Charles Baudelaire famously wrote, beauty is "needed to teach an animalized humanity" and that reason and artifice reform nature.[6] "Fashion," he continues, "should thus be considered as a symptom of the taste for the ideal which floats on the surface of all the crude, terrestrial and loathsome bric-a-brac that natural life accumulates in the human brain, as a sublime deformation of Nature, or rather a permanent and repeated attempt at her reformation."[7] To Baudelaire, a manipulated, artificial body was beautiful and cultured. This fashionable, beautiful artifice was repeatedly countered by alternative and anti-fashion movements that instead viewed the natural body as ideal. By moving closer to nature—allowing the body to be healthful and active, or embracing an artistic, or political reimagining of classical clothing—these reformers featured dress as a means through which the body was liberated to serve a higher function.

In this chapter, we examine how nineteenth-century dress worked with—and against— bodies to illustrate contemporary ideas of beauty, morality, and health. We begin with a discussion of late eighteenth- and early nineteenth-century fashions of new republican governments, showing the extreme volatility of society and fashion alike at that time. The chapter then discusses leg o' mutton sleeves, the cage crinoline, the cuirass bodice—all fashionable elements that stand out in popular memory as attempts to control the body— while exploring the various reform and alternative fashions that countered popular styles. The chapter closes by examining the New Woman and the gradual rise in prominence of many reform dress ideals that developed throughout the century.

EXPOSING REVOLUTIONARY FASHIONS

The end of the eighteenth and beginning of the nineteenth century was a time of great change in fashion and politics in Europe and the United States. In France, revolutions wracked the country, and ripples of political dissent were felt throughout the continent. New systems of government created new power structures, which in turn resulted in long-standing social hierarchies being questioned, challenged, and overturned. This political upheaval was accompanied by correspondingly radical changes in dress. While heavy gowns and structured silhouettes were associated with the repressive governments of the old regime, French citizens sought form-revealing garments with classicized detail to embody their new paradigm. Nascent Empire styles included dresses of semi-transparent white muslin worn with simple jackets and hairstyles close to the head, while men favored slim breeches and dark narrow coats.[8] Relatively inexpensive fabrics and lack of embellishment—save for references to the French nation or minimal classicized detail— suggested support of a new constitution and recalled visual elements relating to ancient democracy.[9]

The undergarments required for these new fashions were correspondingly less restrictive. Earlier eighteenth-century styles, particularly for more formal settings or at court, required a torso stiffened and held upright with stays or a boned bodice. Stays, which frequently included a rigid busk inserted at the center front, facilitated an upright posture and necessitated bending at the hips rather than the waist. Less formal environments allowed loosened stays, but women still generally viewed them as necessary undergarments. By the second half of the eighteenth century, anti-stays texts promoted a more "natural" form of beauty and body carriage, and revolutionary fashions marked the demise of such stiff bodies.[10]

Empire fashions theoretically required little in the way of shaping and restricting the torso through undergarments. Shorter stays, boneless corsets, and proto-brassieres that supported the bust allowed the soft, serpentine line of a *contrapposto* stance rather than the ramrod uprightness of the past century. These styles also emphasized the verticality of the body, echoing the narrow uprightness of a classical column rather than the exaggerated hips and narrowed waist of pre-revolution fashions. For those whose bodies already fit the fashionably thin silhouette, a tight sheath followed the line of the body and offered a minimal amount of coverage for the sheer fashions.[11] Women with fuller torsos, however, had two options: long, narrow corsets or dieting to transform their bodies into the fashionable form.

Empire styles also emphasized fertility and new life, paralleling the contemporary birth of new nations and governments. The long, straight line of the female body was interrupted by a high, full chest, which was at times supplemented with false bosoms. Low necklines further facilitated the semi-nudity of these styles, pushing the breasts nearly out of the dress.[12] By exposing the body and emphasizing the breasts, these fashions glorified the post-natal female body. Men wore skin-tight breeches with narrow, simplified waistcoasts that emphasized their youthful and virile masculinity. And if a man's body lacked volume in the desired areas, lacing, padding, or innovative tailoring could fill out a calf or draw in a waist.

The fabrics used in Empire styles were shockingly sheer, loose, and revealing, creating a number of unprecedented issues relating to immodesty. The slimness of the fashionable body meant that only minimal undergarments could be worn, lest bulkiness appear around the waist, hips, and legs. Without these extra layers, the translucent fabrics of the dress and petticoat clung to the body and revealed its form. This demanded a new garment enter women's wardrobes: the pantalette. Shin-length and separated at the crotch, this bifurcated undergarment allowed women to wear the gauzy, light clothing without allowing inappropriate visual access to their bodies.

While the sheerness of the styles necessitated garments to cover the body, it also meant that accessories were needed to maintain warmth. Items like shawls and light tuckers to cover a bare chest were commonly shown in fashion plates, popularizing accessories that facilitated the continued wearing of lightweight garments. The cashmere shawl, written on extensively by Susan Hiner, both covered and drew attention to the body.[13] Scantily clad limbs, gauze-covered bodies, and exposed décolletages necessitated the warmth offered by the shawls, and the shawls allowed for a modicum of modesty. However, they also facilitated these gauzy fashions and drew attention to the naked arms and narrow bodies to which they clung.

Later writings discussing these fashions associate them with moral looseness, and a number of myths about the indecency of Empire fashions have been perpetuated. For example, early costume historians misinterpreted the styles, suggesting that women dampened the thin muslin to create the sheer, clinging styles. However, no documented proof of this exists. In studying these fashions today, artworks, fashion plates, and actual garments offer insight into the balance between the idealized form and the way these styles were actually worn.

This 1806 fashion plate (see Figure 3.1), though not necessarily representative of the everyday fashions on the streets of France, demonstrates the extreme to which this radical dress was worn by few and envisioned by many. The figure is draped in a delicate white satin dress that creates a columnar silhouette. Her breasts are emphasized with a plunging, wide neckline edged in ruffles. Gravity hardly seems present, as one sleeve of her dress appears on the verge of rakishly falling off her shoulder and a flimsy band of horizontal fabric forms a demi-cup that barely holds her breasts in the dress. A leg delicately extends forward to interrupt the vertical line of the dress, and a petite shoe peeks from underneath the hemline. Embellishments at the neckline, sleeve, and hem of the gown recall the decorative acanthus leaves and swags that adorn capitals on columns in classical architecture.

Similarly, male silhouettes and dress reflected the noble characteristics of antiquity (Figure 3.2). Echoing Greco-Roman sculpture, buff-colored breeches and stockings

FIGURE 3.1: *Costume Parisien*, 1806, France. Private collection.

An 11. Costume Parisien. (473)

Habit à Taille étroite. Culotte et Guêtres de Nankin.

FIGURE 3.2: "Habit à Taille étroite. Culotte et Guêtres de Nankin," *Journal des Dames et des Modes* (May 30, 1803). Rijksmuseum, Amsterdam.

mimic the marble musculature of classical nudes.[14] These fitted garments create a body consciousness, which is further illustrated in this fashion plate by the figure's posture. He stands with a hand in the front pocket of his breeches, calling attention to his masculine attributes and emphasizing his virility. In fashion plates such as this, the relative simplicity of the ensemble draws attention to the figure's form.

Instead, then, of acting as armatures for the trimmings and trappings of status assigned by material wealth, fashionable bodies of the Empire were clothed to represent a political ideal and espoused a natural form of the body. Drawing inspiration from classical sculpture—high waistlines, loose draped fabric, and a columnar form—such garments echoed the contemporary interest in harkening back to the supposed political ideals of antiquity. Aileen Ribeiro argues that these fashions were a kind of reform dress; rather than being developed from an ever-changing fashion system they brought an ideal that was grounded in intellectual thought to the forefront of discourse relating to fashionable dress.[15]

LEG O' MUTTON SLEEVE

As the political environment of the early decades of the nineteenth century settled into more stable social and political structures, fashions and the bodies they shaped returned to more historically familiar modes. Many aristocratic governments were reformed into more republican and capitalist structures that reinstituted social hierarchies, and the freer styles of the revolutions gave way to more controlled forms. The gauzy and transparent fashions of the early nineteenth century gradually became more formal, with the waistline lowering and becoming more defined, fabrics and embellishments becoming heavier, and skirts and sleeves moving further away from the body's line.

This renewed social conservatism brought a restrictive, almost repressive, sense of moral culpability to women. Held as paragons of virtue, it was felt a woman's choice in clothing embodied her morality. Women with undergarments that were not tightly cinched were deemed "loose" women, their clothing both reflecting and contributing to their moral deficit.[16] By forcing the body to be stiff and upright, fashionable dress was seen as integral to mental firmness and integrity. Maintaining and representing unprecedented control over both the body and the mind, these garments shaped women into the ideal silhouette and comportment of the day.

Rather than merely returning to the styles preceding the revolutions, the popular fashions of much of the nineteenth century emphasized the difference in the roles and bodies of the sexes (Figure 3.3). While there were many similarities between the general silhouettes of fashionable dress of men and women, the control exercised over the body varied. Men's clothing showed a more modern fit, with the relatively unchanging suit staying close to the body and facilitating movement[17]—although we must remember that stiff collars, tight cravats, and stirrups that pulled pant legs close to the body operated their own constraints. Women's clothing, by contrast, nipped in and ballooned outwards in almost cartoonish proportions.[18] Waistlines fell from under the bustline to the natural waist and skirts began to blossom outwards, distorting the shape of the female body by emphasizing secondary sexual characteristics.

Enormous leg o' mutton sleeves built up the area around the upper arm, puffing up and out at the shoulder and narrowing at the elbow or forearm. While stiffened, sturdy fabrics could create the leg o' mutton shape, some extreme styles required more

FIGURE 3.3: *L'Eco* 45 (October 1832). Rijksmuseum, Amsterdam.

support, such as wire hoops, horsehair attached to lighter fabric, or—in the case of this British gown from 1830—feather-filled pillows placed inside (Figure 3.4). These sleeve supports required that the arms were held away from the body, or else the desired volume was crushed. It is easy to imagine how immobilizing such garments would have been.

These voluminous sleeves were emphasized through manipulation of the shoulder. High boat necklines and nipped-in waists created a strong triangularity for the torso. Even the pattern on this gown highlights the triangular torso created by the tight shoulders and cinched-in waist, with strong diagonals from the shoulders meeting at a belt clasp at the waist. Shoulders were pushed down with armholes shifted forward and downward, at times as low as the bust line. This shoulder stance was further enforced with low, wide-set corset straps. Creating a diamond shape for the shoulders and torso necessitated a composed and still body for the garments to lie properly. Popular through the 1840s, styles with voluminous sleeves and stiff torsos demonstrate the ideal female submissiveness that was thought innate to their sex.[19]

Noted economist and social historian Thorstein Veblen drew inspiration from the limitations of these fashions in his turn-of-the-century book *Theory of the Leisure Class*.[20] Seeing the conspicuous consumption and waste of his day as the product of centuries of class differentiation, Veblen viewed the restrictive fashions and the lack of economically

FIGURE 3.4: Leg o' mutton sleeve. Day dress, 1830–4, Great Britain. © Victoria and Albert Museum, London.

productive work they demonstrated as overt displays of leisure afforded to women by the wealth of their husbands. "It has come about that obviously productive labor is in a peculiar degree derogatory to respectable women, and therefore special pains should be taken in the construction of women's dress, to impress upon the beholder of the fact (often indeed a fiction) that the wearer does not and can not habitually engage in useful work."[21] Fashion, to Veblen, was a wasteful demonstration and celebration of the excesses of time and resources of the upper classes.

While sloping shoulders and leg o' mutton sleeves contributed to the immobility of these "delicate women," this silhouette also served to highlight a part of the body that came under much scrutiny: the face. With new scientific interests in psychology, increasing urbanization and interactions with strangers in city settings, and rigid codes dictating morality proliferated in printed materials, clothing and the way one carried one's self became paramount for appropriate self-presentation. While physiognomy—a problematic and rather disturbing practice of determining character through viewing details of the face and body—was often used to perpetuate racist agendas and discriminate against those deviating from the white middle class, it also further entrenched the dominant belief that emotions belonged to the feminine realm, and that women's minds and bodies by nature were more controlled by their nervous systems and heightened sensibility.[22]

CAGE CRINOLINE

As the nineteenth century progressed, women's fashion became even more structured and distant from the natural shape of the body. The volume of leg o' mutton sleeves deflated, but in turn skirts expanded away from the body. From the 1830s, layers of petticoats increased, holding skirts at a fashionable distance from the legs and weighing down women's hips. As this volume grew even greater, dressmakers in the 1840s lined the petticoats with horsehair to stiffen them, in an effort to minimize the amount and weight of fabric necessary.

While these layers of petticoats may have created an attractive figure, they also created many problems relating to health and cleanliness. Women often complained of the uneven body temperatures caused by the yards of fabric around their legs, bemoaning that the petticoats provided unreasonable warmth in the summer months and inadequate warmth for the torso in winter. Furthermore, the weight of the fabric was supported exclusively and uncomfortably by the hips, and its long layers tended to "sweep stairs and streets and crossings," picking dirt and debris from city streets.[23]

However, fashion seldom bends to complaints of those who partake in it. Instead it pushes boundaries until a change is unavoidable. As the fashion historian and curator Harold Koda states, "In many historical instances, the details of dress appear to evolve with increasing exaggeration until they are unstoppable and implode. It can be argued that the only mechanism for the demise of faddish style is the physical limit of the body to suffer its intervention."[24] Rather than forcing change in the fashionable silhouette, this outrageous style sparked innovation. Copious layers of petticoats were replaced by an innovative and new foundational undergarment: the cage crinoline. Introduced in the mid-1850s, this garment used concentric hoops of lightweight spring steel connected with fabric tapes to create an armature onto which a single petticoat and a skirt would rest. The thin bands of steel eliminated the weight of layers of petticoats and meant there was much less fabric sweeping the ground. Additionally, the flexible steel could bend slightly to facilitate movement. Many women found "them light and pleasant to wear" and appreciated that they "did away with the necessity for heavy underskirts."[25] Industrial factories created these undergarments in massive quantities, and the cage crinoline was quickly adopted by women across classes and throughout Europe.

Unfortunately, the garment that liberated women from layers of bulky petticoats created myriad new problems.[26] While the circumferences of skirts, particularly in formal settings, had reached impressive sizes when filled out with petticoats, the size of the skirt was limited to the amount of fabric that could be supported by the hips and held away from the body. Now that the light and sturdy steel frame had only to support a few layers of fabric, skirts reached a previously unimaginable volume. Moving one's body gracefully with such a cumbersome yet delicate structure proved challenging, and performing the already limited amount of movement in social situations—for example, sitting gracefully or exiting a carriage—was complicated at best, and catastrophically embarrassing and dangerous at worst.

Harper's New Monthly Magazine's "Dressing for the Ball" (Figure 3.5) illustrates some real and some imagined complications of maintaining the bell-shaped silhouette. Two figures in the foreground demonstrate the perceived ludicrous nature of the undergarments required to form the silhouette. In the center, a woman wears a corset and petticoat, her hips jutting out from her body unnaturally, perhaps suggesting she is also wearing a crinoline support, or that the ideals for feminine beauty were so engrained that

FIGURE 3.5: "Dressing for the Ball," *Harper's New Monthly Magazine* (December 1857): 282. University of North Texas Library, Special Collections.

a woman not wearing a crinoline was still thought to look as if she were. Another woman lowers the frame of a crinoline over the center figure's head, bringing new meaning to the experience of wearing the "cage" crinoline. To the left, another women fills nearly a third of the illustration with her capacious gown. It surrounds her narrow corseted torso, the skirt nearly consuming her body. A hose snakes from underneath her gown, attached to a bellows that another figure uses to inflate the skirt. These extremes in feminine fashion create an uncomfortable and claustrophobic space.

Satirical cartoons—often appearing in the same publications that featured illustrations of popular fashions—mocked the cage crinoline and the women who wore them (Figure 3.6). These drawings take issue with fashionable female dress for a number of reasons, here expressing the frustration with the amount of space and delicate social

THE SAFEST WAY OF TAKING A LADY DOWN TO DINNER.

FIGURE 3.6: "The Safest Way of Taking a Lady Down to Dinner," *Harper's Weekly* (December 24, 1864): 832. University of North Texas Library, Special Collections.

maneuvering required by both women and men in the presence of a wide crinoline. However, the crinoline's spatial reconfiguration of the female body could result in much more serious consequences than mere social discomfort. This was a democratized fashion worn by all classes of women in the crowded and newly industrialized contexts of the nineteenth century. It was certain death for wearers to become entangled in machinery, and the danger of being burnt alive—the large, airy skirts sweeping into open flames and igniting into flaming prisons—was very real. Nor were their effects felt only by wearers, as the amplitude of the feminine form pushed, tripped, and tangled innocent passersby. Some coroners' reports specifically condemned the crinoline as an unwarrantable threat to safety and health.[27] Satire, therefore, had a more serious undertow, lampooning the inflated female form as a moral and bodily warning.

BLOOMER DRESS

Though crinolines and accompanying voluminous skirts were widely popular, voices of dissent arose from various factions that equated this stylish dress with an array of hegemonic powers. From religious organizations to women's suffrage movements to health-conscious activists, reformers located the ills of society in the bodies of women subjected to the vagaries of fashion. Turning away from the "imported, absurd, hurtful, ridiculous fashions from Paris," many reformers wanted women to free their bodies from the suffering caused by fashionable dress.[28] As an alternative to the oppressive styles, iterations of bifurcated garments for women began gaining popularity in the first half of the nineteenth century at private health facilities and in fringe religious groups like the utopian Oenida Perfectionist community.[29]

While reformers from varying backgrounds had been practicing alternative dress for several decades, in the 1850s health and political reformers brought more public attention to dress and the ways that it interacted with the body. Publications from temperance, women's suffrage, and water cure organizations encouraged their female followers to adopt "Turkish pantaloons and a short skirt, leaving the upper vestments to be fashioned according to the taste of the wearer."[30] These various reform groups touted their bifurcated garments as superior to fashionable dress because they were hygienic, conducive to good health, and able to facilitate a woman's performance of her moral duties.

In 1851, the popular press immortalized well-known American women's suffrage activist and dress reformer Amelia Jenks Bloomer, coining the neologism "bloomers." While Bloomer was not the first woman to don a bifurcated garment, she and her fellow proto-feminists decried fashionable dress through much of the 1850s and made headlines for their efforts. In her temperance and abolition newspaper *The Lily*, Bloomer emphasized that popular female fashion made women "have our dresses drabbled in the mud" and that whalebone corsets did not allow for breathing room.[31] Bloomer cast reform dress in these relatively non-threatening terms, with sartorial change as an issue of bodily comfort rather than political protest.[32]

However, not all women's rights campaigners approached dress reform in such moderate terms. Bloomer-contemporary Dr. Lydia Sayer Hasbrouck described fashionable dress as a material assault on the bodies and minds of women. Hasbrouck, who adopted a reformed style several years before Bloomer and continued wearing it until her death in 1910, criticized Bloomer for her lack of dedication to the dress reform cause. Seeing the women in fashion plates as "senseless ninny faces and forms deformed," Hasbrouck demanded that women adopt more practical garments that would allow physical movement and active participation in the world that was only open to men.[33]

Women's rights and health reform frequently overlapped in the issue of reform dress. While Hasbrouck is now most strongly associated with women's rights activism, her formal education came from a hydropathic institute. These health reform spas and boarding houses offered alternative dress, diet, and lifestyles to benefit the bodies of both men and women.[34] *The Water-Cure Journal* promoted a variety of therapies and regularly featured articles on reform dress, focusing on its religious, moral, and health benefits. One anonymous writer equated fashion with "a tyrant trampling upon the laws of Nature, thereby was defacing the image of God, and destroying the health, happiness, and life even of innocent men, women, and children."[35] By turning away from restrictive garments of fashion and allowing the body to look and move in the way God had created it, water cure practitioners understood themselves to be demonstrating morality.[36]

Reform periodicals also addressed the health benefits of alternative dress by writing about and illustrating the differences between fashionable clothing and reform costume for both men and women. The contrast is described in biological and body-centric terms, with the reformist goal being the "cure" of the "disease" of fashion.[37] To these reformers, an artificial, fashioned body was a perversion against health and morality, and a natural, "reformed" body an expression of healthfulness and goodness. In 1851, *The Water-Cure Journal* reproduced a popular portrait of Bloomer shown alongside a poor rendering of a French fashion plate (Figure 3.7).

Bloomer is shown as a realistic, relatable figure, her body and garments rendered three-dimensionally through careful modeling and shadows. The fashionable figure's body, by contrast, is more linear and geometric. Her triangular torso is perched precariously on a rounded cylinder of a skirt, and her body is flat and cartoonish. "Anatomical views" of the figures' respective torsos send the alarming message that tight lacing reshapes and constricts the lungs, ribs, and spine, destroying the body inside and out.

While the visions of early and radical dress reformers did not initiate widespread public change, reform clothing and its more natural approach to the body did inspire subtle shifts in some forms of fashionable dress. Many reformers also focused on men's health and clothing, addressing concerns about the dangerous materials used to produce male fashion—like mercury in hats and toxic dyes used in garments that touched the skin.[38] Reformers like John Harvey Kellogg and Dr. Gustav Jaeger developed significant health systems that offered alternative diet and promoted undyed wool undergarments. However, the general public did not adopt wholesale the reformist paradigm. Compared to the structured, exaggerated forms of popular fashion, alternative dress was not seen as becoming to the female figure. Anne Hollander argues that anti-fashion and counterculture dress—among which reform dress can be counted—has a complicated relationship with popular clothing. She suggests that dress that is not fashionable will not ultimately be adopted if it does not fit the aesthetic of the time; even if it is ideologically appealing, it is only by being attractive that it becomes appealing enough to be widely accepted. Additionally, anti-fashion clothing, even though it proposes to contradict fashionable dress, usually incorporates elements of it. It is "not really revolutionary but evolutionary," and from anti-fashion styles the future of fashion will emerge.[39] Unfortunately for Amelia Bloomer, Lydia Sayer Hasbrouck, and the water cure practitioners of the mid-nineteenth century, bifurcated garments for women would not become popular until much after their time.

FIGURE 3.7: "The American and French Fashions Contrasted," *The Water-Cure Journal* (October 1851): 96. Courtesy of Boston Medical Library in the Francis A. Countway Library of Medicine.

CORSETS

Probably the most discussed element of nineteenth-century fashion—the corset—best epitomizes the control achieved over the female body. This foundation garment was ubiquitous across classes and Western countries, and many nineteenth-century publications note the moral imperative of wearing the corset. Scholars Valerie Steele and Leigh

Summers have published extensively on its history, arguing that the popular understanding of corsets as tools of torture that caused myriad health problems has been exaggerated, though its cultural importance has not.[40] In this section, we explore the development of increasing control over the torso in the second half of the nineteenth century, and contemporary discussions of the morality relating to corset wearing.

While structured undergarments for the torso were not new, corsetry from the second half of the nineteenth century is remarkable in the amount of control it exerted over the body. While previous garments offered support and forced the wearers' bodies into fashionable and appropriate postures, these corsets engaged with the body more forcefully by forming, rather than fitting it. Instead of merely nudging flesh into a smoother line or pushing the chest upwards and upright, these undergarments constricted the torso and forced the waist into a round rather than more natural ovoid shape.

The structure and shape of corsets changed the ways bodies looked through the course of the nineteenth century.[41] For much of the first half of the nineteenth century, corsets were given their structure through boning, which was created by sewing whale baleen into a form of stiff canvas or linen. As the availability of baleen decreased and the price increased, steel was used as an alternative. The length of these garments also varied throughout the century, reflecting the rise and fall of the fashionable waistline. When waistlines were high corsets did not need to shape the hips, but styles popular in the second half of the century required longer undergarments to create the ideal silhouette.

While women's garments had previously been divided into a bodice and skirt, the new princess-line dresses created a literally seamless transition from the shoulders to the feet (Figure 3.8). Without this break at the waistline, flat stomachs and flared hips created a visual foil for the voluminous bustle at the back of the skirt. As waistlines fell and the bulk of the skirt moved to the back of the body, corsets extended further to cover the top of the hips. Controlling more of the body than the earlier, shorter corsets, these undergarments created a more uniform, idealized shape to the bodies they encased. The longer corsets controlled posture, pushed up the breasts, drew in the ribs and waist, and regulated the ratio of the waist to the hips. Commonly referred to as a cuirass bodice, the name and characteristics of this garment recalled the French meaning of the word, a metal breastplate in a set of armor.

Technological innovations facilitated even more restraint. Edwin Izod's 1868 patent describes an innovative steam molding technique that created a shell-like garment by shaping fabric over a model of an ideal torso and baking a starchy glue mixture into the fabric through the use of steam.[42] These corsets were advertised as "adapting with marvelous accuracy to every curve and undulation of the finest type of figure," which gently suggests that the garment would provide the appropriate shape for whatever body it encased.[43] While Izod's technique sounds rather draconian, alternative means of creating undergarments provided similar stiffness for maximum control in shaping the body. With wire, leather, metal, wood, cording, felting, and horsehair used in combination to create a tightly-stitched corset, these materials were no more forgiving than Izod's steam-molded garment. The addition of metal rather than sewn eyelets also offered the opportunity for lacing with greater resistance, making cloth-based corsets increasingly worthy opponents for the unshaped form.

Women's relationships with corsetry were complex and contradictory, illustrating conflicting views of morality relating to the female body. At one extreme, tight corseting was taboo, as it was associated with vanity, overt sexuality, and poor health. However, a lack of corseting allowed the body to be unruly, a sign of loose morals. Corseting and

FIGURE 3.8: Day dress of silk satin and cut velvet, c. 1878, American. University of North Texas, Texas Fashion Collection, Gift of Mrs. Abraham J. Asche. Photo: Laurie Ruth Photography.

the degree to which it was practiced were widely discussed in women's periodicals.[44] For children, does the body need to be trained and be shaped into a civilized form, or should undergarments merely offer support? For older girls, their mothers knew that corsets were needed to make their daughters sexually attractive to draw suitors, but these garments also served a punitive function, creating moral and modest bodies.[45] This paradoxical position—with female bodies wavering between the natural and unnatural, sexualized but modest—demonstrates the complex and problematic treatment of women, their sexuality, and their bodies.

AESTHETIC DRESS

While the silhouette created by the cuirass bodice and the princess-line dress were immensely popular, the Aesthetic Dress movement countered it by promoting a more natural, less restricted female body. Unlike other dress reform garments, the clothing created by this movement resembled mainstream fashions closely enough that it could be worn in public without drawing excessive negative attention. Aesthetic—or artistic—dress, departed from fashionable modes in its construction and treatment of the body. Rather than being low and tight, sleeves in artistic dress came from the shoulder line, echoing the body's joints to facilitate free movement. Additionally, the bodices of the gowns did not require corsetry or the manipulation of the body to achieve the desired silhouette. Understructures for the skirt—like a crinoline or bustle—were unnecessary. Instead, expansive skirts created volume below the waist, echoing the fashionable silhouette but allowing the natural contours and movement of the body to be seen.

Drawing both visual and ideological inspiration from medieval dress, these fashions valued natural and athletic bodies over the stiff, formed bodies depicted in fashion plates. Aesthetic dress incorporated loose fabric draped around the body, which showed thicker waistlines than those created by corseted styles. Overwhelmingly for those practicing Aesthetic dress, corsets were contrary to an enlightened view of the female body; the less-restrained female form was seen as a beautiful living artwork.[46]

This iteration of reform clothing was worn primarily by upper-class artists in England and those who ran in similarly bohemian circles. Companies like the fashionable Liberty of London provided garments to this select but influential group, offering styles that incorporated soft, luxurious fabrics that draped around the body. Images of these fashions were proliferated in photographs of popular figures like Oscar Wilde and actress Ellen Terry, in paintings by James McNeill Whistler and members of the Pre-Raphaelite Brotherhood, and in illustrations by Aubrey Beardsley. An important figure within the Pre-Raphaelite Brotherhood and a frequent model for their artworks, Jane Morris embodied the ideals of artistic dress. In this 1865 photograph (Figure 3.9), Morris dons the unstructured, capacious dress, the silhouette of which required no restrictive undergarments. With her torso undefined by a stiff, constricting corset, she can easily twist into expressive forms. Fabric bunches around her waist, a shocking departure from the armor-like definition created by contemporary corsets and dress.

The rationale for aesthetic dress was informed by discourses of naturalism. Paintings by the Pre-Raphaelite Brotherhood showed figures in outdoor settings, their garments matching the organic colors and lines found in nature. English writer, illustrator, and Aesthetic-dress wearer Mary Eliza Haweis gave voice to this ethic, stating that through all art "nature must not be destroyed, but supported."[47] She wanted clothing to follow the lines and movements of the body, stating that "we might dispense with half our

FIGURE 3.9: *Portrait of Jane Morris*, John Robert Parsons (British), negative, July 1865, printed c. 1900. The J. Paul Getty Museum, Los Angeles.

complicated folds, our whalebones, our scrunched toes, our immovable arms, and many other miseries, and look less like mere blocks for showing off clothes, and more like human beings."[48]

Although depicted in art, Aesthetic dress came into the public eye but did not enter into most wardrobes—perhaps, because of its artistic connections, being viewed as costume rather than a viable style for daily life.[49] Additionally, as the artwork depicting such styles was often viewed as decadent and excessive, the fashions associated with them were increasingly seen as unnatural and deviant, as morally ambiguous as the artistic crowd that donned them.[50] However, some elements of Aesthetic dress were adopted into mainstream fashion. Revolutionary at the time, tea gowns shared many visual and structural characteristics with Aesthetic dress and were increasingly popular in the last quarter of the nineteenth century. Worn in the pseudo-private sphere of the home for afternoon social events attended by both men and women, tea gowns were generally seen as being part of a state of fashionable "undress."

THE NEW WOMAN

Toward the end of the nineteenth century, the center of the fashion world was still in Paris. However, as print media in America expanded and more women's periodicals were published, a distinct American style developed. In France, styles were still primarily defined by the clothing of upper class women—or at least those who had the means to dress as though they were members of the social elite—and the fashions there were slow to move away from the structured, corseted, statuesque figures that dominated the previous decades.[51] In the United States, various reform movements and their associated clothing became more familiar and slowly infiltrated popular fashion. Styles began to suggest a more natural body, similar to the ideals promoted by health reform, women's rights movements, and Aesthetic dress.

The late nineteenth-century New Woman exemplifies a widespread and significant move away from the restrictive fashions of most of the nineteenth century and toward a view of the female body as active. A product of the feminist ideals that had been gaining popularity since the suffragette movements of the 1850s, the New Woman was popularized in literature and art in America and Britain. In his novels, Henry James created female characters who were fiercely independent and exercised an unprecedented amount of control over their own lives. This New Woman was further exemplified by Charles Dana Gibson's drawings of "Gibson Girls," healthy young women with bright eyes and active bodies. They were depicted as sexually autonomous figures, and their clothing corresponded with their vibrant personalities. With minimal decoration and silhouettes that provided less differentiation between male and female bodies, the New Woman's dress flirted with the line between fashionable and reform dress.

While such styles still required foundational undergarments, they were less structured and allowed freer movement. Along with a long skirt, the typical Gibson Girl wore a shirtwaist, a garment with roots in reform dress that mimicked the style and production of men's dress. Under these simplified, pared down garments women often wore health waists. An alternative to the stiff, strapless undergarments that were necessary for previous fashions, these health waists provided support through a corded bodice and straps, becoming so popular that enterprising advertisers began to adopt the label for their more restrictive traditional corsets.

The silhouette achieved through this relatively minimal structure was viewed as integral to new modes of beauty. Symmetry of musculature, graceful proportion, moderation, and "physical endowment in harmony with the mind" were thought to create a beauty reminiscent of classical models.[52] Though this ideal did not require the columnar thinness of Empire styles, it suggested physical conditioning and light exercise to leave "fat enough to round all the surfaces to smoothness, no more."[53] While a waist that was narrower than the hips and bust was considered the ideal, the more radical ratios of earlier in the century were no longer the only acceptable silhouette.

Clothing for athletic endeavors, particularly sports like golf and bicycle riding, became more commonly seen in print publications, further illustrating a shift toward women's bodies as agents of movement. Some clothing for sport, like riding habits for women, had been included in fashion plates throughout the nineteenth century. These outfits, however, generally used fashionable silhouettes and were not worn in public for most casual social situations. Other sport-related clothing has been documented in the second half of the nineteenth century in private gymnasiums, particularly at women's colleges, but again that clothing had a limited functional use and was not worn in public settings.

At the turn of the century, a surge of clothing for newly fashionable sporting activities graced the pages of periodicals in fashion plates and played a dominant role in advertisements. This 1895 Gibson print (Figure 3.10) shows an imagined game between the young, androgynous women of Vassar and the men of Yale. The bloomered Vassar girls charge through the print, the dynamic angled lines that form the folds in their clothing propelling them aggressively across the page. Though the left figure's vest shows the curve of her breasts and a narrow waist, the women's clothing and bodies are virtually indistinguishable from that of the male Yalie.

While masculine, athletic clothing did exist and images of women donning it frequently appeared in American visual culture, this did not necessarily translate to an overwhelming paradigm shift. Patricia Warner Campbell argues that while bicycle suits were prominently featured in the advertisements and pages of women's periodicals, they were not as commonly worn and warmly received as scholars previously assumed.[54] As presented in popular text and images, bicycle culture afforded greater mobility, made possible unescorted travel, and promoted increased physical activity through less structured clothing. The presence of these ideas indicates a significant shift in societal norms, though the freedom associated with female bicyclists at the turn of the century was more symbol than reality.

While bicycles might not have been the development that freed women's bodies from the fickle hand of fashion, an increase in women's education and a resurgence in the ideals championed by Amelia Bloomer and her dress reform counterparts are linked

THE COMING GAME.
Yale versus Vassar.

FIGURE 3.10: *The Coming Game: Yale vs. Vassar*, 1895, Charles Dana Gibson. Private collection.

with reform clothing in the late nineteenth century. Campbell cites women's colleges and the interaction between genders in educational settings as instrumental in the gradual adoption of reform dress by women.[55] In the 1890s, women of the upper classes, and a few women on scholarship, were increasingly pursuing post-secondary education. These women embodied the ideals of the New Woman, where their independence was asserted through their competition with men. While fashion played an important role on college campuses, reform dress and gymnastic costume were more prevalent there than in other settings. Dress reformers hoped that through education women would no longer be enslaved by fashion, and would be freed to serve society in more meaningful ways.

However, the rise of the New Woman was not uncontested, and a rhetoric of the importance of athleticism competed with a discomfort with the empowered female. While popular advice literature strongly suggested regular exercise, a fit body that showed evidence of athletic activity was viewed as neither feminine nor beautiful. And while garments that facilitated physical movement permeated visual culture, their "masculinized" nature and the mobility they allowed made many uncomfortable. These conflicting views of women's roles and less restrictive fashions are evident through many characteristics of contemporary clothing; garments were simplified yet structured, more conducive to movement but still controlled.

CONCLUSION

From the late eighteenth century through the end of the nineteenth century, fashion and its relationship with the body displayed a tension between the natural and artificial. The century began with the radical and sheer styles associated with the French Revolution, with the body allowed an unprecedented natural shape. Gauzy, columnar gowns exposed the line of the body and emphasized the breasts, offering a sartorial interpretation of the contemporary interest in classical aesthetics and democratic ideals.

In a return to more familiar forms and fabrics, fashions of the 1830s and 1840s became more structured and necessitated innovative undergarments to support the capacious skirts and voluminous leg o' mutton sleeves. An unprecedented amount of control was asserted through structured styles, exaggerated features, and the undergarments that were necessary to restrain and reshape the body. This control of the body was equated with moral control, and fashion was seen as both an indicator of, and contributor to, social stability.

Countering these structured, artificial silhouettes were myriad reform movements that offered alternative styles. By shifting the weight of dress, freeing legs from capacious skirts, and restructuring undergarments to create a more natural body, through the last half of the nineteenth century health reformers developed dress that facilitated athletic movements in increasingly public spheres. While other alternative-dress supporters—water cure practitioners or those in artistic groups that donned aesthetic dress—enjoyed brief moments of popularity in the public eye, it took several decades for these changes to evidence themselves in more mainstream fashions.

The longstanding battle between fashionable and reform dress worked toward a meeting point at the end of the nineteenth century, but women's fashions still had several decades before they fully incorporated the ideals of rational dress. The liberated bodies of women in the 1920s owed much to the reformers of the nineteenth century, the men and women who worked toward the freed torsos, raised hemlines, and—eventually—the bifurcated garments that the twentieth century came to take so much for granted.

CHAPTER FOUR

Belief

DENISE AMY BAXTER

RELIGIOUS DRESS IN THE AGE OF MODERNITY

While all modes of clothing or adornment communicate belief systems, religious dress in particular does so self-consciously, expressly revealing, or concealing, associations with religious organizations, systems, and practices.[1] Within the attire of any such group we may ascertain distinctions, as readable as military insignia. Not only does religious dress set its wearers apart from the general community at large, but it may also communicate understandings of gender, rank, and affiliations such as religious order. In many ways we think of this dress as antiquated and unchanging, as if religious leaders, in particular, have always dressed as they now do. Yet while the Roman collar and cassock have their origins in the twelfth century, the antiquated aspects of religious, even Roman Catholic religious, attire should not be understood as not changing with historical and cultural context.[2] As Sally Dwyer-McNulty has pointed out ". . . a priest wearing a cassock outside church or walking in the community would be unusual in the 1850s, required in the 1930s, and curious in the early 1970s."[3] Indeed, the cultural context of the aftermath of the French Revolution, the geographical context of the United States, and burgeoning religions or religious movements all had manifestations in religious dress.

The late eighteenth century was arguably a nadir for Roman Catholicism. To take the example of France, the rise of Enlightenment thought combined with squabbles between Jansenist and Jesuit factions and predated the confiscation of church lands, anticlericalism, and dechristianization associated with the Revolution, during which an estimated 3,000 priests lost their lives.[4] Attendance at mass as well as the continued education of religion within seminaries were essentially curtailed, at least at the height of the Terror, with disruption of rites and material losses following along with the progress of the French armies. During the Restoration that followed the Napoleonic regimes, the trappings of Roman Catholicism accompanied those of the monarchy. In particular, the nineteenth century is marked by a Catholic devotion to Mary, with the Immaculate Conception becoming dogma in 1854 and several significant Marian apparitions in France contributing to the widespread cult of the Virgin.[5] This Marian devotion is seen in the establishment and particularities of dress of new Marian orders. These included the Society of Mary, founded 1817 by William Joseph Chaminade, whose Marianists wore a gold ring on the right hand as a marker "of their alliance with the Queen of Heaven."[6] The Little Brothers of Mary, or Marists, dressed in what the order's founder Marcellin Champagnat referred to as the "livery of Mary," consisting of a frock coat and hat, both in the blue symbolic of the Virgin Mary. William J.F. Keenan notes the reverence in which Champagnat held these garments, directing the brothers "to honour their religious costume as they would clothing gifts conferred upon them by their Divine Mother, the Queen of Heaven" and "instilling in his recruits the belief that their sacred livery of Mary would afford them special protection against both spiritual and practical dangers."[7]

This Marianist affiliation in dress extended to women religious as well, and into the United States context. Following the proclamation of Mary Immaculate as Patroness of the United States by Pius IX in 1847, the American Sisters of Providence renamed themselves the Congregation of Sisters, Servants of the Immaculate Heart of Mary and replaced their black habits with blue ones, to emphasize their Marian devotion.[8] Yet the American situation was very different from that of re-Catholicizing Europe. The Servants of the Immaculate Heart of Mary donned their new blue habits during the height of the Know-Nothing power, during which generically nativist and specifically anti-Roman Catholic secret societies held sway. Explicit anti-Catholic persecution in the United States led to some religious—men and women alike—adapting more normative attire. Yet it was the more traditional dress of women religious in particular, when nursing soldiers, Union and Confederate alike, during the Civil War that proved a public relations coup, rebranding Catholic religious from monsters to angels of charity who might be identified by their dress.[9]

Many native-born religious movements also developed in the United States of the mid-nineteenth century, among them Unitarians, Adventists (Seventh-day Adventists), Jehovah's Witnesses, and Mormons (Church of Jesus Christ of Latter-day Saints), all of whom had various relationship to dress, variously choosing whether or not to display religious affiliation or adhere to norms of fashionable dress. For the Mormons, while founder Joseph Smith set the precedent that his followers should eschew immodest or showy dress, there were no sumptuary codes nor codified regalia. Indeed *the garment*, a special undergarment which is received as part of a rite of initiation, is the only aspect of dress specifically associated with the newly organized Latter-day Saints, and it is explicitly not public facing.[10] Nineteenth-century descriptions of the dress of Mormons by those outside the faith did, however, note a relative predominance of what was variously termed Bloomer—after Amelia Bloomer—dress or Deseret Costume.[11] This mode of reform dress, which is described in greater detail in Chapter 3 of this volume, typically comprises a full skirt, without hoop, sufficiently short to reveal a bifurcated undergarment.[12] More typically, however, Mormon men and women alike wore fashionable dress. This may be understood to be in keeping with church tenets to be in the world but not of it, preparing for Christ's millennial reign. As controversy regarding celestial marriage, or polygamy, gained ground in the 1850s onward, Mormons, like Roman Catholics, might have had good reason not to seek ready legibility through their dress.[13]

LEGIBILE DRESS

This question of readability in relationship to dress is always fraught. In previous generations, sumptuary laws had regulated color or fabric or type of dress. These had various intents. Some were intended to regulate moral or social behavior. Others, such as England's Calico Act of 1720, propelled consumers to select textiles that furthered a nation's economic interest. Equally typically, however, regulations were intended to set guidelines by which one could ascertain from an individual's dress his or her social status, such as Elizabethan restrictions on the rank required to wear silk trimming on hats. Sumptuary laws codified legible sartorial sign systems under which it was illegal to use clothing to present oneself as "better" than one's station. Sumptuary laws were therefore instruments by which the status quo was reinforced, self-fashioning was stifled, and fears of usurpation were quelled.

Regardless of the relative success or failure of these precedents, sumptuary laws were by and large forgotten by the nineteenth century, "freedom of dress" even having been declared in Revolutionary France.[14] Simultaneously, population shifts from country to city entailed increasing encounters between strangers, in the absence of a readily comprehensible sign system by which to identify socially crucial aspects of identity, such as class. Concurrent with this were forms of clothing production and distribution that allowed greater accessibility of modish garments to an ever broadening population. Into the breach came publications rather than regulations, including physiognomic tracts, typological volumes such as the *cris* or physiological guides, etiquette manuals, and the increasingly illustrated popular press.[15]

Philippe Perrot explains the phenomenon in terms of fashioning the bourgeoisie and argues that:

> Bourgeois dress replaced the multiplicity of aristocratic costumes, but beneath its superficial uniformity it created levels of meaning that bred subtle differences and revealed novel qualities to be carefully cultivated. It was between these levels that "distinction" developed, a new value in vestimentary discourse and practices, which would become the cardinal element of a differentiating system that constantly improved as copies threatened its exclusive nature. Fundamentally bourgeois and quintessentially antidemocratic, "distinction" replaced the "grace" and *bel air* of the ancient régime, transformed elegance and etiquette, and complicated the science of style, signification, and appropriateness inherited from earlier days.[16]

The Swiss writer Johann Caspar Lavater proposed and popularized a physiognomic system, by which, through study, the internal might be discerned through an interpretation of the external. His four volume *Physiognomische Fragmente, zur Beförderung der Menschenkenntnis und Menschenliebe* was first published between 1775 and 1778, with French and English editions rapidly following, and later editions and pocket editions published throughout Europe and the United States in the nineteenth centuries.[17] Early editions of the works were luxury objects, quarto volumes with high-quality images from old masters and contemporary artists, such that physiognomy was a practice of connoisseurship through which the eye was trained.[18] Subsequent editions presented the process in a much more practical light. The ready availability of pocket volumes implies that one should carry one's Lavater always, much like a map, in case a reference guide is needed. As improbable as this sounds, the preponderance of underlining and marginalia in extant nineteenth-century copies of the works demonstrates the utility readers found in the text. However, in addition to being a wildly popular pursuit, physiognomy was also frequently condemned, as this defense from an 1818 edition makes clear:

> Nothing is more common than to hear the study of physiognomy condemned as being calculated to mislead men in their judgments of each other, and the impossibility of its being reduced to a science; yet, nothing is more universally prevalent, in all classes of society, than forming judgments from the appearances of the face.[19]

Yet even while the horrific extent to which similar practices of discrimination would be taken by eugenicists are outside the scope of this discussion, it is clear that the need for a legible face and body was being both filled and justified. For while Lavater may have "believed in physiognomy as a science that would help people know truth and love one another," its practice was based in distinctions, of face and body alike.[20]

For the nineteenth-century navigators of urban environments, the distinctions between physiognomy and physiology were blurred, with editions of Lavater being supplemented by guidebooks to various social types. Stemming from texts such as Louis-Sébastien Mercier's and *cris*, these nineteenth-century texts focused on feminine social types, variously *grisette*, *cocotte*, or *lorette*, to name only a few.[21]

These texts, such as Ernest Desprez's *Paris, Ou Le Livre Des Cent-Et-Un* (1832), Jules Janin's *Les français peints par eux-mêmes* (1840) or Louis Huart's *Physiologie de la grisette* (1841, Figure 4.1) augmented interpretations of physical characteristics with those of

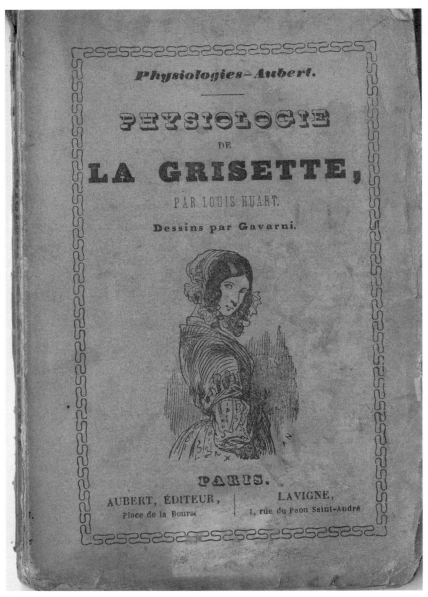

FIGURE 4.1: Paul Gavarni, cover of Louis Huart, *Physiologie de la grisette* (Paris: Aubert, 1841). Author's collection.

clothing and comportment.[22] The implict rhetoric of these guides is a pseudo-scientifically aestheticized and commodity-based conception of the self wherein propriety becomes the new morality and codes of dress are judged accordingly.

One case that points to the extremity to which the belief in the legibility of clothing was taken within the period is that of Dr. Hugh Welch Diamond, psychiatrist and founding member of the Photographic Society of London, who photographed primarily female patients of the Surrey County Lunatic Asylum, the Female Department of which he was resident superintendent for ten years. Diamond saw these photographs as serving two primary medical functions. They would be curative insofar as the might be viewed by patients as a form of accurate self-representation. They would also then record the individual in order to provide guidance for subsequent diagnosis.

It was with the goal of subsequent identification and diagnosis that John Conolly published engravings of the photographs in his 1858 "The Physiognomy of Insanity."[23] In addition to the engravings of photographs of specific diagnoses, such as "suicidal melancholy" or "melancholy passing into mania," some cases were presented in a before and after or stages of treatment layout (Figure 4.2). In examining the layout of puerperal mania in four stages, what appears most striking is that the difference between insanity

FIGURE 4.2: Puerperal mania in four stages, *The Medical Times and Gazette*, 1858. Wellcome Library, London.

and cure seems almost entirely marked by the donning of appropriate, nicely-fitting clothes.[24] The facial expressions and placement of hands appear nearly identical. Similar before and after *carte-de-visite* photographs for Dr. Barnardo's homes purportedly showed orphans in a state of neglect, in tattered clothes and then, apparently, rehabilitated by the homes, insofar as the clothing and grooming demonstrated them to be newly upstanding members of society, never mind the superimposition of narrative on photographs wherein the temporal distance between before and after may have only been the time for a wash up and change of dress.[25]

WEDDINGS AND FUNERALS, OR, MARRYING, BURYING, AND BUYING

While rising out of the Judeo-Christian tradition, this modern conception of morality is based at least as much in concern regarding judgment of others in this world as it is judgment of an almighty God in the next. While not typically in opposition to traditional religious doctrine, socially-held strictures regarding morality were at least equally influentially promulgated from conduct manuals as pulpits.[26] Not only is the nature of morality in the modern age different from in previous eras, but the process by which one might discern not only the qualities of others but of one's self differed as well. Without sumptuary laws to legally codify dress and with the generally diminishing influence of the Church came an augmented social anxiety regarding appropriate sartorial self-representation. Codification of mores then became a more diffuse and increasingly commercialized process, with fashion leading the way. The increasingly commercialized and fashion-driven aspects of socially-appropriate or moral dress is made particularly manifest in the industries that developed around two of the most profound social rituals in the nineteenth century: weddings and funerals. Both have traditionally held familial, religious, and legal significance, and these local, church, and state codifications have long given form to the practices and attire. Yet it is within this period that we see industries developing in order to create and then serve the needs for both these rituals, with appropriate consumption and display in many ways replacing what had been legal or moral obligations.

Weddings

Mlle MARIE DE L. DE MONTF . . . Before I reply to your charming question, please accept our hearty and smiling congratulations. You want, you say, to owe your wedding dress to *La Dernière mode*; but does not our publication owe you many of its successes among your elegant set of acquaintances? I have never had a more agreeable task than to design the outfit you want. Here it is, though too briefly described. Wedding dress in white satin, with smooth crêpe flounces with sharp pleats; cachepoint in white jet; a tunic-scarf in white satin, trimmed with a flounce like those on the skirt, (With a bow on the train and one of the flaps held back at the waist, this tunic will be enchanting.) A train of orange-blossoms going from the waistband and finishing in the bow of the train proper. The bodice has rounded basques, very long in front and very short at the back. A ruff of smooth gauze edged with a garland of orange-blossoms.

When you read here certain details a little different from what our Fashion column defined as the coming style, do not think I have described anything unfashionable.

Wedding dresses, as an earlier column of ours said, are the last to change; they cling
to the established mode. There would be something not quite proper—particularly in
your case, living so far from the capital as you do—in a bride wishing to be in advance
of fashion.[27]

This was how symbolist poet Stéphane Mallarmé responded to a purported bridal attire
query from the readers' correspondence section in the December 20, 1874 issue of
La Dernière Mode. The publication is an unusual one, largely self-financed by Mallarmé
who took on the guises of the various authors, ranging from Le Chef de bouche chez
Brébant to fashion critic Miss Satin. What is most striking in this context, however, is the
widespread understanding that it demonstrates of the wedding dress—and it is a white
wedding dress—as a significant expression of fashion whose design should be considered
in consultation with the latest modes and expert opinion, and the thorny relationship
between propriety and fashionability.

Then as now, the most significant garment associated with weddings was the bride's
gown, which varied with fashions as the century progressed, increasingly codified as
white, frequently reworked for later wearing, and often simply the woman's best dress.[28]
While the general public has always been fascinated by the specifics of royal nuptials,
technology allowed details of the union of Queen Victoria and Prince Albert of Saxe-
Coburg and Gotha on February 10, 1840 to be known faster and in greater detail than
before (Figure 4.3).

Her white dress of Spitalfields silk satin, Honiton lace veil, and orange blossoms
established precedents that were readily reinterpreted.[29] An account in *The Times* the
next day remarked on the "wreath of orange blossom." *The Mirror* published a detailed
and illustrated account on the 16th noting the "rich white Satin," orange blossom
flowers, and the exact placement of the Honiton lace veil. George Hayter's painting of
the day would be engraved by Henry Graves, with a supplemental key to the depicted
attendees.[30]

The advent of photography having occurred only the year before in 1839, no
photographs were taken on the day of the wedding. Yet in 1854, Roger Fenton
photographed Queen Victoria both alone and with her husband in ball attire whose floral
wreath, dress, and veil appeared as those from her wedding, then fourteen years and
eight children earlier. The queen is also known to have worn her reworked bridal lace at
important events, such as christenings of her children, and these images had subsequent
currency as referents.[31]

The trappings of royal marriages had always been items of public fascination, but
Queen Victoria was not only the reigning monarch, but a media celebrity. A thinking
through of Eric Hobsbawm's concept of an "invented tradition" may be on point here.
Hobsbawm defines an "invented tradition" as "a set of practices governed by overtly or
tacitly accepted rules and of a ritual or symbolic nature, which seek to inculcate certain
values and norms of behaviour by repetition, which automatically implies continuity
with the past."[32] While the ceremony bringing together two individuals, and two families,
was clearly not invented within the nineteenth century, the wedding industry, with its
commercially-driven sentimentalized etiquette was. As such, constant external reference
was needed in order to discern its regulations. This came in the form of etiquette manuals,
which offered guidance as to dress, as in the 1852 *Etiquette of Courtship and Matrimony:
With a Complete Guide to the Forms of a Wedding* insistence that "whether or not wearing
a bonnet, the bride must always wear a veil," to questions of appropriate gifts, how to
react as a suitor if you are rejected by the bride's parents, or even, the 1890 *Mystery of*

FIGURE 4.3: Engraving depicting the wedding of Queen Victoria of Great Britain and Prince Albert Saxe-Coburg and Gotha, St. James's Palace, London, February 10, 1840. Photo: Guildhall Library & Art Gallery/Heritage Images/Getty Images.

Love, Courtship, and Marriage Explained chapter concerning "How a Lady should manage her Beau to make him propose Marriage."[33]

Whether or not she knew the details of Queen Victoria's dress, the American bride who wore this (Figure 4.4) gown was demonstrating her own ingenious interpretation. In addition to referring to etiquette texts, the illustrated press, and fashion illustrations, this bride may well have been influenced in her planning by the burgeoning wedding industry, with increasingly frequent product placement for elements of the trousseau, attire, and most significantly the gifts—which were now expected to be displayed along with clear identification as to from whom they had been received—within purportedly informative texts regarding fashionable, yet proper, wedding traditions.[34]

FIGURE 4.4: 1840s American wedding dress. From the collection of Steven Porterfield, courtesy of the Texas Fashion Collection. Photo: Laurie Ruth Photography.

Funerals

Paralleling weddings, and potentially exceeding them in expenditure and the nascent industry to facilitate them, were increasingly detailed and widespread fashions for mourning rituals.[35]

While mourning dress had been worn for centuries, the public presentation of its fashionability became increasingly prevalent in the nineteenth century along with the advent of print and commodity culture.[36] While fabric, color, and accessories might connote mourning, the cut of clothing was expected to follow the latest trends, as in the Empire gown depicted in this 1809 plate from Ackermann's (Figure 4.5) in which mother

FIGURE 4.5: Mourning dresses. *Ackermann's Repository of Arts, Literature, Commerce, Manufactures, Fashion and Politics*, series 1, vol. 2, September 1809. Author's collection.

looks—in elegant profile—at a mourning vase. The young daughter, alone in expressing apparent emotions, mourns only for the doll that has been dropped and is now out of reach.

Royal precedence and independently manufactured strictures for mourning comportment—similar to that for weddings—were presented in print media, both periodicals and etiquette manuals alike to a European and American populace filled with anxiety regarding propriety and the intricacies of the appropriate display of mourning. The timing of the particularities of dress was of utmost concern, with women frequently writing letters to the editor for confirmation of the specifics of practice—when to wear crape, how long, etc.[37] In the American context, relevant magazines included *Harper's, World of Fashion, Ladies Cabinet*, and *Godey's Lady's Book* and references to mourning were so common that, to take a single example, nearly every 1899–1900 weekly issue of *Harper's* included some mention of mourning clothes.[38]

Unfortunately for contemporary consumers, the proliferation of advice was so extreme as to lead to contradictions.[39] As Lou Taylor points out, "[t]radesmen and industrialists with business interests in death made a good living in the Victorian period."[40] For not only were there mourning clothes to purchase, at mourning warehouses such as Jay's (Figure 4.6), but also jewelry—both jet and hair—black-edged mourning-envelopes and stationery, commemorative ribbons, and wool-work memorials, among others.[41] Furthermore, the model set by Queen Victoria in her perpetual mourning for Prince

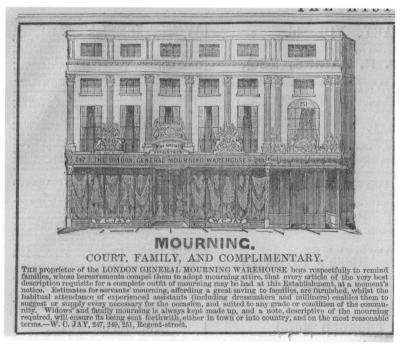

FIGURE 4.6: Illustrated advertisement for London General Mourning Warehouse, W.C. Jay, 247–51 Regent Street, London. *The Illustrated Historic Times*; or, *The London Press*, 1850. Note the reference to the ability to service clients' needs "at a moment's notice." Author's collection.

Albert could not be ignored. The burden of representational propriety through mourning was disproportionately borne by women. While men's mourning dress existed, its particularities and stages were dramatically less extensive than those for women. As Taylor perceptively acknowledges, "[w]omen were used, albeit willingly and even eagerly by most, as a show piece, to display their family's total respectability, sense of conformity and wealth."[42]

PROPRIETY AND THE GREAT MASCULINE RENUNCIATION

At about that time [the end of the eighteenth century] there occurred one of the most remarkable events in the whole history of dress, one under the influence of which we are still living, one, moreover, which has attracted far less attention than it deserves: men gave up their right to all the brighter, gayer, more elaborate, and more varied forms of ornamentation, leaving these entirely to the use of women, and thereby making their own tailoring the most austere and ascetic of the arts. Sartorially, this event has surely the right to be considered beautiful. He henceforth aimed at being only useful.[43]

J.C. Flügel published his account of what he termed the "great masculine renunciation" in his 1930 *The Psychology of Clothes* in which he describes a "sudden reduction of male sartorial decorativeness which took place at the end of the eighteenth century."[44] Flügel does not claim that distinction was not still displayed in men's dress. Indeed, in reviewing the 1864 fashion print (Figure 4.7) we see differentiated forms of hats and coats and

FIGURE 4.7: British fashion plate, 1864. © Victoria and Albert Museum, London.

trousers of solid colors, Tattersall plaid, and stripes. The men's bodies are themselves elegantly displayed. Yet, in comparison to the representation of women's fashions of around the same period in the French print (Figure 4.8), the gentlemen are significantly more drab.

In the era of "masculine renunciation," the variety of men's civilian clothing was reduced, in cut and fabric alike.[45] In its wake came an almost exclusive attention to a

FIGURE 4.8: French fashion plate dating from c. 1855–6. The Metropolitan Museum of Art, New York.

morality of men's clothing based upon its immaculate condition, whereby "[Q]uestionable linen, a rumpled suit, a spattered overcoat were so many signs of a needy and laborious life compared to the clean and neat appearance that suggested, even if it did not prove, affluence and leisure."[46] Under this sartorial regime, therefore, women's bodies were made to signify more so than those of men, differentiations based upon sexual difference rather than class differentiation increased in importance, and the readable female body came to bear the burden of the related imperatives of morality and capital.

In a discussion of the drawings of Elizabeth Siddal that Dante Gabriel Rossetti completed in the 1850s, Deborah Cherry and Griselda Pollock explained, "[t]hey signify in the ideological process of a redefinition of woman *as image*, and as *visibly* different. They appropriate 'woman', as an explicitly visual image—seen to be seen—as a signifier in a displaced and repressed discourse on masculinity."[47] For Cherry and Pollock, then, there is an important distinction to be made between images of women—with their problematics—and woman *as image*. It is in reference to the latter that Abigail Solomon-Godeau charts a renunciation parallel to Flügel's within the realm of visual culture. She argues that during the nineteenth century the female "display nude" replaced the active, heroic and, occasionally, nude male bodies of the history paintings that formed the pinnacle of representational regimes through academic structures.[48] Significantly, while both Cherry and Pollock and Solomon-Godeau base their arguments upon representations of women in either elite or non-elite visual culture, the fashionably dressed woman of the 1850s may equally be considered representation, as a manner of expression.[49] In the now classic terminology of Thorstein Veblen, she is the site of conspicuous consumption.[50]

Fashionable feminine silhouettes ranging from layers of petticoats; cage crinolines; tied back skirts and trains, in addition to the corset, forged the female body into relative immobility, demonstrating defined roles of masculine activity and femininity visibility.[51] As such, the woman of fashion has variously been defined as an "unfree servant" or an "exquisite slave."[52] In short, the readability of women within the visual field was imperative. Yet even while women, essentially exclusively, came to signify wealth, too close an alignment with commerce might mark a woman as herself for sale.

FALLEN WOMEN, *FEMMES GALANTES*, AND FINERY

Taking them as a class of young women, they are surpassed by none in any rank of society for a genteel and beautiful appearance. For the handsome manner in which they are paid by those who visit them, they are enabled to dress remarkably well, which, together with a tint of *rouge*, renders them very fascinating and attractive. Whilst walking on the street, many of them are exceedingly modest in their appearance, and have no particular marks by which they can be distinguished from ladies in the higher walks of life.[53]

The image of the whore, . . . is the embodiment of objectivity, not subjectivity . . . As seller she mimics the commodity and takes on its allure: the fact that her sexuality is on sale is itself an attraction.[54]

Writing in 1840, William Tait pointed to the beauty, modesty, and quality of dress of a class of prostitutes that he refers to as *femmes galantes*. This observation was a source of tremendous anxiety to the author of *Magdalenism: An Inquiry into its Extent, Causes and Consequences of Prostitution in Edinburgh* and many others as well. While the legal and public health reactions to prostitution, or, the Great Social Evil, varied technically from Anglo-American abolition to French regulation, the belief that prostitution was a widespread problem that needed to be in some way addressed was consistent.[55] The issue was seen to be one of the relationship between moral, economic, and social stability, wherein it was believed that "female morality determines public morality which is manifested in either social stability or revolution."[56] The prostitute, as a social type, was understood as a threat to public safety, both in terms of biological contagion such as syphilis, but also social contagion, particularly in her relationship to the concept of commodity. As Hollis Clayson points out, while social concern regarding prostitution has had a long chronological sweep, it is no surprise that near obsessive focus on her as type, individual and image, and the morality of appearance more generally corresponds with the rise of the department store and mass-produced garments.[57] For it is in two modes of her relationship to fashion that the prostitute was particularly troubling (Figure 4.9). First, given the increasingly broad accessibility of both garments and concepts of fashionability through avenues such as fashion plates and magazines, women both virtuous and venal wore the same garments. Second, fashion itself, or a passion for finery, was seen as potentially drawing otherwise honest women into prostitution.

William Tait was not alone in experiencing or at least proclaiming difficulty in discerning the prostitute among other fashionable women. Writing in 1857, William Acton referred to a "numerous band" of prostitutes that he described as "sober, genteelly dressed, well ordered, often elegant in person."[58] A lithograph by Auguste Andrieux published in *Le Charivari* in 1864 asked the question, "What difference is there, at first glance, between

THE HAYMARKET.—MIDNIGHT.

FIGURE 4.9: "The Haymarket, Midnight," from Henry Mayhew, *London Labour and the London Poor*, vol. 4: "Those Who Will Not Work" (London: Griffin, Bohn & Co., 1862). Courtesy of University of North Texas Libraries, Special Collections.

une grande dame and *une petite dame*? Their dress is the same, they go to the *bois* at the same time, they receive the same gentlemen."[59] In his extended study of prostitution in the city of Paris, Alexandre-Jean-Baptiste Parent-Duchâtelet devoted considerable text to the question, "Can and should we compel prostitutes to wear distinctive dress," ultimately concluding that while desirable the policy would be impracticable.[60] This lack of legibility was especially troubling as the mere presence of the prostitute—discerned or not— was perceived as threatening social order. What could, then, be more menacing than a threat that not only was not readily perceived or, more damagingly, might be lauded as a fashionable model as the prostitute forms the lynchpin of the interlocking realms of consumption and fashion? Therefore, as clothing became a more difficult cipher, its importance as an indexical marker of morality increased.[61]

The protection of society was, in fact, a focus of the regulationist argument—the idea that prostitution must exist, but be contained and enclosed to a point where the "decent folk" of society would not be influenced to act in a similar fashion. Indeed, in a climate of conspicuous and vicarious consumption that prized the display of luxury on the bodies of elite women, wealthy women ran the risk of being misread. Furthermore, insofar as even the most purportedly stringent opponents of prostitution, such as Acton and Tait, recognized the beauty inherent in the fashionable display of *femmes galantes*, it was unsurprisingly understood that other women might see them as aspirational models. In Tait's entire chapter on "Pride and Love of Dress," he claims that of all the causes of prostitution that there is perhaps not "one more general or more powerful than ambition for fine dress."[62] Mayhew refers to "the passion for dress" as an impetus to prostitution.[63] For both Tait and Mayhew, these are "fallen women," whose descent from the respectable classes, like those of Theodore Dreiser's *Sister Carrie*, were instigated, at least in part, by outsized sartorial ambitions.[64]

COMMODITY CULTURE AND CATHEDRALS OF COMMERCE

The well-rounded neck and graceful figures of the dummies exaggerated the slimness of the waist, the absent head being replaced by a large price-ticket pinned on the neck; whilst the mirrors, cleverly arranged on each side of the window, reflected and multiplied the forms without end, peopling the street with these beautiful women for sale, each bearing a price in big figures in the place of a head.[65]

Perhaps the reigning belief system of the period was not religious faith, but an increased realization of the power of commodity. In his essay "Marx's Coat," Peter Stallybrass notes that in *Capital* it is a coat that forms the framing device by which Karl Marx explicates the meaning of commodity as that which may be fetish but exists primarily as exchange value rather than material good.[66] Stallybrass points to the poignancy of this. In reviewing the letters and accounts of the Marx family, it is clear that the clothes of Karl, his wife Jenny, and their children, like those of many of their station, spent at least as much time in the pawn shop as they did in the possession of the Marx family.[67] The absence of these garments had a concrete impact on the welfare of the family. For instance, without his own coat Karl Marx could not, in the winter of 1852, make himself sufficiently presentable to enter the Reading Room of the British Library, despite his possession of an entrance ticket. Not only would he be insufficiently warm to make the journey, in the cold and in ill health, but he could not present himself in suitable dress.

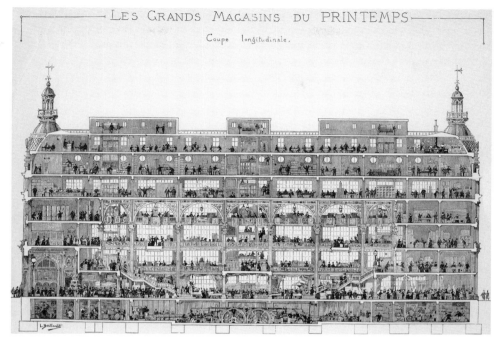

FIGURE 4.10: Printemps department store, Paris, 1885, engraving. Photo: DEA Picture Library/Getty Images.

It is precisely this aspect of commodity consumption, display, and internalization that is this era's legacy. The department store is key to its construction.[68] As Michael Miller explained in regards to the Bon Marché, although the same could certainly be said of Lewis's or Wannamakers or Printemps (Figure 4.10):

> Bourgeois costumes, bourgeois occasions, bourgeois ambitions—the very range of bourgeois life style—were to be found on the store's shelves and counters and floors. The department store was, in short, a bourgeois celebration, an expression of what its culture stood for and where it had come over the past century.[69]

The department store acted as both distribution center and fashion house, and a relationship was forged by which fashion magazines and shops came to shape desire as well as presenting the goods to satiate it.[70] Coded as both feminine and pleasurable, shopping in these new halls of temptation constituted women as consumers, and consumption, rather than production, as the site of identity.[71] While commodity culture and the circulation and fetishism of commodities touched all levels of society, those like Marx felt the materiality of these circumstances differently from the bourgeois. Yet it is the spectacle of bourgeois consumption—whereby the heads of beautifully dressed women are replaced by sales tags within the window of Zola's *Au Bonheur des Dames*—that is the legacy of the period.

CHAPTER FIVE

Gender and Sexuality

ARIEL BEAUJOT

Fashion gives the body significance. It helps people perform their sexed and gendered identities, and it allows them to emphasize their various and varied sexualities. Dress is one of the most immediate ways that people identify one another as being male or female, masculine or feminine. Because clothing lies close to the skin, most do not consider the layers of cultural meaning embedded in clothing and mistake dress as an extension of the natural body, a true revelation of a person's sex, gender, and sexual identity—this despite the fact that many can and do cross dress convincingly. Many scholars have argued that gender is a performance that incorporates careful attention to the choice of clothing. Following the work of researchers such as Anne Oakley, Sherry Ortner, and Robert Stoller we can see that gender is, indeed, a performance, more than it is a fact based on the possession of certain genitals.[1] While these are all scholars studying modern gender phenomena, the gendering of men and women has a long history. The modern dichotomous constructs of gender began around the last quarter of the eighteenth century and was solidified by the nineteenth century. Thinking about gender as a performance, partially achieved through clothing, is particularly imperative for an exploration of the cultural history of dress and fashion because it was in the nineteenth century that clothing became exaggeratingly distinct for each gender— through careful tailoring, corseting, bustling, and crinolining nineteenth-century women's bodies became hourglasses, and men's bodies became long, straight, and cylindrical. Judith Butler pushes feminist theory further and into the realm of queer theory. She explains that we are blinded to the way in which gender becomes naturalized because we have been socialized to see only two gender options: "male" and "female." But these two options operate in the larger framework of heterosexuality. When one does away with this framework, the two genders are no longer seen as natural categories, but "persistent impersonations that passes as the real."[2] Butler provides the example of people dressing in drag and poses the question: "Is drag the imitation of gender, or does it dramatize the signifying gestures through which gender itself is established?"[3] As Butler considers gender she identifies phallogocentrism (the privileging of the male point of view) and compulsory heterosexuality as the cultural constructs that maintain gender dichotomy.[4]

The nineteenth century marks the culmination of a phenomenon that had begun in the eighteenth century: the gender differentiation based on fashion. Before this, clothing had been more often used to convey social class than gender.[5] Women and men of the noble classes of Britain and Europe wore ornate clothing with rich colors and fabrics that created similar silhouettes (Figure 5.1).

From the late Middle Ages until the eighteenth century, the clothing worn by men and women of the upper class was so remarkably similar that it was not always possible to distinguish the gender of the wearer from far away. Anne Hollander traces this shift back

FIGURE 5.1: Note the similar silhouette for men's and women's clothes during the Renaissance. Anonymous seventeenth-century Dutch engraving. Rijksmuseum, Amsterdam.

to a split that happened in the craft of tailoring. In 1675, a group of French seamstresses successfully petitioned King Louis XIV to form a guild of female tailors who would make women's clothing. According to Hollander, "[t]he moment marked the beginning of a fundamental divergence in the clothes of the two sexes that affected the whole eighteenth century, reached an extreme in the nineteenth, and still persists."[6] Up until the last quarter of the seventeenth century, male tailors created the clothing for both men and women. Trained to design, cut, and fit clothing, they formed complementary dress styles, fabric, shape and drape, so that neither gender was more ornamented than the other. Heretofore, women had been employed in the dress industry working on seams, trim, and finishing. With the new guild of women tailors, trained mainly in fancy work and not in how to design and cut clothing, the silhouette for women's clothing became focused on ornamented draped fabric over a bodice, rather than the refined cut now reserved for men's clothing. In this period, we saw the emergence of the finely tailored three-piece suit, and the reputation of elite women's vain obsession with the ornate, lavish, and decorative, and a time when frivolous fashion becomes solidified. By 1775 we begin to see in fashion plates and portraits of the period, the marked gender differentiation in clothing (Figure 5.2).

FIGURE 5.2: By the 1770s we begin to see in fashion plates the marked difference between men's and women's clothing. Top: Gallerie des Modes et Costumes Français, 1778, P.88: Bourgeoise se promenant . . ., Nicolas Dupin, Pierre Thomas Le Clerc, Esnauts & Rapilly, c. 1776–c. 1786; Bottom: Gallerie des Modes et Costumes Français, 1776, T 113: Fraque d'été de toile . . ., Dupin, Esnauts & Rapilly, in or after 1776. Both from the Rijksmuseum, Amsterdam.

The gendering of clothing—men wearing the sober and ever darkening three-piece suit representative of their seriousness and rationality, and women sporting the increasingly large, more colorful and elaborate dress, representing their irrational pursuit of luxury and attempts at beatifying their bodies—though previously present in the Christian world, becomes obvious and real through the tailoring shift of 1675.[7] It is interesting to put this into the context of the changing concepts of sex evident around this same period. According to Thomas Laqueur, *Making Sex: Body and Gender from the Greeks to Freud,* the post-Enlightenment period marked a divergence in Western understandings of sex posited by scientists, doctors, political activists, and writers of fiction alike.[8] Before the late seventeenth century, the one-sex model prevailed. In this model, women and men were considered of the same sex; women were undeveloped males with their sexual organs reversed and contained within their bodies—the vagina being an internal penis, the womb being the scrotum, and the ovaries being the testes. The two-sex model that emerged during the Enlightenment newly proclaimed that men and women were entirely different, dichotomous creatures, with two distinct sets of sexual organs. Laqueur's argument is that the physical makeup of the body, our biologies, are understood in a series of differing ways throughout history. In other words, sex is socially constructed. But for the two-sex model to become common sense there had to be a corresponding shift in cultural interpretation and representation.

The unprecedented changes that happened in the tailoring industry from 1675 to 1775 could be seen as making the two-sex model evident, obvious, and observable. Clothing *showed* that men and women were entirely separate sexed entities because their clothing no longer followed similar stylistic principles. Men's and women's clothing looked so different that no one would assume that the flesh beneath the clothing was not also distinct. The ideas of the natural difference between men and women became increasingly evident in the nineteenth century, especially within the bourgeois class. The middle classes aligned themselves with the separate sphere doctrine, a process that has been aptly historicized by Leonore Davidoff and Catherine Hall who show that over time middle-class men and women develop different roles in the family and the workplace.[9] Looking back at the nineteenth century, we encounter fashion theorists such as Thorstein Veblen (1899) and, later, J.C. Flügel (1930) both of whom reinforce the two-sex model by arguing for a natural difference between the sexes.[10]

Around the time of the emergence of the two-sex model, people's attitudes toward sexuality also began to shift. According to Valerie Steele, a historian of fashion, eroticism, and fetish, the eighteenth century was a period of transition that saw sexual behaviors and attitudes develop toward what they are today.[11] No longer did sexual acts stand alone. People began to think of themselves and others as possessing sexual *identities* based on the sex acts in which they participated. In agreement with Steele, Joanne Entwistle states that "sexuality is a modern construct" and that it was not until the 1860s that Victorians began to create and categorize sexualities like homosexual and bisexual as a form of comparison to the normative heterosexuality.[12] We need now to digress into a discussion of sexual theory because it will give us the framework with which to interpret the connections between gender, sexuality, and fashion. To understand the historiography of sexuality we can review the work of the three theorists that have had the most influence on the field: Sigmund Freud, Michel Foucault, and Judith Butler. The first two authors write about fetish as well, something that Steele connects to dress: "fetishism evokes images of 'kinky' sex, involving an abnormal attraction to items of clothing such as high-heeled shoes and tightly laced corsets or body parts like feet and hair."[13]

According to Freud, sexuality develops in infants and is a core part of our identities.[14] Children go through various phases of psychosexual development where they fixate on certain objects. In *Three Contributions to the Theory of Sex*, Freud argues that one "pathological aberration" resulting from the phallic phase, in which children come to understand gender, is fetishism.[15] Freud's essay "Fetishism" contends that some boys, realizing their mother's lack of phallus, become fearful of castration and therefore imbue all their future female lovers with a stand-in penis in the form of a fetish. For Freud, "the fetish is a substitute for the woman's (the mother's) penis that the little boy once believed in and . . . does not want to give up . . . in his mind the woman *has* got a penis, in spite of everything; but this penis is no longer the same as it was before. Something else has taken its place, has been appointed its substitute, as it were, and now inherits the interest which was formerly directed to its predecessor."[16] Though fetishes can be focused on body parts they are also associated with such dress and fashion items as shoes, velvet, fur, and underwear. Freud believes that fashion items develop as fetishes because the accessory represents the moment before a mother reveals her lack. A shoe fetish might develop when a boy looks up his mother's skirt while lying by her shoe. An underwear fetish develops because this garment represents the moment just before full undress when a womanly phallus remains a possibility.

For Michel Foucault, sexuality is not inherent in us. Rather, it was produced by newly emerging discourses of the seventeenth century that restricted and prohibited certain sexual acts and separated them from what was deemed normative. This resulted in the production of sexuality as an important aspect of our identities, which it had not been previously.[17] According to Foucault, these discourses were further developed in the late-nineteenth century by psychoanalysts (of which Freud is an example) who named and strictly defined the parameters of normative (hetero)sexuality and non-normative sexualities which included fetishists. In fact, Foucault calls fetishism "the model perversion . . . which, from at least as early as 1877, served as the guiding thread for analyzing all the other deviations." It was in the fetish that psychoanalysis "could clearly perceive the way in which the instinct became fastened to an object in accordance with an individual's historical adherence and biological inadequacy."[18] In *The History of Sexuality*, Foucault stands Freudian analysis on its head, seeing his work as the culmination of a longer historical process of naming and regulating sexualities. Instead of seeing sexuality, as Freud does, inherent in individuals from their infancy, Foucault argues that it is created externally through systems of power and knowledge. For Foucault, sexuality has no essence, it is not a natural quality of individuals, but rather it has been produced by writers, thinkers, and psychoanalysis who named and classified it, creating sexual types and placing individuals within them.

Through a close reading of Freud, Foucault, Jacques Lacan, and others, Butler establishes that both sex and gender are cultural constructs with no distinction between them as many earlier feminists have supposed.[19] Instead, Butler explains that sex/gender is created by repetitive performative acts that help to establish sex/gender as natural when in fact it is a "regulatory fiction."[20] In other words, there is no such thing as genuine womanliness or genuine manliness; these are simply masks or mimicries that have no foundation whatsoever.[21] She further states that the binary of sex/gender into male and female, masculine and feminine, is a false dichotomy that helps to establish heteronormativity. Following Lacan, Butler shows the phallocentricity of modern heterosexuality is made to seem real because of the distinctions between the genders: the male phallus needs the female lack in order to conceive of male desire. For Butler, like

Foucault, sexual desire is created rather than inherent, this time through the myth of gender distinctions. The foundational illusion of heterosexuality is established through the sex/gender distinction which is a fiction. Or as Butler puts it, "part of the comedic dimension of this failed model of reciprocity . . . is that both masculine and feminine positions are signified, the signifier belonging to the Symbolic that can never be assumed in more than token form by either position."[22] Sexuality and pleasure in the gendered body are further culturally constructed to focus on certain organs: the penis, the vagina, and the breasts. For Butler, "some parts of the body become conceivable foci of pleasure precisely because they correspond to a normative ideal of a gender-specific body."[23] But in focusing on specific organs for pleasure, other pleasure centers are deadened. Furthermore, there are discontinuities within heterosexual, bisexual, gay, and lesbian subjects and relationships so that gender does not follow sex (as in drag), and desire or sexuality does not follow from gender. It is in these contexts that heterosexual normativity and phallocentricity begin to break down and reveal their constructed status.[24]

Butler's most radical claim is that the very essence of our selves—some call this our identities, our souls, our inner-most thoughts and desires—are culturally constructed through restrictive laws that help give an impression of an inner and outer self. I believe myself to be female, therefore I enact femininity through bodily gestures, clothing, and an attraction to men. For Butler, we have no essence, no inner selves; we are only the products of narratives that give us an impression of coherence and two of the strongest narratives regulating our lives are sex/gender and heterosexuality. In the concluding remarks of *Gender Trouble* Butler argues for a proliferation of gender and sexual desire: "The loss of gender norms would have the effect of proliferating gender configurations, destabilizing substantive identity, and depriving the naturalizing narratives of compulsory heterosexuality of their central protagonist: 'man' and 'woman'."[25]

We might ask ourselves what these theories have to do with fashion. For Butler, the way in which gender, and therefore heterosexuality, is enacted has much to do with the body's surface. Though never explicitly stated in her work, I think it would be fair to say that the effect of the "stylization of the body,"[26] repeatedly referred to in her work, is established partially through clothing that helps distinguish one gender from the other and accentuates the primary sex characteristics of men and women. In contrast, for Freud, clothing, or at least objects and accessories, are often fetishized. Therefore, garments help bring feelings of sexual desire in some individuals. The gendering of the self, so important in Freud's theory of child development, can also be understood as fashion based. Girls/women take on the role of beautifying the self through fashion to ensure that they fulfil their passive gender obligation of being looked at. And boys/men take on the active role of mastery, as bearers of the look. Fashion takes a front seat here in the dual action of display and voyeurism between the genders. Finally, Foucault, a little harder to pin down in terms of fashion, argues for a creation of sexuality through regulation and knowledge. Around the seventeenth century, according to Foucault, newly emerging laws began to separate heterosexuality from other types of sexuality, thereby making sexuality part of the way in which we categorize our selves, rather than simply understanding sex as an act that may take various forms. What we will find as we review the sources on fashion is that often, people sorted out the various sexualities partly through what they wore. By the 1890s, homosexuality was aligned with the fashion of dandyism because of the trials of Oscar Wilde. In other examples, police arrested men with powder puffs as this accessory was thought to be an indication of their homosexual status in inter-war London.[27]

This chapter will review two examples of clothing that will help elucidate the connections between gender, sexuality, and fashion. We will begin by discussing the three-piece suit, a sartorial choice that helped to formulate a specific type of masculinity in the late-seventeenth century that drew on the gender differentiation inherent in the two-sex model, and was based on class differentiation. By the end of the nineteenth century, a particularly well cut and fashionable three-piece suit became the symbol of dandyism, a style of self-presentation that is often interpreted to be evidence of gender performativity by scholars and was increasingly associated with homosexuality after the 1890s. The second example we will review is the corset, sometimes worn by dandies, but especially associated with women in the nineteenth and early-twentieth centuries. This study is about the actual garment—the corset—rather than the attire that required corsets. Here we will see how the corset helped reinforce sex/gender differentiation, and how it was associated with fetishism in the nineteenth century and beyond.

MASCULINITY, DANDYISM, AND THE THREE-PIECE SUIT

The item of male attire most strongly associated with men in the modern period is the three-piece suit consisting of a jacket, trousers, and waistcoat. The first person to analyze the transition from men wearing brighter, more elaborate, and more varied forms of clothing (such as breeches, doublets, cravats, and capes) to the uniform style of the suit was John Carl Flügel. In his 1930 book, *The Psychology of Clothes*, Flügel coined the term "Great Masculine Renunciation" to describe the phenomena of men choosing plain, sober, and inconspicuous clothing, leaving ornamentation to women. Flügel explains this phenomenon using psychoanalytic theory suggesting that the political and social upheavals brought about by the 1798 French Revolution necessitated a sartorial shift. As Flügel has it, the call for "Liberty, Equality, Fraternity" meant that civic-minded men no longer sought to emphasize distinctions in rank and class but rather chose to attire themselves similarly to represent their devotion to the new democratic spirit. "Man abandoned his claim to be considered beautiful. He henceforth aimed at being only useful."[28] In making these claims, Flügel is indicating that the two-sex model (at least when it comes to clothing) originates around the end of the eighteenth century but he also adds psychosocial weight to the idea that sex/gender are givens, and that the essence of men and women is expressed externally through clothing: "modern man has a far sterner and more rigid conscience than has modern woman, and the man's morality tends to find expression in his clothes in a greater degree than is the case with woman. Hence it is not surprising that . . . modern man's clothing abounds in features which symbolize his devotion to the principles of duty, of renunciation, and of self-control."[29]

Flügel goes so far as to use Freudian theory to explain what this change in clothing and mentality meant for men psychologically. He explains that the tendency toward narcissism and exhibitionism in men has moved away from clothing toward "showing off" by being good at one's work, or projecting the narcissistic tendencies onto one's female partner, who vicariously displays the exhibitionism of the man.[30] Otherwise, he suggests that men transfer their (passive) exhibitionism into (active) scopophilia "the desire to be seen being transformed into the desire to see."[31] In this case, the woman and her clothing become fetishized erotic displays for the voyeuristic male. In Flügel's analysis we see how thoroughly Freudian understandings of gender differentiation are entrenched and we see a strong assumption that sex/gender are internal states of identity.

In the last twenty years, historians have begun to question the validity of this proposed watershed moment in men's fashion, some placing it further back in history, and others arguing that the renunciation did not last past the middle of the nineteenth century and that many men were in fact interested in fashion and self-display. Art historian Anne Hollander argues that the origins of the suit were much earlier than Flügel suggested. That is, the suit appeared in the late-seventeenth century rather than the late-eighteenth century (Figure 5.3).

FIGURE 5.3: Seventeenth-century men's suit as seen in Daniël Mijtens' depiction of Charles I, King of England, 1629. The Metropolitan Museum of Art, New York.

As discussed earlier, Hollander shows that the suit came about because of a split in the craft of tailoring which left men and women to design clothing for their own genders, where previously men had designed for both genders, and this had ensured that neither gender had fancier or more frivolous-looking clothing than the other. This ensured that fashion followed the same principles and the sexes therefore appeared sartorially similar. There was at the same time a desire for more somber clothing brought about by soldiers' uniforms and a new vogue in clerical modesty due to the influence of the Reformation and religious wars of the earlier seventeenth century.[32] Presenting a different view, Hardy Amies agrees that the three-piece suit originated in the mid-seventeenth century, but suggests that it came out of the riding suit worn by the aristocracy at their country estates.[33] Like Flügel, Amies sees the suit as a move toward democratization. David Kuchta similarly sees the origins in the later-seventeenth century but he adds to this fact an argument that the reasons behind this sartorial shift are due to the political, economic, and social changes of the period. That is, Kuchta argues that aristocratic men donned the suit after the Glorious Revolution of 1688 to show themselves as industrious, frugal, and able to properly run the nation.[34] While governing was strictly limited to kings, nobility was relegated to more frivolous preoccupations. As governing descended toward those without royal blood, sober demeanor was required. As such, modesty in dress of the rich, landed governing class came to represent their independence from concerns about fashion, vanity, and luxury.

This redefinition of upper-class masculinity and clothing, identified by Kuchta, came at a price for lower- and urban middle-class men and women who were labeled as vain for their luxurious displays. They were supposedly under the controlling influence of their conformity to fashion and therefore politically tainted, unable to see past their pursuit of luxury to do what was best for the nation. This same set of rhetorical devices, this time aimed at excluding the lower classes and women, was later used by the middle class during the nineteenth century when they began to wear the suit in order to claim political legitimacy. The move away from Flügel's thesis of the suit representing Republicanism is important to note. Here the suit represents powerful hegemonic masculinity and is used as a way of excluding unworthy classes and genders from parliament (Figure 5.4). The three-piece suit as understood by Hollander, Amies, and Kuchta also materializes around the same time as Laqueur claims the emergence of the two-sex model.

The effects of the great masculine renunciation were reduced during the period of 1860 and 1914 when merchants aggressively sought out men as consumers and helped to make pleasurable materialism once again acceptable for men.[35] In my own work about men and fashion accessories, I also argue that ordinary men of the middle class and aristocracy were not as impervious to fashion and vanity as Flügel would have us believe. Most men of the nineteenth century were acutely aware of the subtle differences in fabric and fit that differentiated a gentleman from a poser, for example.[36] So what many have relegated to the woman's realm—fashion, vanity, self-display—was in fact a generalized social experience rather than a gendered/sexed experience. And no one figure can better prove the importance of clothing to men of the nineteenth century than the dandy.

Both a real-life individual and a literary character, the nineteenth-century dandy was distinguishable for his well-cut suit of dark home-spun wool and crisp white linen.[37] His three-piece suit conformed to the body in a way only achievable by perfect tailoring. He wore stays and wasp-waisted jackets to emphasize his body's affinity to Greek statuary.[38] Often not of the aristocratic class, the dandy participated in the education, social circle, and leisured lifestyle of that class and was known to be "consumed by a slavish devotion to impeccable correctness in all manners of dress, gesture, taste, and wit."[39] Many scholars,

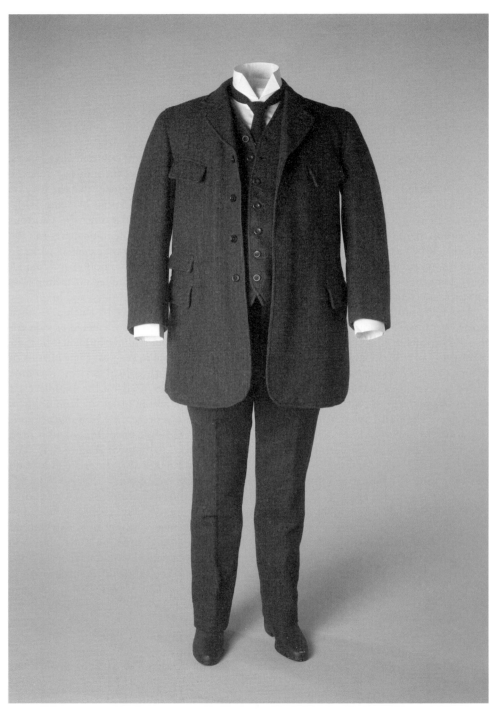

FIGURE 5.4: Man's three-piece suit of gray wool, woven with a herringbone pattern, c. 1890–1901. Image © the Olive Matthews Collection, Chertsey Museum. Photograph by John Chase.

both historians and literary experts, see dandyism as a performance of manliness that becomes evident because dandies do not quite fit into a class (and yet they set the sartorial tone for the aristocracy) and their preoccupation with the minutia of dress and exacting mannerisms (sometimes staid, sometimes flamboyant) put them in what is generally considered as a women's realm of conscious and conspicuous self-display.[40] The dandy has been said to participate in "highly theatrical gender play."[41] Some even argue that they become a "third transgressive sex" that helps reveal the performative aspects of the heteronormative gender construction.[42]

Though there have been many, including such personalities as George Bryan Brummell, Count d'Orsay, Edward Bulwer-Lytton, Oscar Wilde, Benjamin Disraeli, and young Winston Churchill, each dandy is said to be unique in his self-performance. He uses style as a way of confronting the ever-increasing capitalism of his age, to create a personality all his own, and to set himself outside the system of exchangeability, mass production, and class specific self-display.[43] The dandy is seen as a counter-culture figure, one that challenges conventional middle-class masculinity of hard work, restraint, and earnestness, and his disdain for these attitudes is portrayed partly through his choice of clothing.[44] Many dandies, including the famous regency-period dandy George Bryan Brummell (Figure 5.5), renounced colorful and fancy dress for understated clothing, viewed by Flügel as representative of the middle-class mindset.

FIGURE 5.5: George Bryan (Beau) Brummell, illustration from Capt. William Jesse, *Life of Beau Brummell* (London: The Navarre Society Limited, [1844] 1927). Photo: Hulton Archive/ Getty Images.

This might suggest that dandies were believers in the democratizing influence of the Great Masculine Renunciation, but their devotion to uniqueness and conspicuously elegant self-display puts them firmly outside this phenomenon.

By the end of the nineteenth-century, those dandies who were part of the aesthetic movement (and not all of them were) completely threw off their proximity to the middle-class suit, and also aristocratic gentlemanly modesty. Wilde's clothing departs from the earlier dandy dress of Brummel in that it is not subdued and elegant, but unusual and outlandish. Wilde wore single items that pushed the boundaries of the dark three-piece suit: a green *boutonnière*, a bright red waistcoat, or a turquoise and diamond stud.[45] On his 1882 American tour, Wilde wore what amounted to a Regency-style suit: a black-velvet costume complete with knee breaches and shiny shoes with large bows, nicknamed his "Little Lord Fauntleroy" outfit after its resemblance to clothing described in a children's novel (Figure 5.6).[46]

FIGURE 5.6: Oscar Wilde in his "Little Lord Fauntleroy" costume, 1882, *carte-de-visite*. Photo: Napoleon Sarony. The Metropolitan Museum of Art, New York.

This representation was ridiculed in its day for being outrageous and effeminate. One American audience member at his Brooklyn lecture, for example, commented: "He looks like a love-sick young girl."[47] His costume and staging were frequently commented on by the American press, whom Wilde accused of "refusing to take him or his cause seriously."[48]

Many scholars have pointed out the link between dandyism, effeminacy, and homosexual culture.[49] But in fact, these associations did not begin to form in the average Victorian person's mind until the fin de siècle when Oscar Wilde's 1895–6 trials made a link between the aesthetic movement and the underground world of homosexuality. Certainly there was derision directed at dandies because of their association with effeminacy before the Wilde trials, but this had to do with their sex/gender non-conformity and not their sexualities. As Foucault and others have found, it was not until the end of the nineteenth century that same-sex sex began to be considered an aspect of one's psycho-social identity; before this period sex was simply an act that one might participate in with a same sex or opposite sexed partner. Brent Shannon argues that after Wilde is convicted of gross indecency there is a labeling of male-male sexual behavior as deviant and the associations between aesthetic dress, effeminacy, and homosexuality are solidified.[50]

According to Breward, this meant that dandies who self-identified as heterosexual retreated from the aesthetic movement that used dandyism as a form of political, sexual, and social resistance, and moved toward the earlier subdued Brumwellian uniform that represented their engagement with the urban marketplace, refined taste, and comfort with commodity fetishism.[51] It was this later representation of dandyism that was used in advertisements to sell products to the masses.[52] By the turn of the twentieth century, the dandy had become what he had set out to counter: the ideal type for the middle-class masher and the working-class swell. The dandy had become a democrat; no longer did he represent West End refinement, he was now an example followed by all.[53]

THE CORSET, FEMININITY, AND FETISHISM

It is difficult to imagine a more obvious representation of the two-sex model of gender than that portrayed in Victorian dress. While men were busy encasing themselves in dark fabric that made them look like long black tubes finished off with top hats, women used corsets to remake their bodies into a silhouette that accentuated their bosom, hips, and waist. The corset, worn close to the body and able to modify the figure, was seen as enhancing "natural" beauty by Victorian men and women.[54] Typically measuring between 18 and 30 inches most corsets are thought to have constricted the waist by a couple inches, and be restrictive but not uncomfortable (Figure 5.7). Curators at the Museum of Costume at Bath have found that the smallest waist size in the dresses in their collection is 21½ inches.

The Chertsey Museum has found that their average Victorian dress waists are 27–28 inches.[55] Notoriously, some Victorians laced themselves so that they had very small waists. Members of this group, called "tight lacers," claim that they managed to get their mid-sections down to 16 or even 13 inches.[56] Though tight lacing received a lot of press in the period, historians are now agreed that it was a small minority of women and men who engaged in the practice. By the nineteenth century, at least in England, women from all classes wore corsets.[57] The French word for corset is "corp" meaning body, demonstrating linguistically that the clothing worn and the woman's flesh and bone were one and the same.[58] Since corsets of one shape or another were worn from early adolescence on, we can see corset wearing as an essential element of creating the look of femininity. Corseting was

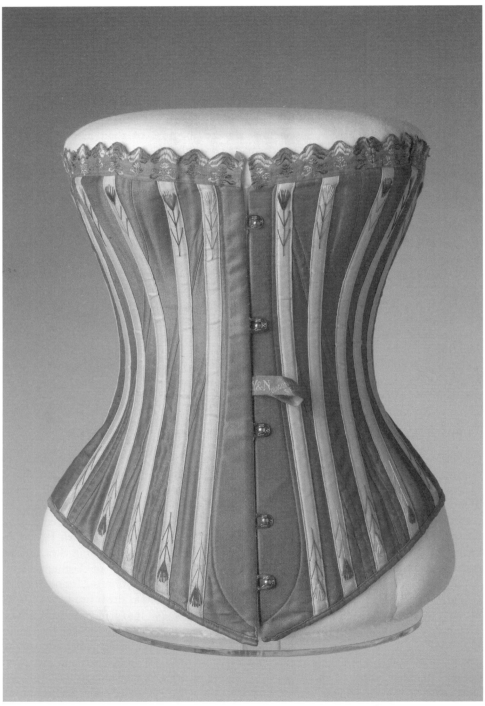

FIGURE 5.7: Corset of coffee-colored cotton sateen by Y&N, c. 1885–95. Image © the Olive
Matthews Collection, Chertsey Museum. Photo: John Chase.

a commitment that women made to differentiate their bodies from men. The thing that makes it especially obvious that the corset helped to form gender distinctions and reinforce the two-sex model are the caricatures that arose when dress reform movements called for an end to the corset in favor of less restrictive clothing for women like the bloomer (Figure 5.8).[59]

The origins of the corset, much like the suit, can be traced back to the aristocracy in the first half of the sixteenth century. During this period, whalebone and other stiff materials were incorporated into bodices to create an upright posture.[60] Aristocratic men of the Renaissance also wore clothing such as stiffened doublets [61] that helped them maintain an upright posture; some men of this period wore corsets to maintain the correct fit and drape of formal military costumes.[62] An especially important fact of this period is that the purpose of clothing was not to distinguish one gender from the other. As explained earlier, it had been more important that clothing created class than gender distinction. The corset, then, was an important element of aristocratic self-fashioning and performance for men and women alike. Corsets, in this early period, connoted rectitude, discipline, and self-mastery. The physical uprightness of the aristocratic body then signified not only the qualities of the individual, but also the virtues of the state.[63] Female monarchs of this period including Elizabeth I, Catherine de' Medici, and Catherine the Great were able to run their nation and live life at court while constricted and upright. In doing so, they crafted a theatrical aura of power through the "seductive look of effortless effort."[64] But as aristocratic culture became more familiar and copied, elements of dress that were

COMING MODES FOR WOMEN
OR WHAT IT WILL END IN.

FIGURE 5.8: Caricature of dress reform where the uncorseted women's dress is similar to men's. In these caricatures we see a fear that the genders would be indistinguishable from one another, as manly women and womanly men promenaded down the streets of the European metropolises. These spoofs are accidentally revealing; they demonstrate that gender is a performance heavily dependent on the wearing of specific garments. Mary Evans Picture Library.

particularly associated with the class became linked to women only—use of color and trimmings, more uprightness and rectitude.[65] This change occurred in the later eighteenth century, during the same period that masculine sartorial choices were shifting toward the suit. Fashion shows a shift in the mindset of the period: class is no longer the primary identity upon which people are differentiated. Now it will be gender. And the two elements of clothing that will help distinguish one gender from the other are the hour-glass-forming corset and the tubular and straight suit.

Early interpretations of the corset by historians and social thinkers cast it as a form of oppression for women.[66] Thorstein Veblen, the American sociologist writing in 1899, called corseting "a mutilation, undergone for the purpose of lowering the subject's vitality and rendering her permanently and obviously unfit for work."[67] Writing in 1977, Hélène E. Roberts argued "[t]he clothing of the Victorian woman clearly perfected the message of a willingness to conform to the submissive masochistic pattern, but dress also helped mould female behaviors to the role of the 'exquisite slave'."[68] According to Roberts, and Veblen, the corset was a form of suppression, creating passivity in women of the nineteenth century. Authors such as these tend to see dress reform as the liberating force that would relieve women from their confining and oppressive corsets in the twentieth century. Once emancipation from constricting and uncomfortable dress was secured, they argue, other forms of emancipation for women would soon follow.

Rather than seeing women of the past as victims of fashion who do not have agency in their clothing choices, some historians have begun to look at the corset as liberating. The most adamant of these authors is art historian David Kunzle who flips the argument that corsets were a form of patriarchal oppression on its head by arguing that the undergarment was a form of emancipation for those women who chose to lace them tightly (Figure 5.9).

As Kunzle would have it, tight-lacers "used their sexuality, and sexualised forms of dress . . . to rise out of a socio-sexual subject position."[69] Kunzle sees women's sexuality as a "subversive force" that represents rebellion from dominance and sexual liberation rather than passivity. In direct response to Roberts's article, Kunzle argues that it was the dress reformers, led by a sexually-repressive agenda, and socially conservative men, led by a patriarchal agenda, that were encouraging female submissiveness. Socially aspirational women of the lower-middle class, on the other hand, were tight lacing to express their sexualities, and reject their maternal and domestic roles for a chance to move up in the social scale.[70]

Anne Hollander takes a much more measured view, reminding us that corseted women did housework and raised children, and that the undergarment provided a good figure and a better drape to fabric.[71] Looking partially at individual women's feelings about corsets, Valerie Steele shows the way that women felt about corsets was much more mixed then Kunzle and Roberts have assumed. Certainly some felt them oppressive (Steele notes the memoirs of Gwen Raverat and Edith Rode and their young struggle against wearing stays)[72] but many enjoyed wearing corsets. They must have, after all, provided the feeling of comfort that proper attire always affords no matter the era.

The corset is an object that helped shape the way that women understood and experienced their bodies, be that in their thinking of gender or their understanding of their sexualities. Through the corset we can appreciate the persistence of gender norms and access one of the physical objects through which gender was understood and maintained. For Foucault, the body is "caught up in a system of subjection" where "power relations have an immediate hold upon it; they invest it, mark it, train it, torture it, force it to carry out tasks, to perform ceremonies, to emit signs."[73] While

FIGURE 5.9: French music-hall singer Polaire wearing the famous wasp waist corset, 1890.
Photo: Hulton Archive/Getty Images.

Foucault's terms seem harsh, and historians like Steele and Hollander have argued that the corset is not a form of female subjection, it is difficult not to see corsets as an object of power, that physically and purposefully changes the female body, in that it was an important undergarment in the creation of distinct gender positions. Returning to Foucault's concept that the body is forced to "emit signs" we can clearly see that the corseted body created ideas of femininity, of gender fragility, of moral uprightness, and of sexual knowledge.

Nineteenth- and early twentieth-century discourses around corseting viewed the female body as inherently flawed.[74] Sexologist Havelock Ellis explains in "An Anatomical Vindication of the Strait Front Corset" in 1910 that when women followed men from four legs to two they became physiologically weakened.[75] Therefore, "the corset is morphologically essential" for women who, according to Ellis, have difficulty with the vertical posture.[76] Some nineteenth-century doctors also advocated the importance of the corset, such as Dr. Sauveur Henri-Victor Bouvier and Dr. Ludovic O'Followell, who argued that the corset was necessary to support women's spines.[77] Corsetières like Madame Roxey A. Caplin also suggested that stays help "the weak and delicate or imperfect," and for these types of women "they are absolutely indispensable."[78] Here we are seeing the social and cultural assumptions about women being weaker than men being confirmed by an undergarment.

Corsets were a symbol of femininity—they shaped the body into the curves that emphasized the secondary sex characteristics of the bosom and hips, and suggested daintiness through the small waist. But this femininity had two sides: corsets helped women feel both moral and sexual at once. This is the paradox about the corset. The binding of the corset suggested that the women who wore them were sexually virtuous. The lacing suggested self-discipline, self-control, and moral rectitude.[79] Any woman who appeared in public without her stays was considered to have loose morals, and no respectable women would do so because an uncorseted woman was associated with prostitution. Though they had a connotation of morality and sexual control this undergarment was also sexualized and the women who wore corsets understood that in doing so they emphasized their sexual allure.[80] As Steele points out, the embrace of the corset around a woman's frame was likely to have been a constant reminder of her body, and also possibly of her sexuality.[81] The act of tying up and untying the corset was associated with the act of sex in the Victorian imagination. A lover who ties his beloved back into her corset is performing an intimate gesture, and a corset being untied was often associated with sexual release (Figure 5.10).[82]

Victorian men and women were well aware of the normative sexual associations of the corset. Much of the controversy surrounding sexuality and corsetry was derived from a sub-section of the population who tight laced. Between 1867 and 1874 there was a series of articles and letters in the *Domestic Women's Magazine* (DWM) about tight lacing.[83] Some historians, Roberts and Kunzle included, have used the evidence presented in the DWM at face value; arguing that the Victorian period was a particularly sadomasochistic era, they assumed that most Victorians laced their corsets to 16 inches or less, creating painful experiences for women.[84] In revisiting these sources, Steele has identified them as atypical for the vast majority of Victorian women. Rather, the letters were representative of a subsection of the population who were corset fetishists.[85] Steele sees the correspondence in DWM as having three strands: "(1) extreme body modification, which involved wearing tight corsets day and night; (2) a sadomasochistic delight in pain and an emphasis on erotic scenarios involving dominance and submission;

FIGURE 5.10: Paul Gavarni, "Ah! par exemple! voilà qui est bizarre!" Photo: Three Lions/
Getty Images.

and (3) corsetry as an element in cross-dressing."[86] She emphasizes the element of
fantasy and play in the fetish correspondence. It is unclear whether or not authors
were men or women, even though many of the stories were attributed to women.
She points out, also, that the dream-like imprecision of individual stories but strong
emphasis on feelings of pain and gratification around tight lacing were similar tropes
to those used in pornographic novels. For Steele, it is best to consider these authors'

writings as sexual fantasies. This description pertains to fetish as associated with a garment (the actual fetish here having more to do with pain and body modification than object fetish as described in the introduction). One DWM correspondent fits quite neatly into Freud's interpretation of the fetish object as substitute for the non-existent female phallus. A letter written by "A Male Wasp Waist" describes his disgust with a woman's natural "flabby waist," preferring instead a "stiff, hard, well-boned waist to hold."[87] Surely this is the wasp waist taking on the properties of the erect phallus. Another way to interpret corset-related fetish is to return to Butler's idea that certain body parts become pleasure centers because they are gender specific. The constricted waist of Victorian women is certainly an example of a gender-specific body part, as, for most of the nineteenth century, the waist was not emphasized for men. Because the waist shows gender difference it becomes an area of heterosexual interest and focus for Victorians.

The corset helps to both form and represent a distinctly feminine body by changing the shape of women so that they are immediately and clearly distinguished from men. The corset was also connected to gendered assumptions about women that became more prevalent as the two-sex model emerged, things like weakness, vanity, and morality. The corset was also associated with female (and male) sexuality. It reinforced the idea of the angel of the house by creating an impression of physical and moral rectitude, while at the same time emphasizing women's secondary sex characteristics of breasts and hips. Some believe that women's sexualities could have come to life because they were constantly aware of their bodies because of the tight hold of their undergarments. And certainly this constriction and possible pain caused by tight lacing sexually excited some Victorians.

CONCLUSION

Clothing has become a way of structuring our understandings of sex, gender, and sexuality in the modern world. During the Renaissance, clothing acted as a form of class differentiation. In this period, clothing was understood as a way of self-fashioning and creating the correct erect aristocratic body. With the slow move from the one-sex model to the two-sex model that came to dominate in the post-Enlightenment era, clothing began to shift from representing class difference to representing gender difference. Because gender was one of the primary ways of understanding the self by the nineteenth century, the clothing that came to signify gender difference was thought of as a natural extension of who people were, or as a second skin. The clothing associated with gender was not considered an element of performance as it had been for class in the Renaissance era. Clothing lay so close to the skin that it was considered a companion to what lay underneath, a true mark of the man or woman, their masculinity or femininity. Never mind that the cut of a suit may emphasize broadened shoulders, a large chest, and straight hips, and the lacing of a corset may cinch the waist, pushing up the bosom and creating fuller hips. And yet there were chinks in the armor of clothing, if that armor protected sex/gender difference. Victorians were fearful of a corsetless woman, whom they thought would revert into one-sex and appear too much like a man. And what to do about those men who dressed more like women, as with Oscar Wilde and his use of color and frills, or the men who wore corsets? These examples help to indicate that gender does not always follow sex and that the normative use of clothing helps to naturalize the gender categories. Clothing was also heavily involved in interpretations of sexuality during the

Victorian period. In the case of the aesthetic dandy and the tightlacer, clothing helps to show the limits of heterosexual normativity. Wilde's 1896 trial solidified the connection between homosexuality and precise and aesthetic male dress choices. Also, the tight-lacing correspondence of Victorian men and women indicated the difference between fetish fashion, primarily associated with sexuality, and normative corseting that also connoted women's moral and upright status. Using the examples of a primarily male-associated garment—the suit—and a primarily female associated garment—the corset—this chapter has explored the role clothing played in the nineteenth-century performance of gender and sexuality.

CHAPTER SIX

Status

VIVIENNE RICHMOND

The tract was one of a series addressed to young women on the sinfulness of dress. In style it was devoutly familiar. Its title was, "A Word With You On Your Cap-Ribbons."[1]

In England, the Age of Empire was also the age of industrialization. Rapid transformation brought urbanization and new occupations with new ways of working and living, demands for political rights and religious freedoms, and changed relationships between the sexes and classes. Mass production and developments in retailing and distribution, such as mail order, increased access to new clothing. Individual wardrobes grew from a small number of mostly home-made and second-hand garments, to larger quantities of mainly factory-produced, shop-bought clothes, laying the foundations for the modern Western pattern of clothing consumption whereby most people have a selection of outfits, purchased new, ready-made—and, often, on credit. Dress styles also changed. The protection from the elements afforded by the sunbonnets and smocks of agricultural workers was unnecessary in factories, mills, offices, and shops. Also, their voluminous dimensions, liable to catch in machinery and injure their wearers, were dangerous in the mechanized industrial workplace. And while often picturesque, their rustic charm was aesthetically incongruous in urban business settings.

This was a time of enterprise and opportunity, but also of challenge and anxiety, as social mobility and the breakdown of traditional communities threatened class boundaries, hierarchies, and privileges. And so while there had been no British sumptuary laws since 1604, "governments and moralists," striving to maintain the social order to which they were accustomed, still "claimed the right to restrain material expression within the lower ranks," especially in terms of dress.[2] But those who wished to challenge such restraint or to assert their working-class identity also took it up as a powerful weapon.

In this chapter I focus on three key ways in which people in nineteenth-century England contrived to use dress as a means of social separation. I begin with an examination of the contentious rise of cotton, "the fibre of industrial revolution."[3] Cotton became *the* fabric of working-class clothes, largely replacing wool, linen, and leather. And, as political consciousness grew among the industrial workforce, it also came to proudly symbolize the disenfranchised working man fighting for parliamentary representation.

The expanded clothing stocks of the majority were part of an overall rise in living standards, but this was a gradual and uneven process. Widespread poverty persisted throughout nineteenth-century England and legislative changes reduced the official aid available to the poor, leaving them increasingly dependent on charity for basic necessities, including clothing. Under the pervasive influence of evangelicalism, which deemed social stratification a part of the divine plan, the provision of humble charity clothing became one of the means by which the wealthy sought to keep the poor in their place and instill in them lessons of thrift and morality. This forms the second part of my discussion.

Industrialization also led to the growth and gentrification of the middle classes, within which women became responsible for the management of the home, while the physical labor of its maintenance was carried out by a growing army of principally female domestic servants, who also became an expression of their employers' wealth and status. However, many middle-class wives, unaccustomed to, and insecure in, their elevated status, were unused to the management of servants. Additionally, as clothing became cheaper and more plentiful, the impossibility of differentiating between maid and mistress was frequently asserted. Finally, therefore, I examine the ways in which employers sought to regulate the dress of female servants, to both proclaim their authority and maintain the distinction between themselves and their staff, and the tensions this produced.

The unique combination of factors that placed England at the forefront of industrialization in the eighteenth and nineteenth centuries made it distinctive. As such, its practices, processes and experiences were not replicated wholesale elsewhere. But the very fact of its industrial precocity and pre-eminence makes it the essential and ideal starting point for studies of the relationship between dress and industrialization, and the ways in which dress can be used to articulate social divisions and anxieties in other times and places.

FRATERNAL FUSTIAN

The nineteenth-century cotton trade shaped the face of a new industrial society, in all its aspects. Fustian, as the fruit of this industry, was emblematic of working men.[4]

Between 1801 and 1911, the population of England and Wales increased from nine to more than forty million, and urban residents rose from approximately one third to more than three quarters of the English population.[5] Employment in agriculture decreased from forty to eight percent of the workforce, many laborers moving to the growing retail, clerical, transport, and energy industries.[6]

New ways of working and living required new dress styles. Uniforms multiplied, becoming a powerful means of asserting corporate identity in a competitive capitalist economy and facilitating the swift identification of public service providers such as policemen and railway porters. More generally, by about the mid 1820s most men, of all classes, had put aside knee breeches in favor of "trowsers," formerly worn only by those engaged in seafaring occupations.[7] Also, even among agricultural laborers, the smock was mostly replaced by a waistcoat and jacket, worn over a shirt.

The expansion and contraction of the fashionable silhouette notwithstanding, changes in working-class women's clothing were less dramatic. Skirts remained ankle or floor length throughout the period and the apron ubiquitous as everyday wear. But the previously visible stays became concealed undergarments, and the bed-gown or gown, with skirt hitched up to reveal the petticoat, was replaced by a dress—often in fact a separate skirt and bodice or blouse—with the skirt allowed its full length. These sartorial transitions occurred at different times, and with numerous variations, according to region and occupation. London dustmen, for example, retained their breeches long after most men had replaced them with trousers.[8] Conversely, at a time of highly gendered clothing, Wigan pit-brow girls engaged in dirty manual labor adopted trousers as practical work-wear and thereby shocked the nation—even though they reverted to conventional contemporary women's wear when not at work.[9]

Arguably, however, in terms of social stratification, the style of garments was of less significance than the fabrics from which they were made. In the early part of the period, working-men's breeches were sometimes made of heavy cotton, but more usually of leather or wool. The coats and jackets that some men wore over their smocks were also woolen, as were many women's gowns. Woolen flannel was commonly used to make underclothes, including men's shirts, but alternatively these might be made of linen, so too their smocks, women's gowns, and the shifts worn under their stays.[10] But as the nineteenth-century progressed cotton largely replaced all these fabrics.[11] "The lower classes," commented a Sussex curate and founder of a local clothing charity in the 1820s, "did not wear linen underclothes, but calico."[12] Calico came in a variety of qualities and prices, but in the basic form most often used for working-class underclothes such as shirts and shifts, was among the cheapest of cotton fabrics (Figure 6.1).

Cotton was not a newcomer in the nineteenth century, cotton cloths having been imported from India since the sixteenth century.[13] They were popular, and neither eighteenth-century attempts to ban the import of Indian textiles, to protect the British wool and linen industries, nor attacks on women wearing them did much to dampen enthusiasm for cotton prints.[14] But it was the establishment and rapid expansion of the British cotton industry, centered in Lancashire, that assured cotton's hegemony. An indication of the industry's growth is given by the quantities of raw cotton for processing imported to Britain which rose from 8.2 million to 360 million kg per annum between

FIGURE 6.1: A scrap of calico used for school sewing practice, 1896. Author's collection. Photo: Monica Randell.

the 1780s and 1850s.[15] In the 1840s, nascent communist Friedrich Engels, visiting Manchester to work in his father's textile factory, declared that cotton had become the fabric of "the working-people." "Wool and linen," he wrote,

> have almost vanished from the wardrobe of both sexes, and cotton has taken their place. Shirts are made of bleached or coloured cotton goods; the dresses of the women are chiefly of cotton print goods, and woollen petticoats are rarely to be seen on the washline.[16]

For Engels, this was a disaster. Although calico, at 5d or 6d a yard, was half the price of shirt linen or flannel, it was neither so hard wearing as linen nor as warm as wool, and might therefore prove a false investment.[17] The difficulty for Engels was that many working-class people did not have sufficient money to allow them to make a choice—it was cotton or nothing. And the air in England, he said,

> with its sudden changes of temperature, more calculated than any other to give rise to colds, obliges almost the whole middle class to wear flannel next to the skin, about the body, and flannel scarves and shirts are in almost universal use.

But "the working class," he continued, was "deprived of this precaution" and "scarcely ever in a position to use a thread of woollen clothing."[18]

However, cotton fabrics were not only cheaper, but easier to launder than woolen fabrics, and therefore more hygienic. Hence, in contrast with Engels, the Radical tailor (and maker of leather breeches) Francis Place had twenty years earlier welcomed "the great change . . . produced by improvements in the manufacture of cotton goods." No longer were women seen:

> without gowns on their backs or handkerchiefs on their necks, their leather stays half laced and as black as the door posts, their black coarse worsted stocks and striped linsey woolsey petticoats "standing alone with dirt."[19]

Cotton was, then, contentious, but its rise was seemingly unstoppable, and as its use spread, cotton came not only to be worn by the laboring man, but synonymous with him. As Engels noted, the majority of working men wore "chiefly trousers of fustian or other heavy cotton goods, and jackets or coats of the same."[20] Fustian, originally a linen fabric, then a linen-cotton mix, and by the nineteenth century increasingly just cotton, was the name given to a variety of hard-wearing, napped cloths including moleskin, jean, and corduroy. The fustian suits of working-class men were "cut loosely without padding," and ranged in color "from white buff and yellow to brown and blue" (Figure 6.2).[21] They therefore made a distinctive contrast both with the dark tailored suits of woolen broadcloth worn by middle-class men, and, where possible, the rising band of working-class clerks and shop assistants, and the courtly robes of the aristocracy. Ermine or velvet at one end and fustian at the other were used to indicate the two extremes of the social hierarchy.[22] For Engels, fustian had "become the proverbial costume of the working men, who are called 'fustian jackets' . . . in contrast to the gentlemen who wear broad cloth."[23]

"Fustian jackets" was not a nomenclature simply imposed on working men by their social superiors, but readily embraced by them in their campaign for political representation. In 1830, approximately 11 percent of the adult male population (and very few women) were eligible to vote at general elections. The Reform Act of 1832 increased this to around 18 percent of adult males, but while the working and middle

FIGURE 6.2: Working men about to board the train at Liverpool Street railway station, London, 1884. The photograph demonstrates the ubiquity, and tonal range, of the trousers, waistcoat, and jacket combination, mostly made of fustian. © National Railway Museum/ Science & Society Picture Library.

classes had joined forces to campaign for reform, the property qualification embedded in the 1832 Act divided this coalition by essentially extending the vote only to a greater number of the middle classes.[24] Other reforms, most significantly the amendments to the Poor Law in 1834, which made it more difficult for unemployed working-class men to gain financial assistance, compounded a growing sense of injustice and spawned the Chartist movement, established in 1838.[25] Chartism was the first large-scale, working-class political organization, and called for a wholesale overhaul of the parliamentary system, including universal male suffrage. Moral-force Chartists sought reform through peaceful means, while physical-force Chartists were prepared to use violence. Although its aims were not achieved until long after the movement petered out in 1848, Chartism was a disruptive force to be reckoned with and fustian its "symbolic lingua franca."[26] "Place *Fustian* in the dock," declared Chartist leader Julian Harney during the 1848 trials of Chartist activists, "let *Silk Gown* charge the culprit with being a 'physical force Chartist' . . . and forthwith *Broad Cloth* in the jury box will bellow out 'GUILTY'."[27] For Harney, clothes' fabrics were an unambiguous shorthand for the distinctions between working man, upper-class judge and middle-class juror.

Fustian, says Beverly Lemire, "marked the first industrial working class. It was their emblem for generations." Initially identified with the working-class Radical, it acquired a wider plebeian symbolism so that, "as the political temperature cooled . . . the fustian jacket entered the wider lexicon as synonymous with working folk, a reflection of thrift and diligence and worthy of respect."[28] A "favourite Saturday evening costume with the mass of working men," stated the "Journeyman Engineer" Thomas Wright, in 1867, "consists of the clean moleskin or cord trousers that are to be worn at work during the ensuing week" (Figure 6.3).[29]

FIGURE 6.3: The display cabinet, c. 1911 of the Hebden Bridge Fustian Society, a manufacturing co-operative established in 1870. The name "Hebden Bridge Fustian Society" is spelled out at the top of the left-hand window, and in the center of the cabinet are displayed the various fabrics it produced, including the "Cords" and "Mole[skin]s" advertised at the top of the front window. Image courtesy of the Jack Uttley Photo Library.

SARTORIAL SALVATION

No country on earth can lay claim to a greater philanthropic tradition than Great Britain. Until the twentieth century philanthropy was widely believed to be the most wholesome and reliable remedy for the nation's ills . . . For every affliction, individual or social, physical or spiritual, the charitable pharmacopoeia has a prescription or at least a palliative.[30]

Poverty, like cotton, was not a nineteenth-century creation. But the urbanization and break up of paternalistic small communities that accompanied industrialization, the congregating of the different classes in different parts of the cities and resulting urban slums, and the mass transfer to wage labor vulnerable to the fluctuations of the trade cycle and the seasonality of much agricultural work, all made it increasingly problematic, both to those in need and those called upon to help them. The absence of an agreed, consistent definition and means of measuring poverty renders impossible any precise assessment of its extent. However, the cost of statutory relief, together with the qualitative evidence of sources such as personal histories, charity records, newspapers, and government reports confirm that it was widespread, with some historians estimating that up to 70 percent of the population may have spent at least part of their lives in poverty.[31] Certainly it was by no means uncommon for an individual to own only one set of clothes—and that not always complete—and to use day clothes also as nightwear.[32]

Statutory assistance was provided via the Poor Law, which had remained largely unchanged since its introduction in 1601. The Poor Law was a parish-based system that allowed the needy to apply for aid which was funded through a rate levied on wealthier residents. Assistance was provided either as "indoor relief," meaning admission to a residential workhouse, or much more commonly as "outdoor relief" by which the recipients remained in their own homes and received aid as money or goods such as fuel, food, and clothing. In the 1780s, poor relief expenditure in England and Wales averaged two million pounds per annum, but by 1818 this figure had risen to nearly eight million pounds, a great deal of which was spent on clothing.[33] But as the cost of poor relief rose, so did protests from ratepayers. The result was the 1834 Poor Law Amendment Act which sought to prohibit the distribution of outdoor relief to able-bodied male workers, and make the workhouse the only form of assistance available to them and their families. Although the prohibition of outdoor relief to the able-bodied was never fully achieved, there was a dramatic reduction in the provision of parish clothing.[34] Additionally, living conditions in the workhouse were made deliberately harsh to dissuade all but the most desperate from seeking admission and the threat of the dreaded workhouse proved an effective psychological deterrent to many who might otherwise have sought parish aid.[35]

Those unable to clothe themselves and their families, and who wished to avoid the workhouse, had to look to charity for help. The overarching influence on nineteenth-century English philanthropy was Anglican evangelicalism, which deemed social stratification an intrinsic part of God's plan and so believed that the aim should not be to eradicate poverty, but only to relieve its worst effects. Evangelicals also believed in ultimate salvation, to be achieved by the rich through the performance of good works to help those less fortunate than themselves. The poor were to be saved by proving themselves deserving through the demonstration of moral rectitude, thrift, acceptance of their lowly social status, deference to their "betters," and self-help.[36] Self-help was the key tenet of evangelical philanthropy, promoted most notably in Samuel Smiles's best-selling book of the same name, first published in 1859. According to Smiles:

> The healthy spirit of self-help created amongst working people would more than any other measure serve to raise them as a class . . . levelling them up to a higher and still advancing standard of religion, intelligence and virtue.[37]

As Poor Law aid declined, there was a proliferation of self-help charitable organizations requiring some form of financial contribution by the poor themselves, rather than the gratuitous distribution of money or goods. These charities also aimed to use the provision of aid as a means to shape the recipient's moral character.

A great deal of charity work was done by middle- and upper-class women. Not only did they often have more time for this than men with business affairs to attend to, but also attention to the domestic needs of the poor was considered an extension of women's "natural" feminine role as homemakers and managers.[38] And since needlework was at "the heart of female culture in the nineteenth century," it "was crucial to women's philanthropy."[39] As such, the production of clothing for the poor, the overseeing of its manufacture by poor women, or the provision of materials for such manufacture, was a major focus of charitable endeavor (Figure 6.4).

For liberal, critical, social commentators, ladies' evangelical charity work was a frequent satirical target. Wilkie Collins, for example, introduced into his 1868 novel, *The Moonstone*, Miss Drusilla Clack, an impoverished, but middle-class, hypocritically self-deprecating, evangelical spinster, bent on the moral reform of the lower orders through good deeds. She belonged to the "Select Committee of the Mothers'-Small-Clothes-Conversion Society," which "excellent Charity" existed

> to rescue unredeemed fathers' trousers from the pawnbroker, and to prevent their resumption, on the part of the irreclaimable parent, by abridging them immediately to suit the proportions of the innocent son. . . . work of moral and material usefulness.[40]

Miss Clack's Mothers'-Small-Clothes-Conversion Society was a fiction, but its ambition to combine "moral and material usefulness" was not and there were numerous forms of clothing charity either established, or converted to, the principle of self-help. Maternity societies lent boxes of clothes and bedding to expectant mothers for the first month of their babies' lives. But while these were originally lent free of charge, increasingly the societies required the mothers to deposit small regular savings throughout their pregnancies, to be returned to them, with a bonus and the loan items, at the time of their confinement. Dorcas societies and ladies' working parties collected funds to buy fabrics with which they made clothes for the poor. Again, these were originally given away free of charge, but increasingly were sold for the cost price of the materials, the purchasers sometimes having to obtain an entrance ticket to the sales from a philanthropic sponsor as a guarantee of their moral and deserving character.[41] From the mid-nineteenth century mothers' meetings were established, regular gatherings where working-class women could purchase fabrics at cost price and sew them into garments under the supervision of lady philanthropists who read aloud religious or other "improving" literature while they worked (Figure 6.5).[42]

Clothing societies were another form of local self-help charity and sprang up in parishes across the country from the late eighteenth century. They endured, in some cases, until the dismantling of the Poor Law in 1929 and were chiefly instituted by Anglican clergymen, aided by a committee of lay helpers. Clothing societies collected the small

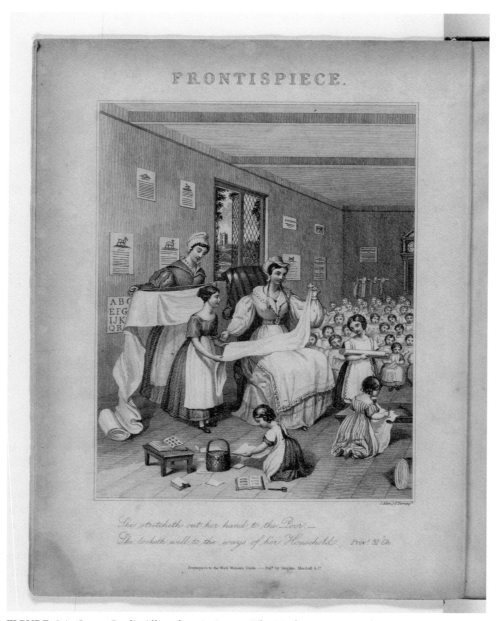

FIGURE 6.4: James Baylis Allen, frontispiece to *The Workwoman's Guide* (1838), an instruction manual for women who made clothes for the poor. The image shows an elite woman supervising a sewing lesson for working-class girls, most probably at a Sunday school. Courtesy of Eberly Family Special Collections Library, Pennsylvania State University.

A MOTHERS' MEETING

FIGURE 6.5: A Mothers' Meeting, *Graphic* 123, April 6, 1872. © British Library, London.

weekly savings of the poor, usually between about 1d and 6d, and returned them at the end of the year together with a small premium donated by wealthier residents. The premium was always to be less than the amount saved by the poor depositor and the combined monies were never given to the poor in cash, only as clothes, fabrics, or a ticket to exchange for goods at a nominated supplier. This was to ensure that the money was indeed spent on clothing, or bedding, and not diverted to another purchase such as alcohol, or the repayment of debts. Fines or exclusion, without reimbursement of the monies saved, were imposed on members who failed to keep up payments, and limiting membership to those who observed certain behaviors further encouraged moral conduct. Hence the societies' rules excluded anyone guilty of a felony, drunkenness, bearing an illegitimate child, or failing to attend church on Sundays (Figure 6.6).[43]

Evangelicalism also deemed different types of clothing and fabrics appropriate for the different classes. *The Workwoman's Guide*, an 1838 sewing manual, contains instructions for making baby clothes for both rich and poor, the latter including the contents of a maternity box. Even when it deems the same items necessary for the different classes of baby, "the quality of the materials, of course, must differ." Hence, "napkins" for the babies of the rich were to "be made of soft diaper, or, if for the poor, old sheeting, table-linen, or strong fine linen answers well."[44]

The aim, above all, was to discourage the purchase of "any smart articles of dress, or finery of any kind."[45] Poor women, in particular, were suspected by many of their social

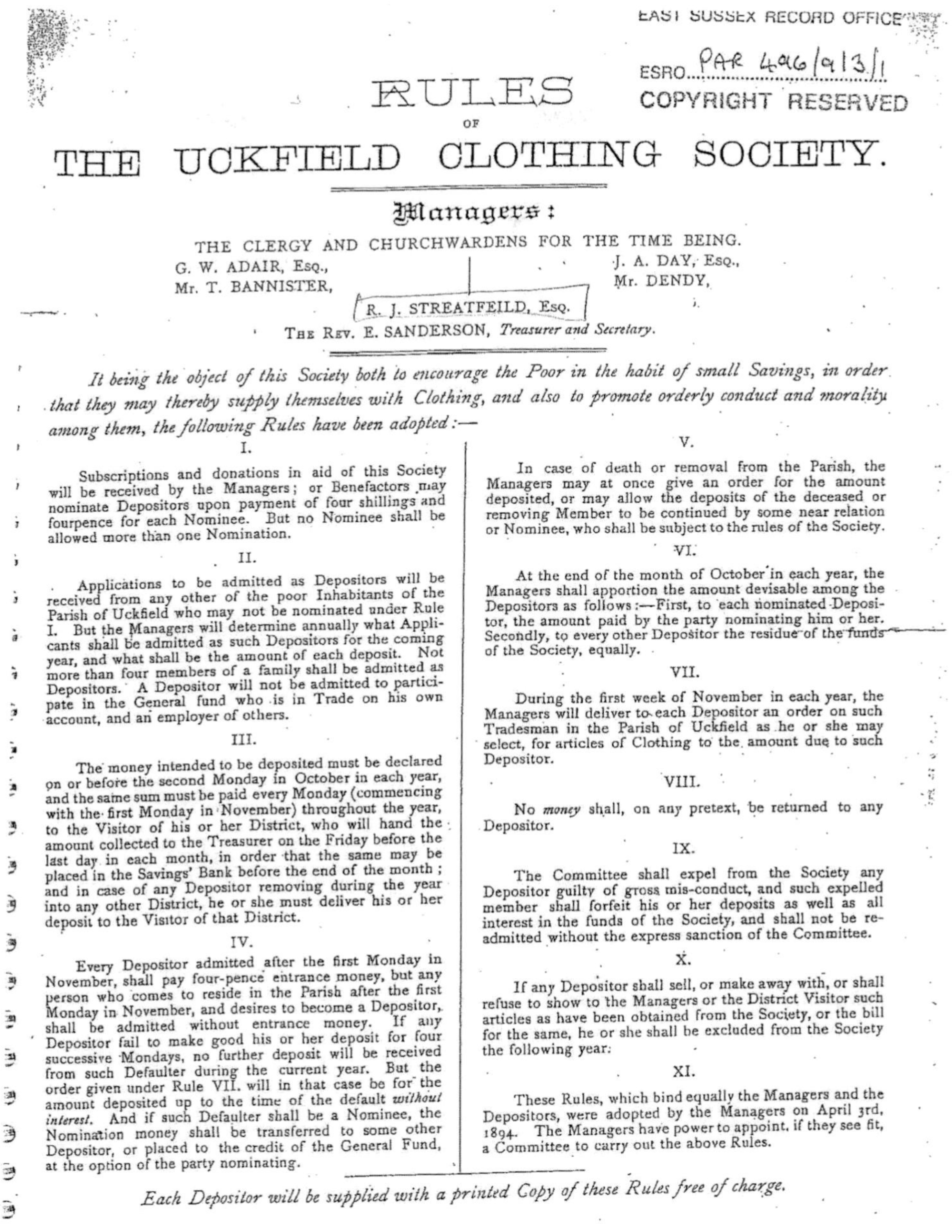

RULES

OF

THE UCKFIELD CLOTHING SOCIETY.

Managers:

THE CLERGY AND CHURCHWARDENS FOR THE TIME BEING.

G. W. ADAIR, Esq.,   J. A. DAY, Esq.,
Mr. T. BANNISTER,   Mr. DENDY,

R. J. STREATFEILD, Esq.

THE REV. E. SANDERSON, *Treasurer and Secretary.*

It being the object of this Society both to encourage the Poor in the habit of small Savings, in order that they may thereby supply themselves with Clothing, and also to promote orderly conduct and morality among them, the following Rules have been adopted:—

I.

Subscriptions and donations in aid of this Society will be received by the Managers; or Benefactors may nominate Depositors upon payment of four shillings and fourpence for each Nominee. But no Nominee shall be allowed more than one Nomination.

II.

Applications to be admitted as Depositors will be received from any other of the poor Inhabitants of the Parish of Uckfield who may not be nominated under Rule I. But the Managers will determine annually what Applicants shall be admitted as such Depositors for the coming year, and what shall be the amount of each deposit. Not more than four members of a family shall be admitted as Depositors. A Depositor will not be admitted to participate in the General fund who is in Trade on his own account, and an employer of others.

III.

The money intended to be deposited must be declared on or before the second Monday in October in each year, and the same sum must be paid every Monday (commencing with the first Monday in November) throughout the year, to the Visitor of his or her District, who will hand the amount collected to the Treasurer on the Friday before the last day in each month, in order that the same may be placed in the Savings' Bank before the end of the month; and in case of any Depositor removing during the year into any other District, he or she must deliver his or her deposit to the Visitor of that District.

IV.

Every Depositor admitted after the first Monday in November, shall pay four-pence entrance money, but any person who comes to reside in the Parish after the first Monday in November, and desires to become a Depositor, shall be admitted without entrance money. If any Depositor fail to make good his or her deposit for four successive Mondays, no further deposit will be received from such Defaulter during the current year. But the order given under Rule VII. will in that case be for the amount deposited up to the time of the default *without interest.* And if such Defaulter shall be a Nominee, the Nomination money shall be transferred to some other Depositor, or placed to the credit of the General Fund, at the option of the party nominating.

V.

In case of death or removal from the Parish, the Managers may at once give an order for the amount deposited, or may allow the deposits of the deceased or removing Member to be continued by some near relation or Nominee, who shall be subject to the rules of the Society.

VI.

At the end of the month of October in each year, the Managers shall apportion the amount devisable among the Depositors as follows:—First, to each nominated Depositor, the amount paid by the party nominating him or her. Secondly, to every other Depositor the residue of the funds of the Society, equally.

VII.

During the first week of November in each year, the Managers will deliver to each Depositor an order on such Tradesman in the Parish of Uckfield as he or she may select, for articles of Clothing to the amount due to such Depositor.

VIII.

No *money* shall, on any pretext, be returned to any Depositor.

IX.

The Committee shall expel from the Society any Depositor guilty of gross mis-conduct, and such expelled member shall forfeit his or her deposits as well as all interest in the funds of the Society, and shall not be re-admitted without the express sanction of the Committee.

X.

If any Depositor shall sell, or make away with, or shall refuse to show to the Managers or the District Visitor such articles as have been obtained from the Society, or the bill for the same, he or she shall be excluded from the Society the following year:

XI.

These Rules, which bind equally the Managers and the Depositors, were adopted by the Managers on April 3rd, 1894. The Managers have power to appoint, if they see fit, a Committee to carry out the above Rules.

Each Depositor will be supplied with a printed Copy of these Rules free of charge.

FIGURE 6.6: Rules of the Uckfield Clothing Society, 1894, East Sussex Record Office, PAR 496/43/3/1. With permission of Uckfield Parish.

superiors of harboring an innate, insatiable, and almost irresistible desire for showy dress, and charities commonly limited their benevolence to "useful and necessary" clothing made of hard-wearing materials. A Suffolk clothing society, in 1833, was typical in allowing its members to purchase only "Calico, Flannel, Stuffs, Checks, Handkerchiefs, Shawls, Cloaks, Fustian ... Waistcoats and Stockings" with their savings.[46] Some societies required the goods to be inspected by the management committee before they were taken home by the poor, to ascertain their suitability, and many retained the right to inspect the goods at will thereafter to ensure they had not been pawned or sold. The same lists of practical fabrics can be found in charity reports across the century, the calico for shifts, and flannel, linsey and grogram for petticoats listed among the materials purchased by a Liverpool clothing charity in 1814 echoed, eight decades later, in the request of a London Dorcas society for donations of "flannel, calico, and warm material for frocks and petticoats."[47] Free agency over clothing choices and the pleasures of dress were to be privileges of the rich.[48]

MAIDS AND MISTRESSES

Uniforms are all about control not only of the social self but also of the inner self and its formation.[49]

While poor women of any age might be suspected of a desire for "finery," it was deemed a particular problem among the young, especially mill and factory workers and domestic servants. The cotton mills and factories of northern England with their massive, thundering, ceaseless machinery were a new type of workplace. Whereas much pre- and proto-industrial production was home-based, factories gathered together large numbers of both sexes, many of them young, away from the parental home and, therefore, parental supervision.[50] Also, wages were higher than in many other manual occupations, and this combination of home/work separation and elevated income offered workers a greater degree of independence which critics considered dangerous. Furthermore, in the heat and humidity caused by the machines and the need to keep cotton damp during processing, operatives often stripped down to their underclothes, prompting suspicions of licentiousness.[51] As a consequence, female factory employees were accused of sexual promiscuity and a lack of deference, as well as a want of thrift expressed most frequently and ostentatiously in the purchase and display of showy dress.

These characteristics are all suggested in the illustration accompanying an 1870 article about the old clothes market at Camp Field, Manchester, in the popular illustrated magazine, the *Graphic*. The image shows a bustling, chaotic market, and in the central foreground a factory girl, accompanied by her friend, absorbed in contemplation of a flounced dress which she holds against her body to assess its fit and appearance. She is observed by two other factory girls and at the edge of the image another tries on some footwear, while two more move gaily and boldly through the throng, devoid of feminine modesty and reserve. It is telling that the *Graphic* considered these young women to be of sufficient interest and novelty to form the focus of the image, and the way in which the scene is presented evokes the exoticism and intimate feminine community of the harem (Figure 6.7).

The novelty, rapid growth, and centrality to industrialization of the cotton industry has made its workers the focus of much historical attention. But they were far outnumbered by domestic servants, the largest female occupational group. The 1851 Census of Great Britain returned 470,317 people employed in cotton manufacture, of whom 247,705

FIGURE 6.7: "The Old Clothes Market, Camp Field, Manchester," *Graphic* 55, December 17, 1870. © British Library, London.

were female, but 754,926 general domestic servants, of whom 675,311 were female. Some 70,000 more women were listed separately as housemaids, and 40,000 as nurses.[52] By 1901, the number of people employed in cotton manufacture in the United Kingdom stood at 545,959, of whom 346,128 were female, while the number of domestic servants had risen to 1,717,217, all but 76,000 of whom were female.[53]

Popular culture has fostered a stereotypical image of Victorian domestic servants working in grand houses with a large staff and paternalistic employers. In reality, the majority worked in much smaller homes where they were either the only servant or one of two or three.[54] For most, it was an arduous, isolated occupation and, with no legal regulation of working conditions, hours were often very long and the accommodation, food, and pay inadequate. Furthermore, girls commonly began domestic service at the age of eleven or twelve, often at a distance from their families, and so at the start of their careers were vulnerable and in no position to dictate the terms of their employment, though many became increasingly defiant as they grew in age and confidence.

Servants were not simply a luxury for the idle rich, but a necessity for the smooth running of even a modestly-sized home in an age of large families, limited domestic appliances, and labor-intensive houses. But the nature of service was changing with industrialization. Previously, mistresses and servants had both carried out much of the work of cleaning, food preparation, and childcare, albeit in a hierarchical relationship. But as the ideology developed that mistresses should manage the home, but not perform the necessary manual labor, the number of female domestic servants increased. And, in addition to their physical work, servants also became symbols of their employers' status and the social gulf between employer and servant widened.

In the late-eighteenth century, the increasing availability of cheap cotton fabrics and servants' proximity to middle- and upper-class fashions gave them the reputation of being fashionably dressed.[55] The impossibility of distinguishing between the maid and her mistress, the latter being so finely clothed, became a common cry, although this was surely an exaggeration. The lady's maid was the servant most likely to be mistaken for a "mistress." Her role was to act as the personal servant to her mistress, looking after her clothes, helping her to dress, and assisting with her toilette. Ladies' maids were therefore to have an extensive knowledge of elite dress and grooming, and commonly received, and expected to receive, as a perquisite, their mistresses' cast-off clothing. However, the fact that the mistress was dispensing with the clothes would usually have meant that they were either no longer in good condition or the fashion had been superseded. Thus, although the lady's maid might be fashionably dressed compared with many of her peers, when in the company of her employer dressed in clothes of a better condition and more recent fashion, she would still have been clearly identifiable as the servant. Furthermore, the lady's maid who attempted to become her mistress's sartorial rival would soon find herself out of work.[56]

Ladies' maids were relatively few in number, being near the top of the servant hierarchy and employed only in wealthier households. Lower-ranking servants, especially the solitary maids-of-all-work, were often paid such pitifully low wages that they were barely—and sometimes not even—sufficient to purchase enough basic clothing, let alone "finery." Also, the marks of labor on their bodies—ingrained dirt, hands reddened and swollen from washing and scrubbing—would have immediately marked them out as maids, not mistresses. Nevertheless, claims that they could not be told apart persisted, and employers' fears about the blurring of social boundaries and loss of authority resulted in a constant stream of didactic literature, extolling the virtues and appropriateness of modest dress for domestic servants. Some of this was intended to be read by the servants themselves, either during the course of their employment or in their formative years, the authors hoping that habits of simple dress and the rejection of "finery" would be inculcated before a girl ever put her foot across an employer's threshold. *Myra's Pink Dress*, for example, written by children's author Emma Leslie and published by the Sunday School Union in 1873, is the tale of a servant girl whose wish to dress like her mistress leads to a child's death and her own familial ostracism.[57]

Other publications were aimed at the growing number of young, and seemingly naïve, mistresses unaccustomed to managing servants. *Trusler's Domestic Management*, for example, published in 1819, warned that "dressy servants" were "women of suspicious character," and that the mistress who left open drawers and cupboards might tempt a servant to steal from them ribbons or other trimmings which, in turn, might lead her to greater crimes with potentially fatal consequences![58]

Like the evangelical female philanthropist, the inexperienced mistress, uncertain how to manage her servants, anxious to assert her superiority and fearful of being outshone, was a figure of fun. In Augustus and Henry Mayhew's 1847 satirical novel, *The Greatest Plague of Life*, Caroline B—ff—n, the daughter of a coal merchant, marries a widowed lawyer and struggles, as a new wife, to maintain authority over a series of unsatisfactory servants. One is the fancifully-named Rosetta, which Caroline changes to plain Susan. She is a pretty girl, while Caroline evidently is not, but arrives for interview dressed "*so thoroughly like what a respectable servant ought to be,*" that Caroline cannot understand why a previous employer dismissed her for being "dressy." But then, on the first Sunday of her employment, "Susan" appears in a:

> starched-out imitation Balzorine gown, of a bright ultramarine, picked out with white flowers—with a double skirt, too, made like a tunic . . . a blonde-lace cap, with cherry-

coloured rosettes, and streamers flying about nearly a yard long . . . patent leather shoes, with broad sandals, and open-worked cotton stockings . . . and net mittens on her hands.

Caroline instructs her to remove all this "trumpery finery" and is gratified to see her later leave the house "no longer dressed out as showily as if she was the mistress instead of the maid." This, though, is by no means the end of Susan's sartorial misdemeanors and she is later depicted setting off on a day's holiday "dressed out to death" (Figure 6.8).[59]

Going out for a Holiday.

FIGURE 6.8: George Cruikshank, "Going out for a holiday," in *The Brothers Mayhew, The Greatest Plague of Life* (1847). Courtesy of University of North Texas Special Collections.

FIGURE 6.9: A general servant, Marylebone, 1872, in print dress, white apron, and cap.
Papers of AJ. Munby, The Master and Fellows of Trinity College Cambridge.

The employers' eventual solution to the perceived problem of "dressy" servants was the introduction of a uniform of "print dress, white apron, and white cap" in the morning, when the majority of the housework was performed (Figure 6.9), with a dark-colored dress replacing the print in the afternoon when the maid might be called upon to answer the door to her employer's visitors.[60] By the 1860s, this had become the standard attire of female servants and was available from specialist shops.[61] But while the 1910 *Every Woman's Encyclopædia* stated that "the mistress will often give the maid material for one black dress, or provide her caps, aprons, cuffs, etc.," it conceded that this was still "a voluntary matter" and servants were generally expected to provide their own uniforms.[62] As most girls entered service because their parents could not afford to keep them at home, they did not have the money to purchase either a ready-made uniform or fabric to make one themselves. In such cases, the uniform might be financed via a loan from the employer, repaid by deductions from the girl's subsequent wages. This was the experience of Kate Taylor, who began work as a general servant in 1904 at the age of thirteen. "I worked," she wrote, "without wages for six months," spending "each evening, Sundays included," sitting behind her employer's chair, sewing her uniform.[63]

Servants passionately defended their sartorial freedom, especially when employers tried to regulate not only their working, but also their off-duty dress. Where *Trusler's* thought "showy dress" an indication of an untrustworthy servant, house steward William Lanceley thought employers made servants deceitful through unnecessary clothing regulation. The requirement of one of his employers, that her servants should dress in "simple attire," he said, "did not prevent them from buying smart clothes," and when one wished to go out in them, "some of the other servants would help her to slip out and would let her in on her return."[64] "Surely," wrote "Three Domestics" to the *Daily News* in 1897, "when our money is well earned we can dress as we like, so long as we are neat and clean in their houses."[65] But many employers did not agree.

CONCLUSION

In recent years, the long-held assumption that the working classes wished only to emulate the fashions of their social superiors has been vigorously challenged.[66] The Chartists' self-identification with fustian is but one example of working-class adoption of a dress style determinedly different from that of the middle and upper classes. For Chartists, fustian was not simply a cheap, practical choice of fabric for manual labor, but a means of celebrating and asserting class allegiance, a potent visual and metaphorical symbol of disenfranchisement, oppression and the determination to obtain political representation. Although very few Chartists would still have been alive by the time universal male suffrage was achieved in 1918, many would have lived to see the advances made by the intervening Reform Acts of 1867 and 1884 which each extended the franchise a little further and justified their proud fustian fraternity.

The effectiveness of attempts to regulate moral behavior through dress regulation are less easily quantified. The vast extent of clothing charity in nineteenth-century England bespeaks the great need—there was scarcely a parish that did not have at least one clothing charity, and most had several. Even as late as 1895, one south London parish magazine was by no means unusual in listing among its monthly activities eight forms of clothing charity, including mothers' meetings, clothing societies and maternity bags.[67] Clothing charities were not only numerous but their surviving records also often show a large and long-standing membership. At first glance, this sort of evidence might suggest a triumph for the moral reformers, the beneficiaries of charitable aid rarely being a position to dictate the terms on which help is given. But this is to assume that the recipients were in need of moral reform and while, as Frank Prochaska says, philanthropy undoubtedly:

> spread middle-class values up and down the social scale . . . most people, however humble, did not need to be reminded that fitness, decency and independence were wholesome.[68]

Historians have distinguished between the "rough" and the "respectable" poor, the latter adhering to a moral agenda broadly in line with that laid out in charity regulations—no drunkenness, crime, illegitimacy—and the "rough" being those who did not.[69] The "rough" were often among the poorest, and were anyway excluded from most self-help charity because they could not afford the necessary financial contribution. The poor who saved their pennies week by week to invest in a clothing society, secure the loan of a maternity box, or buy a garment at cost price rather than hoping to be given one free of charge, were the respectable poor. It is probable that many made use of the opportunities offered by such charities and were untroubled by the stipulated behaviors simply because these already accorded with their own morality.

Self-help charities assisted the poor to supply themselves with the practical hard-wearing clothes they needed for everyday use more cheaply than simply buying from a retailer. But the fact that the sober, industrious, and thrifty poor made use of this facility should not lead us to assume they necessarily shared the extreme evangelical view that decorative clothing was sinful. Indeed, the possession and display of "Sunday best"—fancier clothing for holiday wear—was an important facet of respectability. It demonstrated respect for the Sabbath and the success and economic management necessary to maintain a spare set of clothes, even if they were replaced only at very long intervals, or spent much of the week in the pawnshop.[70] The laboring family that invested in the local clothing society, or bought from the sale of "poor clothing" did not necessarily rely entirely on charity for its clothing, but more probably drew on a variety of sources which might also include buying second-hand, gifts from relatives, and the retention of clothing from more prosperous times. For most, obtaining a little Sunday "finery" from such a source was an opportunity to indulge in the harmless pleasure of self-adornment and brighten lives more commonly characterized by hard work and want.

Similarly, we should not be surprised if female factory workers and domestic servants also took pleasure in dress, especially given the high percentage of young women among their number. In 1851, for example, some 40 percent of female cotton factory workers and domestic servants were under twenty years of age.[71] But it would also be wrong to take at face value the repeated assertion that female factory workers and domestic servants were fixated on "finery." Furthermore, the extent to which factory girls were actually able to indulge whatever sartorial desires they harbored is debatable. Even the higher wages were far from abundant, and although critics claimed they stinted on food to buy clothes, food still had to be bought and household expenses paid.

As the century progressed, and other employment opportunities developed for working-class women, it became harder to recruit and retain domestic servants despite improved wages. In 1876, London footman Herbert Miller investigated this Servant Question, asking "milliners, dressmakers, factory girls and others," why they chose their particular trades in preference to domestic service. They cited its "low and degrading" nature, the "almost total loss of personal liberty" and a factory girl, earning just ten pence a day, claimed to be "above that poor scum what mustn't wear a feather or a ribbon, or breathe the fresh air, without asking somebody's leave."[72] At the same time, while the uniform did undoubtedly become the standard wear for servants, the repeated insistence on the need to regulate servants' dress suggests the ineffectiveness of the message and this may have been due to limited employer enthusiasm for the extremes of dress restriction as well as the servants' own objections.

Most working-class people had few possessions and, despite housing improvements and a growing culture of domesticity from the 1870s, lived in rented accommodation, often of very poor quality. Social life therefore continued to be conducted largely outside the home—at work, in pubs, shops, and streets, where bodies, and the clothes that covered them (or not), were the most prominent signifier of their wearers' status and read as an immediate indicator of their moral character. Today, clothing is but one of the commodities, together with houses, household goods, vehicles, and technological gadgetry, through which people express their identity and status. But in the nineteenth century, clothing played a heightened role, often forming the largest and most valuable of a person's material possessions. Among those with little autonomy, therefore, the freedom to dress as they desired, within the limits of their resources, to display class allegiance through adopting a particular sartorial style, or to brighten drab lives through a little self-adornment, was jealously guarded, and unwarranted interference fiercely resisted.

By the closing decades of the century, with the decline of evangelical influence, it was becoming more widely understood that poverty was a human rather than divine creation, and needed to be addressed through statutory intervention not simply philanthropic goodwill. Also, the expansion of education and career opportunities for middle-class women meant many had less time to devote to voluntary work and clothing charities became more focused on the efficient provision of garments than on moral regulation.[73] Simultaneously the spread of democracy was creating a less deferential society, while rising living standards and cheaper, mass-produced clothes were increasing consumer choice and working-class wardrobes. The fight was not over, but England was becoming less of a sartorial battleground.

CHAPTER SEVEN

Ethnicity

SARAH CHEANG

Dress has played a crucial role in the expression of ethnicity. In all human societies, the body has been dressed and adorned in some way, through the draping and sewing of textiles and animal skins, the wearing of jewelry, and the manipulation of head and body hair. Ethnicity is a grouping of people who share a common culture, and body adornment creates common cultural identities through dress. Even modifications of the body itself, such as the decoration of the skin through tattooing and scarification, and the alteration of body shape such as the wearing of brass rings to lengthen the neck, corsets to pull in the waist, and binding to reduce foot size can be readily associated with particular places, peoples, and historical periods and used to make immediate visual distinctions between cultural groupings. Although the wearing of clothing fulfils many practical and psychological needs, definitions of dress place the greatest emphasis on social signaling, with the main function of dress being proposed as a corporeal display for communication with other humans.[1] The dressed body, therefore, has provided a highly visual and varied means of communicating and experiencing ethnicity and ethnic difference.

Practices of ethnic dress can appear to be separate from fashionable dress in a number of ways, although such distinctions are highly problematic. Ethnic dress is associated with backward-looking traditions, and is "best understood as those items, ensembles and modifications of the body that capture the past of the members of the group, the items of tradition that are worn and displayed to signify cultural heritage."[2] Fashion, when differentiated from dress, refers to a social dynamic of renewal, novelty, innovation and individual distinctiveness that may even operate as a threat to the perpetuation of culture heritage. The idea that fashion practices exist in some kind of opposition to ethnic dress, however, cannot be universally applied, and, as this chapter will show, it was during the nineteenth century that many of the conceptual separations between "modern" fashion and "traditional" ethnic dress took shape. The words "dress" and "fashion" will not be treated as interchangeable. "Fashion" will be used to indicate cultural systems of dress where the key dynamic is style change in the expression of individuality and social identity.[3] This phenomenon of fashion is neither confined to Western cultures, nor totally dependent on Eurocentric fashion systems.[4] Fashion is a process of change whose conceptual structure varies from culture to culture. This chapter is not concerned, therefore, with "ethnic dress" as a category that cannot include "fashion"; neither is it a descriptive survey of nineteenth-century world dress, culture by culture. It is an exploration of expressions of ethnicity in the long nineteenth century through practices of dress and body adornment that often had a close and lasting relationship with notions of fashion.

FIGURE 7.1: Mid-nineteenth-century illustration of female ethnological differences in hair, showing a European, a Patagonian, an "Esquimaux," a "Bisharee" woman, a Fijian, and a woman of the Warrau tribe, South America. From A. Rowland, *The Human Hair: Popularly and Physiologically Considered with Special Reference to Its Preservation, Improvement and Adornment, and the Various Modes of Its Decoration in All Countries* (London: Piper, 1853), pl. I. Wellcome Library, London.

The spread of Western imperialism and the abolition of slavery in the Americas were key societal shifts of the nineteenth century. Race and racism were central to both of these historical contexts, not only underpinning the Atlantic slave trade and its after-effects, but also sustaining Western colonialism with important consequences for perceptions and expressions of ethnic difference. Colonial expansion had seen the rise of Spanish, French, and Dutch empires between the sixteenth and eighteenth centuries, but in the nineteenth century, Britain became the foremost European power. By the end of the nineteenth century, the British "had acquired a quarter of the world, and could behave with privileged immunity in much of the rest."[5] In combination with the legacy of three centuries of European colonialism in the Americas, competition between European nations for possession of lands in Africa, and the existence of quasi-colonial areas of Western imperial interest such as China, there were few places in the world where the effects of Western imperialism were not felt. The nineteenth century also saw a marked rise in the populations of Europe and the Americas, with a corresponding decrease in the percentage of the world's population living in Africa and Asia, which lent sheer numbers to the dominance of the Western world.[6]

Cloth, clothing, and fashions have circulated from culture to culture, country to country, continent to continent for millennia. Nineteenth-century Western colonialism placed pre-existing global trading networks within a new set of imperialistic concerns, as well as forming new inter-cultural flows of fashion that enabled people and material goods to travel. Within the context of imperial power relations, however, these cultural encounters appear to have heightened the need to delineate cultures using dress. The social production of ethnicity is, after all, a boundary-forming activity. As Stephen Connell and Douglas Hartmann explain, "ethnicity is a matter of contrast. To claim an ethnic identity (or attempt to assign one to someone else) is to distinguish ourselves from others; it is to draw a boundary between "us" and "them" . . . An ethnic group cannot exist in isolation."[7] Dress, then, may signal, police, or subvert those boundaries. Fashion has offered a route to self-definition and empowerment, whether through the rejection of cultural stereotypes, identification with dominant social groups, investment in cosmopolitan dress cultures, or processes of creolization.

Dress historians have seen the long nineteenth century as a crucial period in the rise of a particular kind of fashion system. While modern Western fashion has been associated with mercantile capitalism beginning in fourteenth-century Europe, from the late eighteenth century, mechanization enabled the faster and cheaper production of textiles.[8] During the nineteenth century, advances in mass-production also altered many aspects of clothing production; the building of railways and steam ships increased speeds of circulation for goods and people, while an upsurge in publishing expanded fashion knowledge and stimulated the Euro-American fashion cycle still further. The rapid expansion of urban centers and new forms of shopping such as the department store increased the reach of a fashion system that was locked into industrialized capitalist production and consumption with mass mediation. By the early twentieth century, the mass-production of ready-to-wear made the products of this fashion system more affordable and more available. In Paris, the rise of the *couturier* as a fashion designer who could dictate trends (although not always successfully) also increased the symbolic links between fashion change, the creation of contemporaneity, and Western models of modernity. Thus, by the early twentieth century, fashion as a particular type of social dynamic expressed through stylistic change in dress was seen as a specifically modern European cultural trait, inextricably linked with modern "civilization."[9] The cultural and technological systems of

European dress came to define "fashion," in tandem with a set of Eurocentric assumptions about a lack of fashion change and modernity in other cultures.[10] It is clear, therefore, that matters of ethnicity have played a substantial role in shaping the meanings of the word "fashion," in addition to the ways in which fashion as a social dynamic and as a material object was used to mark ethnic boundaries.

ETHNICITY, RACE, AND FASHION

Ethnicity is a term that expresses cultural belonging across many registers. Ethnicity is a collective identity that can sometimes be determined by the physical characteristics of "race" such as skin color, facial features, and hair type; it can also be a nationality, a tribal grouping, or it can be defined by a geographical region or even a religion. This flexibility of definition reflects the ways in which the concept of ethnicity groups people in terms of their claims to a common ancestry or shared culture, but does not dictate the form that shared culture should take. Unlike "race," which is focused on the dividing of humans into categories according to the biological inheritance of particular physical characteristics, ethnicity is a grouping of people who have a collective interest in coming together. Identification of a common ancestry is a result rather than a cause of this coming together.[11] Ethnic boundaries may be defined by quite abstract concepts, but ethnicity is given content and experienced through fashion as well as through the highly politicized, romantic, or pointedly revivalist modalities of ethnic and national dress.

In nineteenth- and early twentieth-century Western cultures, the dominant way of understanding the human species was as a racial hierarchy, in which white people of north European descent were considered the most superior, and black Africans considered the most inferior. Earlier concepts of racial difference were built on religious and philosophical notions of a pre-ordained universal order, and further developed in the appalling context of the Atlantic slave trade which reached its height in the eighteenth century. During the nineteenth century, "race" was further underpinned by scientific studies of the body that focused on the comparative measurement of certain physical differences between peoples.[12] Three main racial groupings were posited (Caucasian, mongoloid, and negroid) and these were then subdivided into a myriad of "racial" sub-categories that enabled the conceptualization of cultural differences between, for example, the French and the English, or the Chinese and the Japanese, as "racial" differences. Ethnography, the study of peoples through culture, formed part of the new discipline of anthropology. Theories of evolution, and Charles Darwin's *The Descent of Man* (1871), were used to provide a scientific underpinning to the argument that non-European humans were at an earlier stage of biological and social development, closer to animals.[13] With European cultures treated as the pinnacle of human development, European fashion cultures were seen as a manifestation, and hence a measure, of modern civilization.

Alternative and earlier attitudes to ethnicity and material culture are worth elaborating on here for what they tell us about the impact of racial theories, slavery, and colonial contexts on the relationship between clothing and ethnicity. In late seventeenth- and early eighteenth-century Illinois Country, Louisiana, native Indian women who married French men were able to officially change their ethnicity, and dress played an important role in these physical and cultural transformations. For example, Marie Catherine Illinoise, born an Illinois Indian, adopted silk taffeta gowns, lived in a French colonial style house, and having been "Frenchified" she could be entered in official records as French.[14] This fluidity was conducted in part through fashion, but was localized and short-lived. In

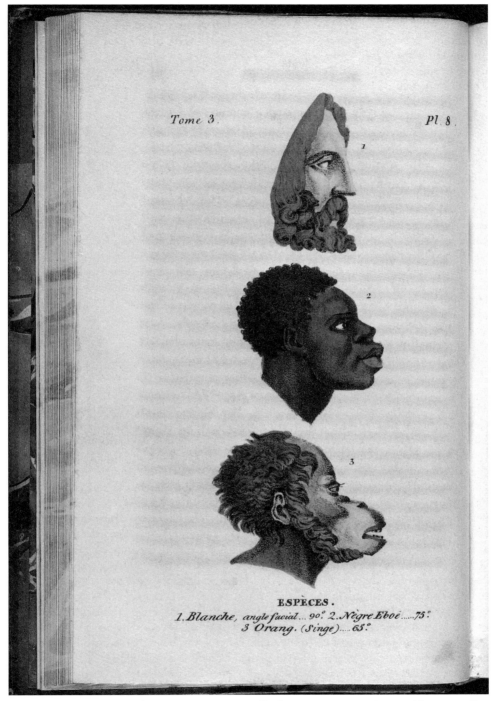

FIGURE 7.2: Julien Joseph Virey, *Histoire Naturelle du Genre Humain*, Aug. Wahlen, Bruxelles 1826, vol. 2, p. 39, pl. 8. Wellcome Library, London.

eighteenth- and nineteenth-century America, European colonizers worried about a potential "descent" into native "savagery" and dressed accordingly to signal their continuing racial "superiority." The Atlantic slave trade also introduced an African population whose horrific position as slaves necessitated a continual racial distancing and fixing to try to justify the cruel exploitation of one cultural group by another. Southern American legislation included dress codes that "functioned to maintain white supremacy in a society based economically and socially on racial slavery. In effect, whites used these dress codes to outwardly distinguish those without power from those who held it."[15] A slave who managed to dress "above" his or her station could have clothing taken away by law.

By the early twentieth century, the "one drop" rule meant that however a person looked or behaved, any kind of sub-Saharan African ancestry (one "drop" of "African blood") could legally categorize a person as black in the United States. In many states, anti-"miscegenation" laws were also passed that forbade marriage between Caucasians and non-Caucasians. Identification as, for example, African American, Native American, Chinese American, or Caucasian American had profound implications for a person's legal rights, and dictated access to occupation, education, land and property, to say nothing of lifestyle. Under such circumstances, ethnic identities cannot be treated as unstable, and boundaries cannot be blurred.[16] Dress, significantly, can be put on and taken off; it is both identity and disguise. Fashion reinforces this instability through its restless cycles of appropriation and impermanence.

FASHIONING RACE: SLAVERY AND BLACK DANDIES

The African diaspora is a term often used to signify people of West African and West Central African descent living in North and South America, the Caribbean, and also Europe as a result of the transatlantic slave trade established in the mid-seventeenth century. In the early nineteenth century, European slave transportation to the Americas ceased, and slavery itself was finally abolished across the whole of the United States in 1865, and in all parts of Latin America by 1888. While free blacks had always had a presence in the Americas, the nineteenth century was clearly a key moment in the negotiation of far-reaching changes in African American identities; dress was a marker of economic deprivation, segregation, and the continuing pressures of racial subordination, as well as offering opportunities for agency by using the body as a site of public display.

During the slave trade, many kinds of ethnic difference between African peoples were supplanted by the single factor of race and blackness. Slaves were forced to wear what their "owners" gave them and denied the means to dress and adorn their bodies as they might have done in Africa, diminishing expressions of collective ethnicities other than race. Enslaved people do not even own their own bodies; the symbolic role of clothing as a marker of humanity, as well as of the social order was startlingly relevant.[17] At the most basic level, beyond even modesty, having sufficient clothing was of great concern to black slaves at a time when the location of black people on the divide between humans and animals was hotly debated in scientific circles.[18] Where there was access to clothing choice, however, fashion's strong links to self-determined individuality meant that dress could be a powerful tool for expressions of African-American consciousness in which European and African dress cultures were brought together.[19]

FIGURE 7.3: American slave market, 1852, by Taylor. Slavery, United States, nineteenth century. Photo: DEA Picture Library/Getty Images.

Within the "natural" order of pre-abolition society, whites were expected to wear finer clothing than blacks, with embellishments such as lace and embroidery—making the clothing of poor whites or prosperous blacks quite problematic in the maintaining of racial boundaries. In their Sunday best at church, Southern white women in their silks and hooped skirts looked, in the words of enslaved Addie Vinson, like "fairy queens" beside black women in their calico dresses, sometimes with skirt hoops made from materials such as grape vines.[20] Slaves who worked in their "owner's" house had better clothes than slaves who worked in the fields, the more intimate contact with white domestic life resulting in the wearing of the white family's cast offs as well as livery. The maintenance of slave appearance—both hair and clothing—was also an extension of the "owner's" domestic interior and followed the dress codes of respectable servants.[21] House servants formed a kind of aristocracy, but this was offset by a lack of freedom in what they wore, whereas field workers had less access to high-quality clothing but more choice in how they wore their garments.

Helen Bradley Foster's 1997 study of African-American clothing in the southern United States makes it clear that while there was no single experience of slavery, multiple histories are united in the empowering value of clothing where other avenues of self-expression were closed off.[22] Slaves were basically dependent on their "owners" for clothing, but it could be mended, supplemented, and embellished through whatever means were at hand. Where slaves were directly engaged in the production of cloth and clothing as part of their work, they possessed the skills to create Sunday best with colorful woven and dyed stripes. Money saved through extra work or received as gifts was often spent on clothing, sometimes to great effect. One man bought cloth that he had tailored into a suit. He wore this suit proudly, eliciting comment that he looked as if he "owned" his master rather than the other way around.[23] This story, whether exaggerated or absolutely true, points to the reasons why control of dress was a source of social anxiety. Dress was a potential disruptor of power structures constructed around ethnicities. Dress also possesses a narrative force, and fashion is a potent language of self-definition and agency in even the direst of circumstances.

Scholars have highlighted the figure of the male dandy as a particular site of engagement with fashion and the construction of African-American identities. Situated initially within traditions of festival cross-dressing that subverted the racial hierarchy and created momentary instability in power relationships, the black dandy is closely tied to the journey from slavery to freedom.[24] North American slave festivals such as Pinkster and Negro Election Day drew from African and European traditions to create new American identities. For example, one early nineteenth-century Pinkster King, an Angolan named Charley, was paraded in a British military uniform of red broadcloth and gold lace, yellow breeches, blue stockings, silver-buckled shoes, and a tricorn hat.[25] African traditional rituals of parody, and the historical incorporation of European clothing into the dress of high ranking Africans, suggest that the wearing of clothing associated with white pomp was not just a comical imitation of whites but resonated with African dress practices that conferred real respect and social order.[26] Dandyism can be seen, therefore, as part of an inheritance of African culture, and as contributing to a distinctive ethnic identity for African-Americans after the abolition of slavery.

In both the northern and southern states of America, and whether free or enslaved, African Americans were criticized for having a "natural" disposition toward showy dressing because they were believed to have a racially-determined lack of self-restraint. This was acceptable during temporary moments of carnival misrule. As abolition took effect, however, what blacks wore took on a new importance and exuberant dressing was interpreted by whites as offensive, presumptuous, and a sign that blacks were increasingly out of control. Asserting the right to dress with style and to walk the streets freely was expressive of a new era for African Americans, while public spaces provided both sociability and an arena in which to see and be seen.[27] A European tourist to New York in 1832, for example, marveled at the dress of African New Yorkers, reporting that the women wore "bonnets decorated with ribbons, plumes, and flowers, of a thousand different colours, and their dresses are of the most showy description." The men were attired in "coats so open that the shirt sticks out under the arm-pits; the waistcoats are of all colours of the rainbow, the hat is carelessly put on one side; the gloves are yellow, and every sable dandy carries a smart cane."[28]

The use of fashion for self-definition while remaining within a system that defined black identities as subordinate and errant, resulted in African-American fashions being criticized as a racial characteristic of pathological excess. Dandyism was ambivalently seen as both an innate African quality and a cross-cultural masquerade, and was open to caricature and mockery on both these accounts. In blackface minstrelsy, fashion was used in relation to music and dance in a performance of "race" that reaffirmed white social dominance through the portrayal of African Americans as non-threatening playful imitators of European fashion. It was this assumption of white fashion authority as social

FIGURE 7.4: "Dandy Jim, from Carolina," sheet music from 1843 showing a free black dressing and acting "above" his station. Mary Evans/Everett Collection.

authority that dandyism disturbed. As Susan Kaiser, Leslie Rabine, Carol Hall, and Karyl Ketchum assert:

> African Americans have not imitated European American style. Instead, they have drawn upon a rich history of aesthetic creativity and innovation from various West African cultures. Forced to adopt Euro-American dress, they have, throughout their history, articulated their own diasporic form of improvisation that appropriates European American style to create an aesthetic of resistance . . . by borrowing from white, European dress to create a more expressive model of fashionability, the idea of style as resistance—both spiritual and political, but no less beautiful—has permeated African-American self-representation.[29]

The notion of fashion as emancipatory rests on the capacity for self-representation. Where self-representation was denied, or where representation was in the hands of the white imperialists, fashion could act as a tool of oppression. On the road to black civil rights throughout the nineteenth and twentieth centuries, the symbolic role of Africa became increasingly important in articulating an identity that was not wholly defined by slavery. However, in Western discourse, the idea of "Africa" was over-determined by a set of orientalist ideas that used non-European cultures in particular ways to ultimately secure a sense of European superiority.[30] "Savages," understood as "our contemporary ancestors," were studied in order to peer into humanity's "past," but it was observed that contact with the "civilised races" had made the study of "primitive" clothing "complicated."[31] Just how complicated it is to reconcile the ideologies of nineteenth-century European fashion and modernity with the material realities of global fashion flow can be seen in the history of Dutch Wax textiles in Africa.

The creation of a symbolic opposition between Western and African dress systems is at odds with the ways in which European nations were producing textiles expressly for African markets that were very actively engaged with the global circulation of textiles. For example, West and East Africans had, in fact, been eager participants in the global market for Indian cottons since the sixteenth century, as were Europeans from the seventeenth century.[32] Eighteenth-century British manufacturers, who were trying to compete in this market by imitating Indian textiles, found that West Africans were highly discerning consumers, seeking both quality and novelty, and preferring the colors and finish of Indian products to any European copies.[33] As European textile production expanded due to industrialization, manufacturers continued to look for patterns that could be sold in Africa. In the second half of the nineteenth century, Dutch traders with imperial links to Indonesia found that although Javanese batik cloth did not sell well in Europe, it was favored in Africa. The intense colors and the potential for a wide range of motifs (both familiar and unfamiliar) appealed to West African tastes, and the double-sided patterning made batik cloth a good fabric for forms of dress that were wrapped or tied around the body as well as stitched. This stimulated methods of imitating the characteristic cracked effect of the wax resist process, using machine-printed techniques. Dutch Wax cloth, as it became known, was therefore inspired by a Javanese aesthetic and technique, featured European, Indian, Indonesian, and African motifs, and was manufactured in Holland, England, and Switzerland directly in response to the demands of African consumers. By the end of the nineteenth century, Dutch Wax cloth had become a key part of West African fashion identity. Its consumers in Ghana, the Ivory Coast, Nigeria, and Zaire had an eye for change, wanted global products, and were wearing textiles that both expressed

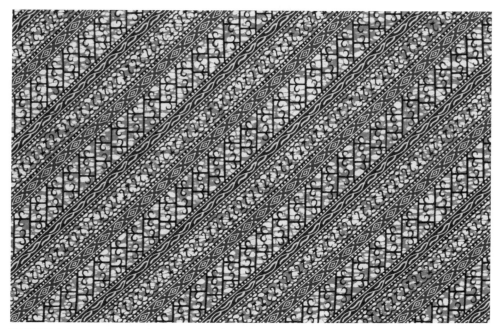

FIGURE 7.5: Dutch Wax cloth introduced in Ghana, Africa in 1929, originating from a classic Indonesian design. Vlisco Netherlands B.V.

African ethnic identities and confounded the notion of neat cultural separations through dress—their clothing was in fact highly cosmopolitan in nature.

The example of the history of Dutch Wax cloth for African markets highlights the problem of "authenticity" when seeking textile designs that might represent Africanness and demonstrates that coherent ethnic identities can be expressed through fashion without having to rely on indigenous materials and motifs, and without adopting European forms of dress.[34] There was no golden age of culturally "pure" peoples and neither was fashion in Africa, as in America, a matter of copying, or being simply on the receiving end of, European fashion.[35] The history of printed cloth in Africa also reflects the cosmopolitanism of fashion history, which has the capacity to add an extra dimension to the cultural "stuff" of ethnicity. Ethnicity as a form of social organization is highly emblematic of cultural differentiation, yet expressions, experiences, and feelings of ethnicity are not absolutes but negotiated social strategies and on-going social processes involving both insiders and outsiders to the group. During the nineteenth century, the racism entrenched within the power structures of Western imperialism resisted this flexibility and self-determination, producing rules of dressing that attempted instead to clearly and cleanly delineate ethnicity in the imperial field.

IMPERIAL RULE AND DELINEATIONS OF ETHNICITY

Ethnic identification may be emotionally charged and powerfully embedded into people's lives and yet deployed or engaged with selectively, as a social resource.[36] Colonial rule involves a specific set of tensions between the desire to change and the desire to preserve native cultures, and dress is used to police ethnic boundaries in ways that are highly contingent. In British India, the social reforms of the "civilizing mission" included an assumption that British clothing was superior and modern, and could play a role in bringing India "up to date." However, Indian interactions with British dress codes were highly charged. Certain social groups adopted European dress, such as Christian converts, wealthy urban merchants, and English-educated elites.[37] For many Indian men, British clothing styles functioned as a way of getting ahead, and combinations of European and Indian dress were worn, such as European tailored jackets or leather shoes with south Asian *dhotis* and sarongs. Some wore either Indian or European clothing depending on the social situation. As Emma Tarlo explains: "Changing one's clothes to suit the occasion allowed an Indian man to maintain, if necessary, two distinct sartorial identities."[38] Ridicule and "indecency" in British social contexts could be avoided by wearing European dress, while changing to Indian dress at home provided a positive act of preservation, loyalty, and respect for Indian culture. The decision of where to the draw the line between Indian and British identities was being played out using dress as the primary social marker of cultural adhesion, but was also fraught with dilemmas. Full European dress accomplished a potentially offensive abandonment of caste identity, and there was also the practical problem of when and how to make the clothing changes required when moving between Indian and British spaces. Anglo-Indian hybridity could also threaten the colonial status quo and suggest spaces for native resistance, for how could the British justify their presence in India if the Indian people appeared equally as "civilized" and at the same time remained "Indian"?[39]

Alongside the promulgation and restriction of British dress, there were also attempts to delineate and therefore fix certain forms of Indian dress. John Forbes Watson of the India Office published an eighteen-volume collection of Indian textile samples (1866), with an accompanying volume entitled *The Textile Manufacturers and the Costumes of the People of India* that gave precise information on the fabrics and how they were worn.[40] These were distributed to textile manufacturers in Britain with the expressly commercial aim of supplying Indian markets with industrially produced British textiles.[41] In the process, however, Forbes Watson's textile collections provided a specifically dress-related contribution to the British classification and fixing of Indian ethnicity. During the nineteenth century, comprehensive studies of Indian languages and customs, and archeological and architectural surveys of India enabled the British to map, and, in a sense, to "own" Indian heritage. Following the 1857 "Indian Mutiny" against the British, it seemed imperative for the British government to understand Indian society in even more detail and thereby exert more direct control. *The People of India* (1868–75) was an eight-volume collection of photographs compiled by the British India Office that attempted to document the physical appearance of all cultural groups in India, the better to know, govern, and profit from them.[42] As Bernard Cohn writes, "The British rulers were increasingly defining what was Indian in an official and "objective" sense. Indians had to look like Indians."[43]

The "Indianizing" of Indian military uniform was one way in which the British attempted to reiterate sartorial markers of ethnicity and hence control Indian society. Sikhs, for example, who fought in the British armies, were given distinctive dress uniforms that incorporated large red turbans, sashes, lower body garments, and footwear more in keeping with native Indian dress than British military styles. Sikh men of the Punjab were considered one of the "martial races," a people with "natural" qualities of the manly warrior, and this accent on ethnic difference in the service of the British empire continued even during the First World War in the uniforms issued to Sikhs in khaki on the Western

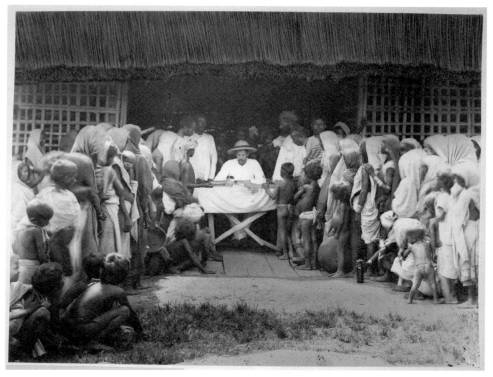

FIGURE 7.6: A shod European man pays bare-foot Indian tea plantation workers, West Bengal, 1880s. © British Library, London.

Front.[44] Above any concession to religious observances, the "correct" beard and large standardized turbans communicated ethnic information that served British interests.

The demonstration and maintenance of colonial rule through the adoption or enforcement of certain Indian customs can also be seen in the "shoe controversy." It was understood that shoes were not worn by most social groups in India, whereas shoe-wearing in northern Europe was seen as the norm. These dress codes were used in an assertion of European and Indian identities that produced a subordinate social status for colonial natives. Indians were not allowed to wear shoes in the presence of the British, whereas the British wore their shoes everywhere, including in Indian sacred spaces where shoes were not permitted.[45] At both ceremonial and everyday levels, shoe-wearing was used to safeguard ethnic boundaries and assert ethnic hierarchies. A revealing exception, however, was made for Indians who had adopted European dress. So as not to hybridize (or render in some way ridiculous) the appearance of British dress, shoes might be worn with European dress in the presence of the British at formal public occasions.

The pressure for British men and women to dress in accordance with British codes of conduct was set against its opposing position of "going native." By asserting their superior status through the wearing of shoes, the British were in effect unable to take them off in public without suffering a lowering of their status—a lack of shoes was interpreted as a humiliation belonging only to the colonial subject. Colonial spaces were, therefore, threatening boundary points at which ethnic identities needed to be most emphatically articulated. The intermingling of ethnic dress codes was associated with sympathy for native Indian causes, or even inter-cultural marriage, while the strict adherence to British dress signaled a physical, cultural, and social distancing of the colonial rulers from their native subjects.[46] For British men, the wearing of Indian dress was prohibited by the British East India Company from 1830. The British memsahibs, who were important conduits of Indian material culture when in Britain, were likewise expected to project a strict Britishness when in India.[47] On the Indian side, late nineteenth-century Indian women were discouraged from dressing in European blouses, petticoats, and shoes that would complicate Indian national identity at a time of nationalist struggle for independence.[48] Therefore, while colonial contact zones had the capacity to increase inter-cultural fashion exchange, this occurred in tension with an active resistance to transnational dress practices because "racial" and national boundaries had a very real relation to power and agency.

Clearly, regulations on dress, whether officially enshrined, regulated through etiquette manuals, or tacitly acknowledged through careful observation of group practices, affected the British throughout the empire. Dressing for dinner in evening gowns and tailcoats was a compulsory requirement for British social elites in Nigeria, well into the early twentieth century, even when no other Europeans were present.[49] These rigid and often impractical dress rituals persisted in imperial spaces, even after they had been discontinued back home, connecting fashion, dress, and display to deep anxieties around distinct cultural identities and colonial authority. When a British woman donned her corset in Africa, she was keeping up morale, and maintaining racial and colonial hierarchies through demonstrations of self-discipline and codes of decency that had a lasting influence whenever narratives of ethnic domination came into play.

INDIGENOUS PRODUCTS, CRAFT, AND INDUSTRY

Ethnicities defined through fashion and racial discourse, geographical region, national identities, and east/west dichotomies were often focused around distinct place names and fantasies of the people that produced them. Kashmiri shawls were an Indian product that became particularly significant in nineteenth-century European culture, prompting both fashion change and industrial innovation. The history of the Kashmir shawl highlights the symbolic importance of indigenous materials, techniques, and motifs, both Indian and European, within the production of ethnicity through fashion. It also illustrates the importance of industrial production to the creation and maintenance of Western fashion meanings, an importance that persists into the twenty-first century.

Finely-worked Kashmiri shawls, known as pashmina, have formed part of social and political systems for centuries, from transactions between the elites of India and Persia, to gift-giving among Europeans, to tributes paid to imperial powers. The Kashmiri city of Srinagar was a center of production for shawl cloth from the fifteenth century onwards.[50] The cloth served in India as hangings, furniture, and floor covering as well as garments, mainly for men, and it was also used by rulers as gifts or payment. Kashmiri shawls were traded within Central Asia, China, Russia, and the Ottoman Empire, where they were adapted according to local needs. For example, from the sixteenth century in Iran, Kashmiri shawls were in demand as a more elite and finer product than Persian shawls, and it was the practice to tailor the woolen fabric into fitted clothing for both men and women.[51] The long narrow shawls employed a woven floral decoration concentrated around the borders, reflecting their use as *patka* (waist sashes).

FIGURE 7.7: Early-nineteenth-century Kashmir shawl. © Victoria and Albert Museum, London.

The undercoat of the Tibetan (or Changthangi) goat provides the wool known as *pashm* for the making of pashmina. This is the wool that is also known as "cashmere," from older Anglophone spellings of the place name Kashmir. The Tibetan goat owes the special properties of its long coat to extreme winter conditions and for this reason they are cultivated at high altitudes in Ladakh, a mountainous region of Kashmir adjoining Tibet. The *pashm* is spun into a very fine woolen thread that can be used to produce shawl cloth that has more fibers per strand than other types of wool, trapping more air to produce uniquely light-weight but warm textiles. At Srinagar, the *pashm* fibers were combed, washed, and color sorted, drawn out into thread using a drop spindle, and then woven on horizontal treadle looms using a twill weave. Decorative patterns and motifs were woven into the cloth, a method of production that was highly skilled and time-consuming, although embroidered decoration was used from the early nineteenth century which speeded up production.[52] Kashmiri weavers altered their designs to cater for their various markets, consciously engaging in inter-cultural trade and actively responding to external influence.

European histories of the Kashmir shawl have tended to privilege Western fashion above any other form of cultural dynamic in the production and consumption of the shawls. The result is a "rise and fall narrative," beginning in the eighteenth century with the pashmina's "discovery" by Europeans, and ending around 1870 when shawls were no longer part of mainstream European fashion. Such a framework is driven only by European fashion demands and places no importance on pre-existing and competing trading circuits within India and the Middle East.[53] The pashmina has been viewed as the traditional product of remote peoples employing their traditional crafts since time immemorial until their talents were harnessed by Europeans. A less Eurocentric approach might see the people of the Kashmir valley as having actively created a world center of shawl production through their entrepreneurial skills in organizing a monopoly over the collecting of the *pashm*, their funneling of this raw material into the Kashmir valley, and their spinning and weaving it with the greatest expertise to create a valuable luxury export.[54]

During the eighteenth century, Kashmiri shawl cloth was seen and worn by the British in India. Travelers, East India Company servants, and officials stationed in India began to bring back shawls as gifts for women to wear in Britain, often by special request.[55] Napoleon's military campaigns in Egypt also brought the shawls to France, so that by the late eighteenth and early nineteenth century, this North Indian product, and its *buta* teardrop or pinecone decorative motif, had an increased presence in Euro-American fashion systems through a number of channels. Such was the interest in these expensive imports that from the 1770s, wool centers in England and Scotland that were capable of light-weight production began making copies of Kashmiri shawls. In early nineteenth-century France, "Kashmir shawls" were also woven on the new Jacquard looms that increased the speed of weaving complex patterns, especially after the 1860s when power looms came into use. This enabled French-made versions of the shawls to dominate the market alongside other European hand-loom woven versions and also printed shawls. European-made shawls cost less than the shawls that were made in Kashmir, creating a mass-market fashion for people of middle income. Scottish production at Paisley near Edinburgh meant that the *buta* motif that adorned the Paisley shawls has been known in Britain as "paisley" pattern ever since.

The consumption of Kashmiri shawls, and arguably their Paisley versions also, brought India and Kashmir into the domestic realm. The shawls connected British people to "global circuits of production, distribution and exchange" and offered an interaction with the exotic spaces of empire.[56] Fashion was acting as a catalyst of both novel distinction and naturalization. Foreign fibers and designs, once fashionable, were transformed from "alien practice" to "European fashion" even while they retained their ability to signal "India" and its riches. This is perhaps no more poignantly seen than in the images made of the Great Exhibition of 1851. This landmark international exhibition was held in London as a showcase of British technological ingenuity, artistic output, and cultural prestige, in which the riches of India were given pride of place among the imperial exhibits.[57] Lithographic prints show European women as they wandered among the displays, seeing and being seen while wearing an eye-catching and enveloping expanse of *buta* patterns across their backs. Indian weavers were imagined as the naive providers of traditional cloth for their social "superiors," and the contrasts between European and Indian shawl production were explicitly drawn along the lines of ethnicity, as an article printed in *Harper's New Monthly Magazine* in 1850 made clear:

> The loom on which a Cashmere shawl is woven is of the rudest and most primitive description, the warp being supported by two sticks, and the woof entirely worked in by the human hand. This slow laborious process permits a neatness and exactness of finish beyond the power of any machinery to rival; and when we take into account a

life-long practice in the art, and—remembering the Hindoo "castes," which usually limit a family to the exercise of a single craft—in most instances the family secrets and traditions which have been preserved, we cease to wonder at the perfection of the work. These Asiatic weavers, temperate in their habits and readily contented, receive a wage of from three-halfpence to two pence a day; . . . There is something very kindling to the imagination in the thought of these swarthy weavers, attired perhaps in our Manchester calicoes, laboring patiently for weeks and months to produce a fabric worthy of rank and royalty, without other than most vague or false ideas of the scenes in which their work will be displayed.[58]

The 1870s marked a point of decline for large shawls within mainstream European fashion systems. Changes in skirt construction from the bell-shaped crinoline to the rear-projecting bustle are argued to have necessitated changes in the shape and nature of outwear, while the social dynamics of fashion change meant that the wide availability and ubiquity of cheap shawls prompted the need for a new garment by social elites. Authentic Kashmir shawls, however, maintained their value in Europe regardless of any rise and decline in Euro-American fashion trends due to their cost and rarity, and the notional space of Kashmir seemed to gain a renewed importance. An "authentic" Kashmir shawl signaled individuality, global knowledge, spending power, and social distinction. Imagined as an idyllic paradise at the foothills of the Himalayas, the natural splendor of Kashmir became bound up with a new, more romantic vision of the shawls as articles of artistic beauty, in opposition to the European versions of mass fashion.[59] The "real" Indian shawls continued to have value because the traditional hand-crafted textiles of Kashmir were positioned outside of the Western fashion system as it developed in the nineteenth century—they were geographically and conceptually beyond a notion of fashion that was to be characterized by spaces of urban modernity, mechanized production, and commodity culture. The continued consumption of Kashmiri shawls throughout the nineteenth century thus helped Victorians to "culturally map" the Empire and was sustained by particular constructions of "fashion" in which differences between east and west, colony and metropolis, hand and machine were crucial.[60] There is also evidence that the material qualities of a unique indigenous product remained very important—Kashmiri shawls maintained their value as much for their light weight as for their pattern and provenance.[61]

Kashmiri shawl production for European markets should also be placed within the far broader and varied context of seventeenth- and eighteenth-century shawls that responded to Mughal floral fashions, and nineteenth- and twentieth-century local Indian style changes. Both before and after the fashionable period for Indian-style shawls in Western markets, Kashmiri shawls enjoyed popularity and fashion change within domestic markets. In the late nineteenth century and early twentieth century, production locations were altered due to the migration of weavers who continued to make Kashmiri shawl cloth for the garments of Indian and Persian men and women.[62] Where shawl histories written from a Western perspective depict the collapse of the Kashmiri industry as Western fashion styles changed, attending to the existence of multiple fashion systems reveals the Eurocentric bias inherent in such an account.

GENDER, NATIONALITY, AND MODERNITY

Contemporary notions of the modern political nation state have their roots in eighteenth- and nineteenth-century European culture, in the context of bureaucratic government (as opposed to feudalism or absolute monarchism), industrialization, capitalism, and particular notions of citizenship.[63] In this same historical period, there developed an explicit gendering of fashion in relation to morality. From the early nineteenth century, men's dress was characterized as plainer than women's, which was held to reflect male rationality and female irrationality.[64] This did not mean that European men were not interested in fashion and personal appearance, or did not enjoy style change in their dress.[65] Rather, discourses of fashion were intertwined with the dominant norms of masculinity and femininity, constructed as opposing ideologies in which male dress played down any flamboyance, while in female dress decorative effects were given free rein. Within many nineteenth-century cultures, women were positioned as the "natural" guardians of tradition through associations with motherhood and the home, but also the "natural" consumers of fashion owing to an apparent interest in passing fads and a preoccupation with personal beauty. In moments of cultural crisis, the dress of women could play an important role in securing core national values, but new fashions could also draw criticism, for example in the history of the Argentinian *peinetón*.

The *peinetón* was a tortoise-shell comb worn as a large decorative headpiece for women of European descent in Argentina during the 1830s. Following independence from Spain in 1810, white women in Buenos Aires could be seen wearing a fusion of English, French, and Spanish fashions clearly expressive of their European heritage, but combined and elaborated to form a new Argentinian national identity. While decorative Spanish hair combs had been introduced into Argentina during the eighteenth century, nineteenth-century post-colonial Argentinian fashions sought to achieve cultural distance from Spain. Regina Root argues that the Spanish hair comb may have been combined

FIGURE 7.8: Water color by Carlos Enrique Pellegrini, showing women holding court in their *peinetóns*, Buenos Aires, Argentina, 1831. Iberfoto/Mary Evans.

with an 1820s French fashion for strikingly tall hairstyles involving combs, enabling the Argentinian *peinetón* to develop into an elaborate headdress that could enhance the wearer's height and also extended outwards like a fan.[66] At a time of unequal legal and social rights for women, the enormous comb asserted feminine Argentinian post-colonial cultures and also increased feminine public visibility; women not only took up more visual and physical space everywhere they went, but also began going into places that had previously been reserved for men. New codes of conduct were mockingly suggested to enable men to safely negotiate the obstructive presence of *peinetón*-wearing women in the street—the men were to pass on the left. Both satirical and serious critics asserted that the combs were a corrupting influence on society and would cause the breakdown of family values. The cost of the combs was said to cause families to suffer, their high visibility subverted the Christian virtue of modesty, and their brazen size led women to be intrusive in general. Women's participation in national politics and the shifting of gender roles obtained leverage through fashion change; their challenge to male social dominance was correspondingly discouraged, using anti-fashion rhetoric that focused around the immorality of fashion. The example of the *peinetón* is a reminder that the fashions that conveyed ethnicity were still contested, and that a pervasive patriarchy, along with colonialism and social status, was an important part of the social power structures informing the ways in which ethnicity could be expressed through dress.

In Japan in the late nineteenth century and China in the early twentieth century, rather than a process of direct negotiation of colonial or post-colonial relationships with Europe, it was the drive to modernize and the question of what that modernity should look like that most strongly underlay changes in dress cultures for women. European and American military forces, practicing "gunboat diplomacy" to access trading rights, catalyzed far-reaching social changes in Japan and China. Both countries were in effect "opened up" to the west by force, disrupting the control that the Japanese and Chinese had previously been able to exert over cultural exchange.

The story of Japanese "modernity" is usually told as a reaction to trading treaties that were signed in 1854 after American Commodore Perry threatened the Japanese with a naval invasion. As a consequence of increased trading, European items of clothing such as bowler hats for men and woolen shawls for women were quickly adopted into Japanese dress cultures, while by the 1880s the kimono had become part of Western dress cultures as an artistic tea gown, dressing gown, or as fancy dress.[67] The period known as the Meiji Restoration (1868–1912) saw the reinstatement of the emperor as ruler of Japan. This new government emphasized modern reform and industrialization modeled on Western societies to counter any threat of colonization and to strengthen Japan's global position, especially in relation to China. From 1871, European dress codes were used in the emperor's court; European style uniforms were introduced for the military, occupations such as the postal service, and in schools. Western attitudes toward nakedness and exposure of the body, synonymous with civilized behavior, together with the gendering of unbifurcated garments as feminine, made some forms of traditional clothing problematic.[68] In the creation of a new identity for Japan as a "modern" nation with a higher ranking on the Darwinian scales of evolution, discourses of fashion that regulated the body according to notions of the contemporary had an important role to play.

It was not, of course, the case that Japanese dress was simply discarded and replaced by European dress, or that Japanese dress styles were experienced as antithetical to modernity. First, as outlined earlier, a modern Japanese look was obtained by incorporating European imported elements into Japanese fashionable attire. For example, images of the newly

FIGURE 7.9: Empress Shoken, consort of Emperor Meiji, in European dress on the cover of the British magazine *The Queen*, 1889. © British Library, London.

rebuilt Tokyo district of Ginza in the 1870s show a busy, gas-lit street "populated by a cosmopolitan mix of pedestrians, rickshaws and carriages alike, and even an omnibus," where men mixed "*haori* (jacket worn over kimono) and *hakama* (lower garment resembling a divided skirt) with bowler hats and Western shoes. These sartorial elements were key visual motifs expressing the Meiji ideal of *bunmei kaika*, civilisation and enlightenment."[69]

Second, although by the 1880s the Meiji empress had joined the emperor and his court in wearing full European dress, late nineteenth-century images of Japanese men in Western morning suits and Japanese women in dresses with bustles depict only a very wealthy elite, whose European clothes were an impractical match with Japanese furniture. As was the case in India, full European dress might only be worn when occasion demanded and be discarded at home. Furthermore, the drive to adopt European dress as daily wear was not evenly felt across gendered identities. The differences between men's and women's kimonos in construction, color, decoration, and methods of wearing were not easily

FIGURE 7.10: Woman wearing a *qipao* in 1920s China. Photograph attributed to Fu Bingchang. © 2007 C.H. Foo and Y.W. Foo. Image courtesy of Historical Photographs of China, University of Bristol.

legible to foreigners. This meant that Japanese male dress styles could look dangerously effeminate when judged by European standards, producing a crisis of masculinity that was solved through the adoption of dark tailored suits, leather shoes, and short haircuts. However, the values of rationality and progressiveness associated with Western dress, which made European clothing suitable for uniforms and the doing of business, diplomacy or warfare, were more fitting for models of masculinity than femininity. In the early

FIGURE 7.11: Emperor Hirohito and his wife Nagoko, 1926, in ceremonial dress that shows the continued importance of the kimono as a symbol of Japanese womanhood. Photograph from "Die Nachkriegszeit," no. 108. © Mary Evans Picture Library/Alamy Stock Photo.

decades of the twentieth century, the kimono was still held to embody "the Japanese sense of beauty and femininity."[70] Until the 1930s and 1940s, the kimono remained the most appropriate garment for Japanese women, leaving women to visually and corporally represent traditional Japaneseness in dress.

It should not be supposed that there was no fashion in Japan before the advent of the Western fashion, or that kimonos could not simultaneously be the provinces of Japanese tradition, fashion innovation, and modernity. While the kimono is a draped garment constructed from rectangles of cloth of a fixed size and does not tend to demonstrate fashion change in terms of structure and shape, choice of fabric and accessories offer ample evidence of a dynamic fashion system. As well as trends in color and pattern, the collars, edgings, and underlays of the kimono and the obi sash were sites of fashion trends. European art nouveau- and art deco-inspired design motifs show further evidence of the ways in which early twentieth-century kimono-wearing could create a space for European acculturation that read as Japanese, modern, and feminine.

In early twentieth-century China also, men moved toward a Westernization in dress by mixing European-style hats with Chinese clothing. A series of disastrous mid-nineteenth-century Chinese military defeats had resulted in the acquisition of territories and trading rights by Euro-American powers. By the early 1900s, China risked being carved up between the Western powers as Africa had been in the 1880s. The two main ethnic groups in China, Han and Manchu, had differing dress styles. In general, however, men wore long robes, and women also wore robes, trousers or long skirts, and jackets.[71] Han women were particularly distinguished by their feet, which were dramatically restricted in size through tight bandaging from childhood.

In 1911, the Qing emperor was deposed, and a new republic was declared. As in Japan during the Meiji period, republican China sought to assert itself as a modern nation, and new republican styles of dressing for Chinese women involved the development of a new kind of garment. Loose-fitting robes and jackets became tighter, trousers and skirts rose to calf length, and leather shoes with heels replaced cloth shoes. In the 1920s, the *qipao* or *Cheongsam* emerged through a modification of men's robes for women.[72] The *qipao*'s high collar and side fastenings marked it out as derived from Chinese dress, but a tighter fit on the body and shorter sleeves resonated with European forms of feminine dressing, to produce a garment for women that crossed both ethnic and gender boundaries. The practice of foot-binding declined and high-heeled shoes were provided as a suitable replacement.[73] Although foot-binding had been discouraged by nineteenth-century Western Christian missionaries and women's rights campaigners as uncivilized and detrimental to women's health, it was not until the articulation of a new kind of national identity was at hand that Western styles of dress and Western body aesthetics were appropriated by Chinese women as the way to express a new Chinese modernity through more cosmopolitanism dress cultures. The new *qipao* garment went on to become a symbol of Chinese nationality with sexual overtones because it became increasingly form-revealing, but it was viewed within early twentieth-century Chinese dress cultures as a potentially threatening new androgynous look for women because of its relation to the male robe. "In tune with Western influences and aesthetic standards" and yet distinctively Chinese, the *qipao* was a contentious symbol of national identity that perhaps owed its success as both national and everyday dress to its development within overtly global fashion cultures.[74]

CONCLUSION

In 1931, anthropologist Ruth Benedict wrote that whereas in "simpler" cultures "dress is geographically differentiated, in modern civilisation it is temporally differentiated."[75] Benedict was reflecting on the trajectory of Western modernity from the Renaissance onwards. In ascribing fashion change only to "modern civilization," she echoes the forces that were at play when African Americans were able to disconcert and make a statement of independence through fashion, when Indian and Japanese men asserted or challenged "racial" status using European modes of fashionable display, when Chinese women donned the *qipao* and signaled a new Chinese nation, and when British women enjoyed the modernity of machine-made shawls and the exotic qualities of the Kashmir product. At stake here are the definitions of modernity, civilization, and fashion change. Whether non-European cultures were celebrated for their "simplicity" or viewed as in need of "updating," dress was a potent vehicle with which to assert and experience the nineteenth-century forces of imperialism and industrialization that produced key shifts in gender and ethnic subjectivities. Ethnic identities expressed through dress were formed in relation to theories of race that might be challenged through engagements with fashion.

Clearly, the nineteenth century was a crucial period for the spread of European dress and fashion cultures, and was intertwined with the mechanisms of colonial and "racial" domination. This was not simply a history of copying or one-way transmission, and it is wrong to assume that cultures without a European cultural heritage had no fashion change of their own. When African or Japanese dress incorporated new motifs and fabrics during the nineteenth and early twentieth century, this was a continuation of pre-existing African and Japanese fashion cultures. However, colonial, post-colonial, and semi-colonial relations necessitated strong, self-conscious assertions of national identity. These operated in tension with the ways in which the dress cultures of different ethnic groups are frequently combined in fashion's pursuit of the new, whether we are dealing with bowler hats in India and China or kimono dressing gowns in Britain and the US. The material cultures of ethnicity contain many such boundary crossings and are testament to the way in which human societies do not exist in isolation from each other. The important point here is to recognize the mechanisms that mediated such exchanges. Fashion was a crucial part of the expression and construction of nineteenth-century ethnic identities, and needs to be understood as operating in a range of registers, and in relation to Eurocentric understandings of fashion, dress, and Western imperialism.

CHAPTER EIGHT

Visual Representations

JUSTINE DE YOUNG

'Suddenly, into their vision, came a dramatic parade of pictured mannequins who moved in and out of the garden trees, and sauntered on the graveled garden paths, wearing the very newest clothes that had been invented by Poiret that week. . . . Goddesses from the Machine . . . it was difficult to believe that these visions of lovely women and costly robes moving among the trees were produced by a machine.'[1]

Thus a *New York Times* reporter described the effect of a film shown by the celebrated *couturier* Paul Poiret during his 1913 lecture tour of the United States. The wonder produced by the event signals the unfamiliarity of what is today one of the most common visual representations of fashion: the filmed fashion show. Yet the most common visual representations of fashion today—the fashion editorial or advertising photograph, the fashion show, and film (whether news footage or fiction)—were largely or entirely unknown in the nineteenth century.

Notably Poiret chose to bring the film rather than the models and clothes themselves—a triumph of representation over reality. Indeed, this chapter will explore precisely these sorts of *mediated* experiences of dress filtered through an artistic lens like painting, photography, or film, rather than direct experiences of dress, such as those achieved by viewing, trying on, or wearing a garment. As such, it will not address other important contemporary means of *directly* observing dress like vaudeville shows, which sometimes featured a fashion revue, and theatrical productions, where actresses since the nineteenth century sometimes wore couture ensembles, or viewing fashion in parks, on the streets, in department stores or their windows.

While the chapter will examine different forms of visual representation of fashion separately, it is important to remember that all the arts inevitably influenced each other and most remained operative throughout the entire period. The following discussion will largely focus on France as in the nineteenth century it quickly came to be seen as the fashion capital of Europe and many innovations in art, advertising, retail, film, and the press originated there, but similar representations of fashion could be found across Europe and America.

PAINTING, 1800–60

Author and critic Charles Baudelaire famously wrote: "There are two ways of understanding portraiture—either as history or as fiction."[2] Late eighteenth-century portraits had been a bit of both. An invented hybrid costume blending classical drapery with contemporary elements was typical—thus the flowing robes of a goddess would be worn with a gray powdered wig. With the French Revolution, such aristocratic and artificial conceits grew unpopular and the fashion became for more "natural" and truthful depictions and as a consequence greater fidelity to contemporary dress. A good example of this new fashion and new style of portraiture is François Gérard's 1805 portrait of Madame Juliette Récamier (Figure 8.1), who during the Directory (1795–9) became famous as one of the *merveilleuses*, women known for their willingness to push the fashion to the extreme.

In Gérard's portrait, we see Mme Récamier dressed in the Greek-revival style of the day with sensuously bare arms and a rich ochre-colored cashmere shawl draped across her hips as she sits on an Etruscan-style couch.

FIGURE 8.1: *Portrait of Juliette Récamier*, François Gérard, 1805. Oil on canvas; 225 × 148 cm. Musée Carnavalet, Paris. Photo: Art Media/Print Collector/Getty Images.

Napoléon would realize the power of this new imagery and commissioned immense history paintings of recent events, like Jacques-Louis David's thirty-two-foot long *Coronation of Napoléon* (1805–7) that offer a snapshot of dress at the imperial court. Notably David also painted a portrait of Mme Récamier in a similar dress and antique setting, but a dispute between the sitter and artist left it unfinished—prompting Récamier to seek out Gérard, one of David's students. If David was the favored portraitist of the French imperial court, Thomas Lawrence and Francisco Goya created works of similar style for the courts of England and Spain.

David's great rival and the other great French portraitist of the first half of the nineteenth century was Jean-Auguste-Dominique Ingres. His 1826 portrait of Madame Marcotte de Sainte-Marie (Figure 8.2) gives a good sense of his style and of the shift in

FIGURE 8.2: *Portrait of Madame Marcotte de Sainte-Marie*, Jean-Auguste-Dominique Ingres, 1826. Oil on canvas; 93 × 74 cm. Musée du Louvre, Paris. Photo: Fine Art Images/Heritage Images/Getty Images.

contemporary dress styles—one can hardly imagine a greater contrast to the near nudity of Mme Récamier than the body-enveloping silk dress of Mme Marcotte de Sainte-Marie.

Ingres carefully records all its details, from the large *gigot* sleeves to the silver chain of her lorgnette, from her ultra-fashionable Apollo knotted hair to the stiffened gauze collar with two buttons visible on the right, but four on the left. Baudelaire describes well the effect of such precision, writing that Ingres "fastens upon [his sitters'] slightest beauties with the keenness of a surgeon, he follows the gentlest sinuosities of their line with the humble devotion of a lover . . . The works of M. Ingres are the result of an excessive attentiveness, and they demand an equal attentiveness to be understood."[3] Indeed, the work of Ingres and his students Hippolyte Flandrin, Henri Lehmann, and Eugène-Emmanuel Amaury-Duval in their careful exactitude represent the *ne plus ultra* of the visual representation of fashion and set the standard for portraiture until the mid-century.

FASHION ILLUSTRATION

About a dozen journals included some fashion coverage in eighteenth-century France, but more than 400 journals featuring fashion would be published in the nineteenth century.[4] The *Journal des dames et des modes* (1797–1839) dominated the early French fashion press until 1818 and covered not just fashion, but art, literature, science, business, and industry. The editor, Pierre de La Mésangère, placed a strong emphasis on quality illustration, hiring talented young artists like Horace Vernet and Paul Gavarni. La Mésangère claimed the plates all took inspiration from real women at society events, insisting upon their accuracy and respectability. In reaction to a writer shocked at the amount of décolletage on display in one plate, he wrote:

> We have again received a letter in which our comparisons are faulted for exaggerating the character of Parisian costume to the point that they amount to caricature. People claim that they cannot possibly portray the dress of respectable women. We dare to protest that our figures are all taken from life and that we take trouble to select our models from highly considered balls, the most respectable society, in short from gatherings where no one is admitted whose dress arouses suspicion of her morality.[5]

As Mésangère suggests, early fashion plates initially recorded fashions seen at society events—they were models for emulation, rather than clothes for sale. After all, this was in the era when there was little ready-made clothing, when most garments were individually made by dressmakers or the women themselves. The first fashion magazine in England solely devoted to fashion, the *Magazine of Female Fashions of London & Paris* (1798–1806) in every issue featured plates of both English and French fashion, sometimes as worn by celebrated beauties like Lady Hamilton or Madame Récamier, other times simply specifying the time and place the dress was seen.[6]

Yet looking at one of Vernet's plates for Mésangère (Figure 8.3) one can see how the confusion over their "truth" value could arise. While Vernet did produce witty caricatures of contemporary fashion (see Figure 8.5), the *Incroyable et Merveilleuse* drawings, issued as a series of prints for collectors, were part of his serious fashion plate work.[7] Early fashion plates like Vernet's continued representational formulas that emerged in the eighteenth century. In them one finds a single male or female figure against a blank background (or the barest suggestion of ground beneath the figure's feet), with a caption describing the fashions below. In this plate, an elegant gentleman poses wearing a top hat, ruffled shirt front, yellow waistcoat, and buff-colored breeches topped with leather

FIGURE 8.3: Incroyable no. 14, Horace Vernet, fashion plate from "Incroyable et Merveilleuse," engraved by George Jacques Gatine, Paris, 1814. © Victoria and Albert Museum, London.

gaiters. His accessories nearly steal the show as he carries a green umbrella, wears a fob-seal attached to a gold chain at his waist, and has a telescope in his coat pocket.

Contemporaneously to Vernet's plate, the English fashion magazine, *La Belle Assemblée* (1806–68), became likely the first fashion periodical to attribute the fashions depicted in its plates to a named shop, that of Mrs. Mary Ann Bell.[8] In France, it was only in the 1840s that shop names regularly began to be attached to the illustrated fashion plates.[9] This shift was not welcomed by all readers, however; the advent of explicit advertising in the *Journal des dames et des modes* in 1837 apparently prompted mass cancellations.[10]

Petit Courrier des Dames (1828–44) broke new ground by systematically featuring both front and rear views of a dress, tweaking the single figure plate format by including in the background a second figure in a dress of the same cut, but often of a different color. This convention proceeded for some time, but was eventually replaced by the dual frontal view of two different costumes. Héloïse Leloir, working for *Le Follet* (1829–82), *Le Bon Ton* (1834–84), and *Le Journal des demoiselles* (1833–1922), was a key early creator of the fashion plate with elaborate background, which arose in the late 1830s. The plates began to resemble genre scenes of everyday life, with implied narratives and detailed settings. Jules David, who created nearly all the plates for the dominant *Le Moniteur de la mode* (1843–1913), which was itself published by a dress shop, also favored a more detailed and at times aristocratic setting for the fashions pictured. An 1850 plate from *Les Modes parisiennes* (1843–80) is a good example of this new representational formula (Figure 8.4).

In it, we find an elegant couple walking arm-in-arm, descending the steps into a garden; behind them a palatial chateau, classical statuary, and a reflecting pool attest to their aristocratic origins. The caption below helpfully informs readers the woman's clothing is the product of Mme Célestine and the man's of the tailor Humann. While many early fashion magazines similarly addressed both male and female fashion, men gradually disappeared from mainstream fashion magazines by the mid-1860s.

La Mode illustrée (1860–1937) is remarkable for the priority it gave to fashion illustration in all its pages. Over the course of the 1860s, text slowly retreated into a secondary role, weaving around dozens of illustrations of dresses, hats, needlework, home décor, sewing machines, and the like that soon filled the pages. For example, one August 1869 issue featured black and white illustrations of three women's garments (a cape, a scarf, and an elaborate collar—all of which were included in that week's dress patterns), four household objects (a watch holder, a magazine holder, a basket for scarves, and a match box—shown open and closed), and an example of embroidery for the ornamentation of a scarf (including both an instructional view and the completed look). Notably, the plates and advertisements in the illustrated press and in the most popular fashion journals tended to promote the clothing and goods available at large department stores or *magasins de nouveautés*; to see fashion plates featuring dresses by famous *couturiers* like Charles Frederick Worth, one had to look to smaller journals, like *Le Printemps* (1866–1910). The fashion plates produced by artists for *La Mode illustrée*, *Le Moniteur de la mode*, and other leading journals of the 1860s and 1870s represent the heyday of French fashion illustration. As we'll see, beginning in the 1880s less inventive illustrators would come to rely on and emulate studio photographs of dresses with often stilted results. Moreover, the prominent bustle silhouette of dresses led to the adoption of profile views, which further reduced the liveliness and interaction of the earlier plates.

FIGURE 8.4: Compte Calix, *Les Modes Parisiennes*, no. 382 (June 23, 1850). Author's collection.

Of course, it bears remembering that fashion illustration was not just found in nineteenth-century fashion journals and fashion prints for collectors, but also in the broader press. For example, the satirical *La Vie Parisienne*, which often commented on fashion and included advertisements for women's dresses, reported on what famous women were wearing at fashionable holiday spots. One whole page in the August 11, 1866 issue was devoted to illustrating the five outfits the unnamed Princesse X (almost certainly Pauline de Metternich, a fashion star at the court of Napoléon III) wore on August 5 at Trouville, a seaside resort. A bathing costume, a daringly short morning dress (helping set the brief trend for almost calf-height skirts that lasted only from 1866–8), a dress to watch the races, an elegantly trained walking dress with parasol and an evening dress hidden beneath an ample cape are all carefully sketched. *La Vie Parisienne* presents this update on one of Worth's most important clients as straightforward news, but the journal was more famous for its witty caricatures of dress.

CARICATURE

The expansion of the fashion press in the nineteenth century was paralleled by an expansion in the caricature press as decreasing print costs, increased literacy and leisure time, and a growing middle class eager to read about elite fashion—but also to laugh at it—emerged.[11] Caricature pushes the tendencies of fashion and art to extremes and many early fashion illustrators like Vernet also produced caricatures of fashion (Figure 8.5).

In one caricature from the ironically titled "Le Supréme Bon Ton" (the supreme good taste) series, we see several women wearing fashionable poke bonnets—hood-shaped hats with large projecting rims to shield the face called "les invisibles" in French—in close conversation with gentlemen suitors. Captioned "Les Invisibles en Tête-a-Tête," while a "tête-a-tête" is typically metaphorical, here it has become literal as the pairs of figures are literally head to head as the men's heads are lost in the exaggerated barrels of the bonnets. The bonnets were a particular favorite of caricaturists in the teens, but male fashion was not immune from the caricaturists' wit as the size and shape of men's hats and the height of their shirt collars (as seen uncaricatured in Figure 8.3) earned them equal mockery. One anonymous French caricature of just such a scene was copied by English caricaturist James Gillray and reissued in England. Just as there was a busy market in copying French fashion plates in other countries, the same was true in terms of caricature—as the fashion at this point had become quite similar across Europe caricatures could easily be copied and recaptioned in other countries. That is not to say that caricaturists were blind to national difference. The French caricature series *Le Bon Genre* (again an ironic title) juxtaposed English and French fashions side by side, with both open for mockery, but the English always managing to come off a bit worse. Conversely, English caricaturists like Isaac Cruikshank and Gillray took particular pleasure in lampooning the extravagances of French fashion.

In a century of dramatic political and social change, dress remained a safe and reliable subject for caricaturists, particularly as interest in fashion grew over the course of the century. There was even a short-lived French journal devoted to fashion caricature: *Aujourd'hui: journal des modes ridicules* (1838–1841).[12] Talented caricaturists J.J. Grandville, Gavarni, and Honoré Daumier all worked for Charles Philipon, whose journals *Le Caricature* and *Le Charivari* were particularly important in the first half of the nineteenth century, only later supplanted by *Le Journal amusant* and *La Vie Parisienne*. Fashion also was a popular source of comment and critique in caricatures by André Gill,

FIGURE 8.5: "Les Invisibles en Tête-a-Tête. Le Supréme Bon Ton No. 16," Horace Vernet. Paris: Martinet, c. 1815. Engraving, hand-colored, 31 × 43 cm. Photo: Hulton Archive/Getty Images.

Cham, Paul Hadol, STOP, and Albert Robida of the painted portraits and genre scenes exhibited at the annual Paris Salon. In England, *Punch, or The London Charivari* with caricaturists like Max Beerbohm and Georges du Maurier kept British readers laughing at men's and women's fashion.[13] It would only be photography's eventual dominance and the eclipsing of illustration (particularly after World War II) that led to the decline of fashion caricature in the press.

PHOTOGRAPHY, 1840–1900

With the introduction of commercial photography in 1839, portraiture soon became a popular use for this new technology and thus photography offers an extensive corpus of images that represent contemporary fashion. These images, however, unlike later fashion photography, were almost never taken to promote the fashions worn. Early photography instead served more personal and private purposes, though this would soon change. Caricaturist and writer Félix Tournachon, known as Nadar, in 1855 opened a commercial photography studio that specialized in photographing famous artistic and political figures. Collecting celebrity photographs was a popular hobby (as collecting celebrity portrait statuettes had been in the 1830s). André-Adolphe-Eugène Disdéri developed a calling-card size, full-length portrait format he called *cartes-de-visite*, which became especially popular with collectors in the 1860s. The full-length format meant that more of one's dress was seen than was typical in a conventional half-length portrait and thus dress had a large impact on one's impression of a figure given the small size of the image. Other important portrait photographers who took an interest in fashion included Adolphe Braun and Léopold Ernest Mayer, Louis Frédéric Mayer, and Pierre-Louis Pierson in the 1850s and 1860s, and Jacques-Henri Lartigue, Constant Puyo, and Robert Demachy later in the century.

Photographs could not record the vibrant colors of clothes in this era, but they did succeed in capturing the texture, sheen, and draping of the fabrics in a way that rivaled the descriptive talents of painters like Ingres.[14] Indeed, Nadar, not surprisingly argued for photography's superiority: "For me the question of Monsieur Ingres's talent as a portraitist was settled the morning Daguerre made his marvelous discovery, and today photography gives us a *dessin* that Ingres could not have delivered in one hundred sittings and a color that he could not have given us in a hundred years."[15] As we will see, photography had a profound influence on the practice of portrait painting, but, at the same time, the conventions of portrait photography themselves were heavily indebted to painting.

One sitter who uniquely exploited the possibilities of photography to capture and reveal her famed beauty (and her extensive couture wardrobe) was Virginia Oldoini, the Countess de Castiglione, an Italian aristocrat who was even briefly the mistress of French Emperor Napoléon III (Figure 8.6). Beginning in 1856, she commissioned a series of inventive and unusual portraits from Mayer Frères et Pierson that showcase her beauty, chic, and obsessive self-regard.

In this example—one of over 400—we see her seated in an enormous crinolined gown with plunging décolletage, her hair in an elaborate updo. Unlike most portrait sitters of the day who relied on guidance from the photographers, it's clear the Countess orchestrated and directed these elaborate portraits, which cast her as everything from the Queen of Hearts to a nun. Her appetite for *haute couture* may have bankrupted her husband, but the photos demonstrate well the power of the new medium to represent the self and, of course, fashion in a way and quantity that painting could not.[16]

Photography made new visual representations of fashion possible, particularly with the invention of stereoscopy, which created the impression of three-dimensionality by presenting a left-eye and right-eye view of the same image side by side. One short-lived fashion magazine, *La Stéréoscope* (1857–9), even used this new technology to present the latest in fashionable dress, including stereoscopic images with its issues. Stereoscopic views staging scenes of everyday life of the fashionable elite also became popular in the 1850s and 1860s; actors and actresses in the latest fashions would pretend to take tea, play cards, or read offering a voyeuristic view of how the other half lived.[17]

La Stéréoscope aside, fashion journals in the second half of the nineteenth century did not typically include photography as printing limitations meant that photographs could not easily be reproduced with the text. It wasn't until 1880 that *L'Art de la mode* (1880–1967) became the first journal to reproduce a fashion photograph in its pages, and photographs only became common in the twentieth century, when advances in halftone printing made it more feasible and economical.[18] During the fin de siècle, journals like *La Mode pratique* (1891–1951) began to rely on photography as the foundation for their fashion plates, but the images were so heavily retouched that their origin as photographs can be difficult to discern.

FIGURE 8.6: Elvira (Countess de Castiglione), 1861–7, Pierre-Louis Pierson (printed 1940s). Photograph; 36.8 × 41.6 cm. The Metropolitan Museum of Art, New York.

PAINTING, 1860–1920

The limitations of photography were such that nineteenth-century portrait photographs were almost invariably studio shot using natural light; perhaps not surprisingly some portrait painters of the time began to favor the outdoors—achieving light effects contemporary photographers could not. At the same time paintings of modern life, known as genre scenes, became increasingly popular with painters and the public. The popularity and monumentalization of genre painting in the 1860s meant that modern dress loomed large at the annual Paris Salon as painters sought to record life in the newly transformed city. The Second Empire (1852–70) saw the entire fabric of the city change as Napoléon III placed Baron Haussmann in charge of a vast public works project that created the Paris we know today. New sites of fashionable display—boulevards, parks, department stores— and a rising middle class hungry for fashion knowledge led to an explosion of the fashion press. Not surprisingly painters soon adapted their subjects to follow suit.[19]

In the 1860s and 1870s, avant-garde artists Édouard Manet, Pierre-Auguste Renoir, and Claude Monet often chose to depict fashionable dress in large, life-size genre scenes. One particularly ambitious such scene was Monet's *Luncheon on the Grass* of 1865–6 (Figure 8.7), which reprised an earlier subject by Manet that had scandalized Parisian viewers by depicting two contemporary men picnicking with one naked and another scantily clad woman.

FIGURE 8.7: *Luncheon on the Grass* (left panel), 1865–6, Claude Monet. Oil on canvas; 418 × 150 cm. Musée d'Orsay, Paris. Gift of Georges Wildenstein, 1957. *Luncheon on the Grass* (right panel), 1865–6. Oil on canvas; 248.7 × 218 cm. Musée d'Orsay, Paris. Acquired as a payment in kind, 1987. Photo: Peter Willi/Getty Images.

Monet's picnic lacks the provocative nudity of Manet's work, but instead centers on four women in the latest summer styles, with three gallant gentlemen in attendance and an amply provisioned picnic. The painting captures the brilliant colors of contemporary dresses and sun-dappled outdoor light effects that photography could not hope to record and at a scale that was simply impossible; the enormous painting stretches nearly 14 feet high by 12 feet high (it is now in two separate panels as it had to be cut down due to damage). Monet's work is daring not only in its size, modern subject matter, and treatment of light, but also in its looser style of brushwork, which lacks the careful detail of an artist like Ingres. Yet even artists with more traditional painting styles like James Tissot, Alfred Stevens, and Auguste Toulmouche became known for producing similarly fashionable scenes of modern life.

Parallel to this revolution in genre painting, avant-garde artists were also re-envisioning the modern portrait. Who was being painted and how they were depicted, the scale of the works and what they were wearing shifted. While full-length portraiture had previously been the reserve of royalty or the aristocracy, Gustave Courbet, Manet, Monet, Renoir, and other Realists boldly portrayed lower and middle-class figures life-size. Aristocratic portraiture by court favorites like Édouard-Louis Dubufe and Franz Xaver Winterhalter continued to favor extravagant evening wear, but these avant-garde portraits showed all sorts of dress—from the drab dress of a street singer to the light summer frocks of Monet's *Luncheon*. The Realists and Impressionists pioneered a form of intimate portraiture that even pictured sitters in informal clothing like *peignoirs*—typically worn without a corset only in the presence of the most intimate of friends—that would have been formerly unthinkable in public portraiture.[20]

These new subjects and styles of art of course both responded to and themselves influenced contemporary fashion illustration and portrait photography. Edgar Degas's incisive portraits of his family and friends reveal an especially profound engagement with photography. But all artists were trying to figure out the role of portrait painting in the age of the photograph. Writing in 1865, philosopher Pierre J. Proudhon praised the possibility of paintings conveying deep psychological intensity, as Degas's best portraits do: "A portrait . . . must have, if it's possible, the exactitude of a photograph, but, more than a photograph, it must express life, the habitual, intimate thought of the subject. While unthinking light, instantaneous in its action can only give a rapidly interrupted image of the model, an artist, more skillful than light because he reflects and feels, can imbue a prolonged sentiment in the face."[21] John Singer Sargent and James McNeill Whistler would produce striking portraits in the 1870s and 1880s that achieved such effects, while more fashionable portraitists like Léon Bonnat and Carolus-Duran would more often focus on the details of dress.

Yet, by the mid-1880s, the avant-garde would mostly lose interest in representing modern fashion as Post-Impressionist artists like Paul Cézanne, Paul Gauguin, Vincent Van Gogh, and those who came after them largely rejected city life in favor of the rural or the exotic. One notable exception to the trend is the work of the pointillist artist Georges Seurat, whose monumental 1886 *Sunday Afternoon on the Isle of the Grande Jatte* depicts an island on the Seine and popular leisure spot (Figure 8.8).

FIGURE 8.8: *Sunday Afternoon on the Isle of the Grande Jatte, 1884*, Georges Seurat, 1884–6. Oil on canvas; 207.5 × 308.1 cm. The Art Institute of Chicago. Helen Birch Bartlett Memorial Collection, 1926.224. Photo: DEA Picture Library/Getty Images.

We see a cross-section of Parisian society enjoying their day off in the sunny park: from a promenading couple with a monkey to two men in uniform, a woman fishing, and a child running through the grass. In contrast to Monet's relatively faithful (if loosely brushed) translation of his picnickers' clothing into paint, Seurat concentrates on shape and color, editing out the ruffles, bows, and buttons that would have invariably ornamented contemporary clothing. While still interested in depicting modern life, he, like his peers, has prioritized the painting's style and technique over accuracy, marking a dramatic shift in painting as a useful representation of contemporary fashion.

ADVERTISING POSTERS

Seurat's strong emphasis on silhouette was characteristic of both contemporary fashion illustration and especially advertising posters. While text posters were common throughout Europe in the early nineteenth century, France led the way in producing large-scale illustrated posters. The earliest advertising posters in the nineteenth century were wood engravings, but color lithography enabled the explosion of images in the fin de siècle. By mid-century, colorful, high quality images could thus be produced quickly in large numbers and at a low cost, but restrictive regulations and taxation during the 1850s initially limited the proliferation of posters in France.[22] New leniency in the 1860s saw the rise of massive department store campaigns targeted at both men and women (in contrast to contemporary fashion plates where men now rarely appeared).[23] Advertising images that featured contemporary fashion ranged from small trade cards to window placards and life-size posters on the sides of buildings. The famous Morris advertising columns put in place by Haussmann typically featured theatrical rather than commercial advertising, but liberalization of press and bill-posting laws in 1881 led to a further explosion of poster printing.[24]

Jules Chéret, one of the first great poster designers, opened his lithographic print shop in 1866, producing a large repertoire of images featuring attractive women regardless the good or venue being advertised—from cabarets and dance halls to oil lamps and cigarette papers.[25] He developed a highly recognizable style and his female figures, dubbed "chérettes" blended fantasy and reality. Seurat was himself enthralled by the joy and gaiety of Chéret's posters, and his works after the *Grande Jatte* of the circus and dance hall reveal that influence.[26] Indeed fine art and the poster became closely aligned at the end of the century. Chéret's style, like that of his contemporary Henri Toulouse-Lautrec, became highly generalized, conveying exuberant silhouettes more than actual details of the dresses worn. Posters moved in an increasingly stylized and graphic direction as artists like Théophile Steinlen and Alphonse Mucha prioritized striking visual effects over exact faithfulness, which often heightened their visual power, but reduced their informative value as representations of actual fashions.

An 1880s poster for the department store Au Moine St.-Martin exemplifies the sort of poster Seurat undoubtedly had in mind when composing the *Grande Jatte*; both works feature fashionable promenading couples in the right foreground, as well as mothers with playful children (Figure 8.9). The poster advertises a department store on the Rue Turbigo, a new street built by Haussmann, and the poster emphasizes that fact by placing the store's façade at its center.[27] The building not only features the typical uniform Haussmannian façade, but also the classic lampposts and broad

FIGURE 8.9: Au Moine St.-Martin, R. Franck, c. 1880–5. Poster, Imprimerie Dupuis et fils, Paris.

sidewalks his renovation of Paris had made so familiar. While one might imagine that a poster for a department store would emphasize the quality and variety of goods on offer, this poster (and many like it) focuses not on what is *inside* the store, but what is outside of it.

We see the bustling boulevard filled with hundreds of tiny figures dwarfed by the massive store, which seems to occupy the entire city block. One unaccompanied woman hails an omnibus as it drives by, emphasizing the ease of access to the store; while an Au Moine St.-Martin delivery carriage appears nearby, piled high with packages, alerting viewers to the ease of conveying purchases home. Single men and women, couples, mothers and children swarm in front of the department store's large glass display windows, stretching from the labeled Place de la République to Les Halles. Notably these two monuments not only help identify the store's location, but also stress its modernity, as the Place de la République includes a monument to the Third Republic at its center by Léopold and Charles Morice. The statue to the newly created Third Republic (founded after the fall of the Second Empire in the Franco-Prussian War of 1870–1) features a figure of La République in classical dress.[28] The distinctive iron and glass architecture of Les Halles, the central markets of Paris built in the 1850s by Victor Baltard, further underscores the exciting newness of the district and the convenient location of the store.

The Au Moine St.-Martin poster combines the two most common styles of department store posters: those that present the impressive building with lively street life before it, as well as those which feature large figures surrounded by text. The promenading couple in the foreground attract our eye, while the little girl in her striped dress gesturing animatedly draws our attention toward the store. Her mother, who wears an even more elaborately striped ensemble, bends forward toward the figure of the Third Republic—subtly linking the two as patriotic Parisiennes and symbols of Paris.

SCULPTURE

Indeed, it was the fashionable modern Parisienne who soon eclipsed the classical goddess as the symbol of the Third Republic and of France. At the 1900 World's Fair, a monumental sculpture of *La Parisienne* in contemporary dress by Paul Moreau-Vauthier was erected atop the Port Binet main entrance gate (Figure 8.10). It was lit at night and stood 5 meters

FIGURE 8.10: *La Parisienne*, sculpture by Paul Moreau-Vauthier, atop the monumental Port Binet entrance to the 1900 Exposition Universelle in Paris, *L'Illustration* 58, no. 2981 (April 14, 1900). Harvard University.

tall while resting atop the 35 meter gate. The fair attracted 48 million visitors, making this painted sculpture perhaps the most prominent visual representation of fashion in the century.[29] The gown and mantle are believed to have been inspired by Jeanne Paquin, one of the leading *couturiers* of the day (the House of Paquin was founded in 1891).[30] Paquin also served as the president of the Fair's fashion section, which included more than thirty dioramas of contemporary and historical fashions displayed on wax figures. Moreau-Vauthier's monumental *Parisienne* wears a blue coat edged in faux-ermine and stands as a proud assertion of the city's status as fashion capital of the world.

That such a representation of the city would be in contemporary dress was highly unusual as sculpted allegorical figures representing the city until then had almost always been seen in classical garb. Indeed, to represent contemporary fashion in sculpture at all was highly unusual as nineteenth-century sculptors tended to favor allegorical, historical, mythological, or animal subjects. Any figures that did appear were typically nude or in classical drapery. Portrait sculptures were typically restricted to busts, which offered limited fashion information beyond favored styles of collars. Full-length sculpture was typical only for royalty and "before about 1830, people of note disliked the idea of posing for a sculptor in their everyday clothing."[31] Thus Antonin Moine's 1833 marble sculpture of *Queen Marie Amélie*, exhibited at that year's Salon (Musée Carnavalet), is remarkable for its enthusiastic embrace of contemporary dress. Though still creating only a portrait bust, Moine captures the queen's full "farrago of finery: the immense coils of her coiffure, her lace-lined hat of huge brim and lush ostrich plumes, her great rope of carved ivory beads, her shirred blouse and collars and bows and ribbons and scarves and epaulets."[32]

The 1830s also saw a brief vogue for collecting portrait statuettes of famous actors, dancers, and royalty (a role *carte-de-visite* photography would soon occupy). Parallel to the popularity of genre painting in the 1860s and 1870s, Aimé-Jules Dalou became known for his intimist images of modern women, producing sculptures of mothers of different classes nursing—from urban *bourgeoise* to a rural peasant—as well as women reading and embroidering. Italian realist sculptors Augusto Rivalta, Adriano Cecioni, and Vincenzo Vela created many scenes from everyday life, including fashionable ones like a woman putting on a glove. Juan Roig y Soler created a striking and unusual sculpture of an anonymous *Woman with Umbrella* (1884) atop a fountain in Barcelona. Yet such sculptures were the rare exceptions, which makes the *Parisienne*'s appearance atop the monumental entrance to the Exposition Universelle even more surprising.

FASHION SHOWS AND FASHION NEWSREELS

Paquin, who had such prominence at the 1900 World's Fair as head of the fashion section and organizer of the Palais du Costume, was also a key figure in the early history of the fashion show, as she was among the first to host shows on a regular schedule. Other *couturiers*, like Lucile and Poiret, with eyes toward the international market also helped shape the fashion show into the seasonal, ordered procession of models along a stage-like walkway with curtains, music, and lighting that we know it to be today.[33] As Caroline Evans's careful research has revealed, all major couture houses were staging fashion shows at set times by 1910.[34]

More informal modeling had become common in the nineteenth century with the rise of couture houses like Worth, but as unscheduled private displays catering to suit a single client, not the theatrical events we think of today.[35] Like these private viewings, the early staged fashion shows, even those catering to foreign department store buyers, remained largely exclusive and private events until well into the 1910s as *couturiers* sought to protect their designs from copyists and thus restricted the representation of their clothes and the event in the press.[36] Thus in terms of the visual *representation* of fashion rather than the reality of it, the fashion show didn't become a viable means of gaining fashion knowledge for the general public until roughly 1910, when newsreels began to regularly show French fashion models—called mannequins—and brief clips of fashion shows with models displaying the latest styles.

While invitations to in-person fashion shows were often restricted to elite clientele, the shows when filmed were made available variously to be screened in department stores and also in newsreels. The earliest surviving fashion newsreel dates to c. 1900; it depicts a model wearing a large hat standing on a rotating platform that slowly reveals the hat's features as viewed from all sides. Such turntable-style displays were popular in early newsreels and mimicked the display strategies employed in department store windows (there featuring wax rather than live models).[37]

French film studio Pathé-Frères in their 1909 film *Paris Fashions* transported viewers to famous sites of fashionable display in Paris: the races at Longchamp, the Bois de Boulogne, and the broad boulevards near the Arc de Triomphe.[38] That same year Pathé began producing the weekly *Pathé Revue* which included a few items of fashion on each reel, later expanding its fashion reporting in a series of fashion short films for its *Pathé Animated Gazette* in 1911. From 1910, Gaumont included fashion in its *Gaumont Journal* newsreels, which by 1912 often used named actresses as the models for looks from Lucile, Laferrière, Callot Soeurs and Drecoll. Lucile, Paquin and Parry allowed cameras into the couture salons, while Poiret—the other major designer of the period—instead made his own fashion films as we saw at the start of the chapter.[39] By 1915, Pathé boasted that its newsreels were seen weekly by ten million people.[40]

Fashion shows were also photographed and described in the press. Perhaps the earliest known photograph of a fashion show in progress is the series of three photographs printed by the *Daily Mirror* in May 1908 of a Lucile fashion show in the garden of her London couture house (Figure 8.11). The photographs are shot from the apparent vantage of an attendee, creating the illusion of exclusivity, and at close enough range that a reader can see the details of the gowns presented. Four Lucile looks are visible on the runway, but the fashionably-dressed viewers of the show also occupy significant space in the coverage. The standing models, who adopt a similar pose, appear in contrast to the seated onlookers; thus, we see the early origins of one of the most common visual representations of fashion today: the couture runway shot.

FASHION PHOTOGRAPHY AND FASHION ILLUSTRATION IN THE TWENTIETH CENTURY

Published in Paris, *Les Modes* (1901–37) was the first fashion journal to regularly feature photographs, often shot by the Reutlinger Studio in Paris, and included both half-tone photos and tipped-in color photographs on glossy paper.[41] *Haute couture* designers including Worth, Paquin, Doucet, and Callot Soeurs were all featured. Reutlinger photographs and those by competing studios, such as Felix, Talbot, Bissonnais et Taponnier, and Manuel Frères, typically followed the conventions of portraiture and fashion plates in presenting full-length views of women in the arguably more artificial setting of the photography studio. An alternative to such static and traditional studio shots were more candid society photographs of the latest fashions as worn by the rich and famous. In France,

LONDON·MODELS·PARADE IN THE LATEST·GOWNS.

SUMMER FASHIONS EXHIBITED ON MANNEQUINS.

Following the Parisian method, Messrs. Lucile, of Hanover-square, gave, on Thursday, a special show of no fewer than seventy-seven gowns of the latest fashions. They were worn by models who displayed the fashion and fit of the creations to possible purchasers by walking round the garden at the back of the premises, where a dainty tea was provided. (1) A Directoire dinner-gown. (2) The latest creation in summer frocks. (3) Two of the mannequins displaying the costumes.—(DAILY MIRROR photographs.).

FIGURE 8.11: *Daily Mirror* (May 23, 1908) p. 9. Volume editor's collection.

the Seeberger family became particularly famous for capturing the latest *haute couture* as worn by the finest society outdoors in Paris and elite holiday destinations like Deauville and Biarritz. Beginning in 1909, their photographs appeared regularly in *La Mode pratique*, as well as *Les Modes, Le Jardin des modes, L'Album du Figaro, Fémina, L'Art et la mode, Vogue* and *Harper's Bazaar*.[42] Designers also began sending their mannequins to these highly visible sites. In the spring of 1908, three models wearing extremely form-fitting Margaine-Lacroix gowns that revealed the whole line of the hip and were slit up to the knee, leaving their legs covered only by filmy petticoats, caused a sensation at the Longchamp racetrack (Figure 8.12). *Illustration* put them on its front page, dubbing them, à la the *Incroyables et*

FIGURE 8.12: *L'Illustration* 66, no. 3403 (May 16, 1908). Retouched photograph. Harvard University.

Merveilleuses drawn by Vernet in the previous century, "Les Nouvelles Merveilleuses," and labeling the dresses as *Directoire* gowns. It is precisely this sort of press furor and public interest that Pathé sought to exploit with their 1909 film *Paris Fashions,* which visited similar sites of high fashion.

Poiret, who opened his couture house in 1903, was not only an early innovator and adopter of the fashion show, but also promoted his work through illustration, photography, and film. A particular marketing genius, he, for example, staged an elaborate party, where guests had to come dressed in his own unique Orientalizing designs and which attracted considerable press attention. Poiret commissioned exquisite fashion plate albums from leading illustrators of the day like Paul Iribe, whose *Les Robes de Paul Poiret racontées par Paul Iribe* (1908) harkened back to the glory days of fashion illustration. This album of ten plates with no text was issued in an edition of 250 and cost 40 francs, thus returning the fashion plate and fashion news to its elite origins—perfect for a designer trying to emphasize the aristocratic *caché* of his designs.[43]

In 1911, Poiret collaborated with early fashion photographer Edward Steichen to create soft-focus photographs of models wearing *Directoire* revival dresses set in his elegant *Directoire*-era *maison de couture* (Figure 8.13). The images accompanied an

FIGURE 8.13: Edward Steichen. Color photograph. *Art et decoration* (April 1911). © 2016. White Images/Scala, Florence.

article by Paul Cornu, "L'Art de la robe," which also featured illustrations by Georges Lepape. The photographs—eleven in black and white, two in color—were published in *Art et Décoration*, marking the first collaboration of designer, photographer, and magazine editor.[44] Steichen creates images full of atmosphere and drama, while also showcasing the beauty of the gowns and their harmony with the setting. See, for example, one of the color images, which shows a model at a doorway about to let in her friend, whose scarf-wrapped head is visible through the window. The delicate green and gold filigree of the décor is repeated in the details of the dress, which revives the empire-waisted, shift-style dress seen in Gérard's portrait of Madame Récamier (Figure 8.1). The turban-style headdresses, both jeweled and feathered, were of the sort Poiret mandated for attendance at his "Thousand and Second Night" orientalist costume party.

In 1912, Poiret along with the other leading *couturiers* of the day (Worth, Paquin, Doucet among them) launched the *Gazette du Bon Ton* which featured luxe illustrations rather than photographs of the latest couture designs. The opening editorial of the magazine offered a history of fashion plate illustration in France, explicitly citing the *Journal des dames et des modes* and Vernet's plates (Figure 8.3) as inspiration for this venture before promising a close alliance between *couturier* and artist to produce "portraits" of their creations.[45] Each issue featured inventive illustrations and color pochoir plates by leading illustrators of the day, among them Iribe, Lepape, Bernard Boutet de Monvel, Georges Barbier, and André Marty. Subscriptions cost 100 francs a year, thus again aiming to restrict access to an elite audience. Yet photography was gaining ground. Beginning in 1913, Condé Nast began publishing photographs by Baron Adolph de Meyer, later hiring him as the first full-time photographer at *Vogue*. Like Steichen, he produced moody pictorialist photography, influenced by his mentor Alfred Stieglitz, manipulating lighting, focus, and printing techniques to produce atmospheric and aesthetic effects. His work for the magazine alternated between evocative society portraits and editorial fashion spreads focused on a single topic like tea gowns. With de Meyer at *Vogue*, the era of the fashion-plate-style staged studio photograph was over and the modern editorial photoshoot was born.

FILM

The year 1895 saw the birth of film as a mass entertainment with short films being shown to paying audiences for the first time.[46] As these brief early films centered on daily life, they rather incidentally featured modern dress, but soon filmmakers produced works with fashion-centered plots like the American 1904 film, *A Busy Day for the Corset Model*, which included scenes of mannequins modeling.[47] While early silent films often presented rags-to-riches tales which saw the film stars don elite fashions of the day—a fantasy of wish fulfilment for the mostly working class audience—early films poked fun at fashion as well. *The Directoire Gown* (Essanay, 1908), for example, targeted the body-hugging silhouettes that had caused such a stir at the Longchamp races (Figure 8.12). As the film's star in the titular gown makes her way down the street, "men are uncontrollably drawn to her and follow her; firemen abandon a fire, men leaves their wives, and some jump out of windows for a glimpse of the gown and her body."[48]

In a 1910 article on "Dress and the Picture" in *Moving Picture World*, the author notes that the theatrical stage had long been a site of fashion innovation and speculates: "We may yet live to see the time when fashionable women will go to the moving picture theater to study the latest modes. Who knows?"[49] It would be only four years later that he would get his wish, with another critic declaring: "Dame Fashion has finally consented to become a photoplay fan . . . modishly gowned ladies are obtaining their ideas of dress in the Motion Picture theater. Many a fashionable dressmaker also visits the Motion Pictures with the same interest and purpose, namely, to see the latest in frills and foibles."[50] Indeed, the inclusion of high fashion in the films of the day sought to expand the audiences for film to include the middle class.

French film studios like Pathé Frères dominated production in the first decade of the twentieth century—only a third of films shown in the US were domestically produced.[51] The arrival of World War I soon challenged that dominance, however, both through the disruption of European film production and growing nationalist sentiment. To counter criticism of its films as too exotic or foreign, Pathé began film production in the US, shooting in studios in New Jersey. Likewise, the Canadian-born Lady Duff Gordon, though based out of England, opened a branch of her couture house, Lucile, in New York in 1910. This made her perfectly positioned to outfit the new American movie stars filming in New York and New Jersey like Alice Joyce, Clara Kimball Young, Billie Burke, and Pearl White, as well as prominent stage actresses.[52] Early films depicting contemporary stories relied on actors to supply their own costumes, so the fashionability of the clothes on display varied according to the cast.

While Poiret was an important early adopter and innovator in his use of film to present his designs to the public and famously costumed Sarah Bernhardt in the 1912 film *Queen Elizabeth*, his closing of his design house in 1914 and enlisting in the French army left a void that other designers like Lucile eagerly filled. Lucile is thought to have dressed actresses in more than 100 films between 1913 and 1922.[53] *The Perils of Pauline* (1914), shot in New Jersey with an American cast, was one of the first films on which Lucile worked (Figure 8.14). A serial drama (Pathé's first), Pauline's adventures played out in a

FIGURE 8.14: *The Perils of Pauline*, dir: Louis J. Gasnier and Donald MacKenzie.© Pathé-Eclectic 1914. From the core collection production files of the Margaret Herrick Library, Academy of Motion Picture Arts and Sciences.

twenty-part series of short films released every other Monday from March to December 1914. These dramas, popular in the 1910s, grew out of the serialized fiction of the nineteenth century and remained linked to printed companion stories published in newspapers and women's journals. As Pathé had a relationship with the Hearst newspaper company and Hearst financed the film's production, it was heavily promoted in the press. Lucile herself was also linked with Hearst as since 1910 she had contributed a syndicated weekly fashion column and from 1913 a monthly column in *Harper's Bazaar*, "The Last Word in Fashions."[54]

Pauline, the heroine, is a writer for *Cosmopolitan* (notably a Hearst publication) and insists she must live a life of adventure to improve her writing. *Cosmopolitan* itself profiled Pearl White, the actress who played Pauline, in conjunction with the film's release, including two stills from the movie, interspersed with five full-length shots of some of the costumes she wears. The article's synopsis captures well the range of Pauline's adventurous exploits: "Heiress to a fabulous fortune, shadowed by lovers, pursued by villains, held up in cripple motor-cars on the wild road to the aviation-meet, and booked for flight in a 'fixed' aeroplane that turns turtle and falls from the sky a hideous wreck— these are mere every-day incidents in the fiction-career of the beauteous and popular Pathé heroine. Such is Pauline, of 'The Perils'."[55] In the film she faces countless dangers, but also wears a tremendous range of outfits from sportswear to evening wear—even dressing up as a jockey at one point. One particularly elegant ensemble (See Figure 8.14) combined a lampshade tunic with stylized roses and fur trim—signature elements of Lucile's 1914–15 couture collection.[56]

Promotional materials for the films featuring Lucile's gowns often highlighted that fact; for example, a full-page advertisement in *Motography* for the film includes a studio shot photo of White in a luxurious fur-edged coat, elaborate hat, and enormous fur muff with the caption: "Miss White's Gowns are by Lady Duff-Gordon, the famous 'Lucile'."[57] As the celebrity of actresses grew, they were increasingly used as models in fashion coverage. In 1915, *Motion Picture Classic* began a regular fashion feature illustrating the latest fashionable styles as worn in the movies by actresses as well as numerous studio portraits of actresses in designer dresses. Elite fashion was available on screen for all to see, as one critic pointed out in 1914: "the fashion leader of Pleasant Corners, Ind., has just as good an opportunity to view the latest modes as worn by the movie actresses, as has the fashion leader of a larger city," which helps explain why Poiret and other French designers felt it important to found *Le Gazette du Bon Ton* as a bid for continued exclusivity.[58]

By the 1920s, as film production after World War I moved out to California, the close connection to *couturiers* lessened and film studios, recognizing the importance of dress, created official costume design departments. "Goddesses from the machine" had entranced the public and would continue to figure prominently in the representation of fashion into the present day. Thus the most common visual representations of fashion in the nineteenth century—painting, illustration, caricature—had by the twentieth been replaced by the forms we know today: the fashion show, fashion photography, and film.

CHAPTER NINE

Literary Representations

HEIDI BREVIK-ZENDER

In *The Sorrows of Young Werther* (*Die Leiden des jungen Werthers*) (1774), the debut novel by celebrated German author Johann Wolfgang von Goethe (1749–1832), the main character adopts a distinctive manner of dress consisting of a blue jacket, a yellow waistcoat, and matching yellow breeches (Figure 9.1). Modern readers might find nothing particularly noteworthy about Werther's wardrobe, but in Goethe's day the outfit symbolized the young man's dissatisfaction with accepted social norms, for his scruffy clothes set him apart from the formal court system in which he circulates, making him appear somewhat a counter-culture rebel. When his suit eventually wears out, Werther instructs his tailor to make an exact new copy, hoping to use fashion to reproduce memories of significant moments during which he had worn the originals. "I struggled with myself before I decided to discard my plain blue dress coat, which I wore when I first danced with Lotte," the protagonist records. "I have had a new one made, exactly like the first, down to the collar and lapels; and also another yellow waistcoat and a pair of breeches."[1] Clothing is clearly important to Werther. But the importance of Werther's clothing actually extends far beyond the novel's pages.

For although Werther's outfit is not itself a crucial element of the plot—a tragic story about a distraught youth who kills himself after realizing that he cannot be with Lotte, the woman he loves—the novel was an overnight sensation and reportedly spawned a morbid practice whereby scores of readers, empathizing with the protagonist and struck with "Werther Fever," dressed up in blue and yellow ensembles and took their own lives, thereby enacting what one psychologist studying the phenomenon of copycat suicides later called the "Werther Effect."[2] If scholars now question whether a rash of sartorially inflected deaths really did occur,[3] there is no doubt that Werther's recognizable outfit came to emblematize the artistic restlessness and fervent internal turmoil associated with romanticism, a core western aesthetic movement of the 1800s that was launched around the time that Goethe's novel began circulating.

"Few writers have ever surpassed Goethe in global fame and influence," one scholar recently declared.[4] The famous blue jacket, yellow waistcoat, and breeches of his troubled protagonist thus offer a fitting introduction to this essay on fashion and literature, which will focus on novels, arguably the nineteenth century's most thriving genre. In sartorial terms, if accounts are to be even partially believed, Werther's uniform inaugurated a cutting-edge (albeit macabre) style of dress: *Werthertracht* or "Werther costume" was featured in fashion periodicals, an "eau de Werther" perfume hit the market, and Werther-inspired accessories, including fans and buttons, enabled enthusiasts to wear episodes from the novel on their bodies,[5] all these practices attesting to the impact fashion in literature could exert on society. Goethe's morose style icon also evokes the notion of

Walking Costume.
Time of the French Revolution.
after Debucourt
1792.
Plate LXXX.

Cassell, Petter, & Galpin, London

FIGURE 9.1: *Werthertracht*. Werther's yellow breeches and blue coat may have been an inspiration for this late-eighteenth-century French fashion plate. *Modes et costumes historiques*, 1864. Photo: Culture Club/Getty Images.

fashionability as it relates to popularity, for *The Sorrows of Young Werther* was a must-read bestseller that appealed to a rapidly expanding readership, one made possible by new technologies of mass-printing that allowed for the distribution of literary texts to grow exponentially throughout the 1800s. Finally, as Catriona MacLeod notes, by 1800 Goethe's novel had been translated throughout Europe.[6] This transcultural transmission of literature paralleled a growing interconnectedness among global peoples that fashion registered materially as, for instance, textiles or tastes in cuts of dress in one place cross-pollinated with those in another, by-products of increased travel and trade. If such global contingencies could occasion creativity and inspiration in fiction and fashion alike, they also were linked to imperialism, a term having dark connotations due to its traditional modes of domination, colonization and violence. These themes are equally present in literary works featuring dress in a period that this volume has entitled, not coincidentally, the Age of Empire.

WOMEN, FASHION, AND BRITISH GOTHIC ROMANCE

The early nineteenth century was a golden age for women authors in Great Britain, an era represented by now well-known names such as Jane Austen, Charlotte and Emily Brontë, and George Eliot. These writers often used fashion to describe social conditions upon which imperial England was organized, such as differences in class that the clothing of the period efficiently conveyed and reinforced. Perhaps in part because fashion was seen as "feminine" and an acceptable subject for women to discuss, garments were a recurring theme in their works. However, in trying to infiltrate a literary scene dominated by men, female authors also used garments to critique patriarchal attitudes and assumptions of the basic inferiority of women, both as citizens and as writers.

Through costume, much information, from a character's economic status to his or her moral fortitude (or lack thereof), could be instantly communicated. Take, for instance, the clothing-obsessed Mrs. Allen of Jane Austen's novel *Northanger Abbey* (1817), who is mentor to the story's protagonist—the impressionable debutant Catherine Morland— and the chaperone who launches Catherine into England's upper-crust marriage market. "Dress was her passion," Austen writes, initially describing Mrs. Allen's preoccupation with muslins, ribbons, and the like as a "harmless delight in being fine,"[7] but then using fashion to reveal faults in her character, such as when Mrs. Allen enters a crowded room "with more care for the safety of her new gown than for the comfort of her protégée."[8] By indicating that Mrs. Allen prioritizes her outfit over Catherine, Austen implies that the older woman's fixation on clothing is not "harmless" but instead a sign of shallowness and self-absorption. Links between objects of adornment and superficiality are amplified in another character in *Northanger Abbey*, the conniving Isabella Thorpe, who masquerades as Catherine's friend only to procure a marriage proposal from her brother. If Catherine is too naïve to discern Isabella's manipulative nature, Austen reveals the truth to readers by way of clothing. Early in the novel, Isabella cajoles Catherine into accompanying her to a hat boutique across town. Yet it is not millinery that interests Isabella, but two eligible bachelors that she spies leaving the building and whom she hopes to pursue:

> In a few moments Catherine, with unaffected pleasure, assured her that she need not be longer uneasy, as the gentlemen had just left the Pump-room. "And which way are they gone?" said Isabella, turning hastily round. "One was a very good-looking young man." "They went towards the church-yard." "Well, I am amazingly glad I have got rid of them! And now, what say you to going to Edgar's Buildings with me, and looking at my new hat? You said you should like to see it." Catherine readily agreed. "Only," she added, "perhaps we may overtake the two young men." "Oh! Never mind that. If we make haste, we shall pass by them presently, and I am dying to shew you my hat."[9]

This fashion pretext—viewing a new bonnet with a companion, an activity considered respectable for genteel young ladies—obscures the truth, which is that Isabella aggressively seeks to lure a man. Later, when endeavors to snare one wealthy suitor end disastrously and Isabella attempts to rekindle a spark with Catherine's brother, hats resurface in her wheedling letter to Catherine, which bemoans that the new look of the season is for "hats the most frightful you can imagine"[10] and also mentions a turban, a chic style in early 1800s Europe, that Isabella mean-spiritedly describes as flattering atop her own head but "wretched work" when worn by another person (Figure 9.2).

Symbols of destructive qualities associated with fashion, among them superficiality, fickleness and deceit, hats in *Northanger Abbey* underscore Isabella's snobbery and

FIGURE 9.2: Turban, c. 1820. This spectacular turban *à la turque*, uncommonly voluminous in size, may have appealed to a showy dresser like Isabella Thorpe. Brooklyn Museum Costume Collection at The Metropolitan Museum of Art, New York.

duplicitousness. However, Austen's repeated references to decorative headgear in relation to the novel's anti-heroine also point to a very real problem that women in similar circumstances faced in early 1800s Britain. That is, having no profession and no inheritance, Isabella's best chance at acquiring financial security is to find a rich husband. To do so she uses the best tool available, namely, her physical beauty, which she enhances through the strategic deployment of attractive clothes and hats. Indeed, Isabella lets it slip that she wears the turban because it had pleased her former love-interest (although apparently not enough, since he leaves her with a sullied reputation, rendering her disgraced and far less marketable "damaged goods"). Perhaps this is why the seemingly self-absorbed Mrs. Allen treats her gown with such care: a generation before, she too may have been acutely aware of the causal relationship between sartorial tactics and female economic stability. With regard to women's financial wellbeing in a rigidly stratified society according them few legitimate opportunities to generate income, fashion could be far from a frivolous matter.

Northanger Abbey, imbued with the author's sparkling prose and clever humor, was Austen's deliberate parody of the gothic novel, the latter a genre of romantic fiction that, in contrast, embraced a serious and often melodramatic tone more in line with Goethe's *Werther*. *Jane Eyre* (1847), Charlotte Brontë's tale of a plain-featured but determined orphan cast into an unkind world of shadowy drama, exemplifies literary romanticism and has immediately recognizable differences from the lighthearted novels of Austen. Yet, despite their contrasting styles, Brontë also made use of dress to comment on the female condition in northern England and, incidentally, to connect the titular character's story to broader issues to do with British colonial imperialism.

Unlike Isabella Thorpe, who relies on eye-catching finery to attract male attention, Jane Eyre shuns opulent attire, associating it with superficiality and abhorring the idea of being made an object of male desire and possession through showy dress. Brontë demonstrates this midway through the novel when Jane, happy to have her affections returned by her brooding employer Mr. Rochester, nonetheless feels strong discomfort at her fiancé's attempts to adorn her in fancy clothing:

> Mr. Rochester obliged me to go to a certain silk warehouse: there I was ordered to choose half-a-dozen dresses. I hated the business, I begged leave to defer it: no—it should be gone through with now . . . With anxiety I watched his eye rove over the gay stores: he fixed on a rich silk of the most brilliant amethyst dye, and a superb pink satin . . . With infinite difficulty . . . I persuaded him to make an exchange in favour of a sober black satin and pearl-grey silk . . . Glad was I to get him out of the silk warehouse, and then out of a jewellers shop: the more he bought me, the more my cheek burned with a sense of annoyance and degradation.[11]

Preferring her utilitarian and modest brown frocks to gowns of rich and brightly colored silks, Jane tenaciously resists being "degraded" as a repeat version of Rochester's conspicuously dressed former lovers. Tellingly, Brontë juxtaposes fashion with masculine tyranny, deploying strong vocabulary—Jane "hates" the new gowns and "begs" to leave— to convey an unequal power struggle which, in the nineteenth century, favored the white male Rochester over women like Jane as well as racial others whom oppressive colonial imperialism relegated to positions of subordination.

Thus, as Catherine A. Milton observes, Brontë performs an "oriental allegorization"[12] when Jane next goes on to compare herself to eroticized female slaves in an Eastern harem and Rochester to the master "sultan" who owns them:

> I ventured once more to meet my master's and lover's eye . . . He smiled; and I thought his smile was such as a sultan might, in a blissful and fond moment, bestow on a slave his gold and gems had enriched . . . "You need not look in that way," I said; "if you do, I'll wear nothing but my old Lowood frocks to the end of the chapter. I'll be married in this lilac gingham" . . . He chuckled; he rubbed his hands. "Oh, it is rich to see and hear her?" he exclaimed. "Is she original? Is she piquant? I would not exchange this one little English girl for the Grand Turk's whole seraglio, gazelle-eyes, houri forms, and all!"[13]

The master-and-slave scenario is put forth playfully by the two characters, but at the same time Jane is "anxious," possibly due to her uneasy realization that marriage, even to a man she loves, will lead to Rochester's possession of her not just legally but sexually, too. Pushing back against the role of erotic harem slave and threatening him with her drab English schoolgirl uniforms ("old Lowood frocks") and unsophisticated "lilac gingham" dress, Jane stages her opposition to Rochester's domination over her with frumpy clothing (Figure 9.3), also subverting any impetus on his part to advertise his own wealth and prestige through his future wife's expensive apparel.[14] In this passage, Brontë's layering of exoticized allusions over Jane's domestic plight inject the novel with an orientalist flavor popular in Western literature from the nineteenth century, when fabrics, decorative objects, and furnishings from or inspired by those produced

FIGURE 9.3: Although still made of fine silk this relatively modest brown dress would probably have been more to Jane Eyre's liking than the extravagant garments that Rochester tries to have made for her. The Metropolitan Museum of Art, New York.

in colonies abroad were greatly in vogue.[15] What is more, the comparison of Jane and Rochester to sultan and seraglio girl anticipates the arrival in the narrative of an "exotic" character as yet unknown to Jane: Rochester's first wife, the Jamaican-born creole Bertha, whom Rochester has kept captive in his attic since her descent into madness.[16] When Bertha escapes one frightful night to Jane's room and dons the veil that the protagonist is meant to wear to her wedding, a link between Jane's circumstances and that of peoples subject to the aggressions of British imperialism is made through a garment. Milton notes that "Bertha's appearance in Jane's bridal veil is both terrorizing and poignant, as she is the visible, undeniable evidence of the dehumanizing position of the colonized female subject."[17] Although their circumstances are not identical, subjugation of both the racialized other (represented by foreign-born Bertha) and the objectified, submissive British spouse (that Jane defies becoming) overlap in the shared veil, a filmy, transparent item of dress that allows readers to "see through" to similarities in the two women's situations.

"MONDERNITY," MASCULINITY, AND THE DANDY FLÂNEUR: YANGZHOU—PARIS—LONDON

While Austen and Brontë were confronting issues to do with the female condition against the backdrop of British imperialism, China was simultaneously undergoing what Antonia Finnane has suggested we understand as "mondernity," or "the modernity arising out of the incorporation of hitherto more or less self-sufficient or even notionally isolated states and societies into *le monde*, with concomitant developments in communications, production, finance, and technology and an accompanying cultural hegemony in colonized societies."[18] Examining fashion in literature from China, a place with its own history of empire-building, suggests how nineteenth-century modernization was being narrated in both unique and similar ways across the globe. One illuminating example is the 1848 novel *Courtesans and Opium* (*Fengyue meng*),[19] penned by a writer identifying himself as "The Fool of Hanshang," Hanshang being a district in the bustling east-coast city of Yangzhou. Categorized by scholars as a "courtesan novel" in the "talented scholars and beautiful women" genre,[20] *Courtesans and Opium* chronicles the adventures of a group of young men in Yangzhou's thriving brothels and opium dens, offering these stories as a cautionary tale to readers who might, like the narrator, find themselves similarly tempted by such dangerous—and exciting—corruptions. Chief among these are the pleasure boats filled with prostitutes, "wearing vivid colors and with their faces fully made up,"[21] who attract keen attention from the young men who gather in the city's central thoroughfares to play dice, drink tea, and seek out female companions.

Like *Northanger Abbey*'s Isabella Thorpe, the prostitutes in *Courtesans and Opium* recognize the power of striking clothes and ornamentation to impact a woman's financial lot in life, for they rely on such sartorial enticements to invite interest from paying customers. At the same time, the pleasure-boat women are the very personification of presumed links among finery, feminine sexuality and indecency, links that Brontë invokes when Jane Eyre, virtuous and virginal, rejects as sexually and morally improper the luxurious dresses that Rochester wishes to have made for her. Calling up the ugliness that external trappings of beauty can conceal, *Courtesans and Opium* provides a sympathetic perspective on the sufferings of courtesans, misfortunes that are only partially camouflaged by the "vivid colors" and cosmetics that they wear. There is, for instance, the prostitute Phoenix, whose blunt account of being forced by her husband and his family into sex slavery at the tender age of twelve draws attention to the sober reality of her oppressed position.[22]

The clothing, accessories, jewelry, and make-up of the prostitutes are richly described throughout the novel, however, it is not merely the courtesans who don flashy attire but also men: male fops who, according to the narrator, "like nothing more than dressing up in brilliant clothes of the latest fashion"[23] when they assemble in town to socialize and enjoy the city's entertainments. As mentioned earlier, the nineteenth century gave rise to an orientalist aesthetic in the west, a vogue that, at times, was further specified through localized terms such as "chinoiserie" or "japonaiserie." Dapperly dressed men in this Yangzhou novel point to analogous western influences on Chinese dress, a phenomenon that has been called "euroiserie"[24] or "occidenterie"[25] whereby, for instance, fabrics such as European wool became integrated and reinterpreted into daywear of those living in cosmopolitan Chinese cities. Such cross-cultural sartorial hybridity is expressed in the dress choices of one male character of *Courtesans and Opium*, Lu Shu, who readies himself to visit his friend Yuan You as follows:

> He changed into a fashionable, high, bridge-shaped hat of broadcloth, vermilion in color with best-quality tassels; clad himself in a lined robe of double-blue corded silk and a silken belt with dragon and tiger hooks of white jade from which were suspended a watch, a fan, an ornamental purse, a small knife, and so on. Over this he wore a lined jacket of natural-colored silk.[26]

If Lu Shu's robe is, by tradition, an eastern garment, the author provides the important detail that his hat features "broadcloth," a textile that, since at least the eighteenth century, had been imported to China from England.[27] Lu Shu's fashionable ensemble, which incorporates British cloth and a decoratively worn western watch, with typical Chinese elements of dress like silk fabrics and his robe, creates a look that is neither Chinese nor European but distinctly "Yangzhou style" (Figures 9.4 and 9.5). His outfit can be read through Finnane's concept of "mondernity," that is, as a narrative description encouraging readers to understand nineteenth-century modernities in geographically distant regions not as completely isolated from one another but rather as interconnected phenomena.

To consider writings from Yangzhou as part of a larger "mondernity" enables correspondences to be perceived between men decked out in stunning attire in *Courtesans and Opium* and male protagonists appearing in other literature produced during this same period in distant parts of the world. The figure of the well-dressed dandy, a man who turns himself into an attractive aesthetic object, provides a revealing point of comparison. Paola Zamperini offers this useful portrait of men, like the finely clad Lu Shu, in late Qing Chinese courtesan novels:

> What all these men have in common is their association with the courtesans and prostitutes, an amateurish approach to modernity and progress, either in the form of unconditional embrace of anything Western and foreign, or of total obtuse refusal of anything not Chinese; a very unstable social and economic situation, going from extremely poor to extremely rich in a matter of days or even seconds; a constant displacement, manifested in their restlessness, in their travels, in constant changes of careers; a tendency to addiction (to sex, drugs, gambling, and to self-created delusions in general); a strong sexual drive, often without the means to carry it to its conclusion; a very ambiguous moral status, saintly one moment, and utterly perverted the following; and a general incapacity to cope with the changing world around them.[28]

17.82.2

FIGURE 9.4: Robe of State. Qing dynasty, 19th century. China. A lavishly decorated silk robe and ornamental dragon buckle accessory might have been desirable wardrobe pieces for a dandy like Lu Shu. The Metropolitan Museum of Art, New York.

FIGURE 9.5: Belt hook in the form of a dragon, China, middle Qing dynasty. Image courtesy of Los Angeles County Museum of Art.

Although Zamperini's summary includes factors specific to late Qing fiction, such as male protagonists' rejection (or, alternately, full embrace) of things western or Chinese, parts of her description could equally apply to the dandies that were proliferating in French novels during these same years. One thinks of well-dressed bucks such as Eugène de Rastignac in Honoré de Balzac's novel *Père Goriot* (1834–5) or Georges Duroy in Guy de Maupassant's *Bel-Ami* (1885) (Figure 9.6), dapper Frenchmen who, through similar attention to self-fashioning, parallel the fashionable young fellows from *Courtesans and Opium*.

FIGURE 9.6: Portrait of a known elegant French composer and dandy Albert Cahen d'Anvers, Pierre-Auguste Renoir, 1881. Oil on canvas. The J. Paul Getty Museum, Los Angeles.

Take, for example, the dandy protagonist of Balzac's *Père Goriot*, a novel in *The Human Comedy* (*La comédie humaine*), a sweeping collection of ninety-odd novels, short stories and essays that occupied Balzac from the 1830s until his death in 1850. In keeping with the *bildungsroman* or "educational novel" format popular in the nineteenth century, *Père Goriot* charts Rastignac's arrival in the capital city from the French provinces, his experiences of the glamorous seductions of Paris, and the lessons he learns from the savvy city dwellers he encounters, all of which form his identity and the principles by which he then determines to live. In line with Zamperini's description of male characters in Qing fiction, Rastignac gambles and accrues fortunes just as quickly as he loses them, is sexually passionate, and, ultimately, morally ambivalent. What makes him a dandy is the way in which he turns himself into an aesthetic being, a process in which clothing plays an important role. Balzac, who wrote for the fashion press in addition to penning fiction, inserts garments liberally into *Père Goriot*, using luxury clothing and accessories to critique not just Rastignac but other superficial social climbers, characters for whom external appearances trump inner truth, and for whom ostentatious elegance, which they equate with power, is desired to the point of financial and ethical ruin. Balzac's criticism of human pettiness, greed, and corruption is expressed through one of Rastignac's dubious mentors, the criminal Vautrin. Vautrin's dream of becoming a plantation owner in the American South renders him an eager representative of France's imperial appropriation of oversea lands and economies; moreover, through Vautrin, villainous greed connects to fashion.

This is shown midway through the novel when Vautrin divulges to Rastignac his cynical but pragmatic view on the importance of fashionable appearance to success in high society:

> If you really want to be somebody, here in Paris, you've got to have at least three horses, with a light carriage for the morning and a covered gig at night ... and that's just for the wheels. You'll be totally unworthy of your great destiny if you don't spend, say, three thousand francs on your tailor, six hundred francs on perfume, a hundred at the boot-maker's. And as for your laundress, why, she should cost you another thousand francs. Fashionable young men simply can't spend too much on their linen, you know: isn't it precisely there that they're most frequently inspected?[29]

Vautrin's remarks, and his sexual/scatological allusion to a man's unclean linens (through the metaphor of "dirty laundry"), relate masculine high fashion to besmirched morals, a link already hinted at earlier when Rastignac sheds the impoverished garb that he normally wears and selfishly spends his sisters' and mother's savings to purchase a fancy new wardrobe for himself. After the main character dons one of his brand-new outfits and finds it dazzlingly transformative, Balzac comments, "seeing himself well dressed, with proper gloves and well-fitting boots, Rastignac forgot his virtuous resolution."[30] By the end of *Père Goriot* the ambitious protagonist finds, as Vautrin had predicted, that prioritizing outer trappings of luxury, and particularly handsome clothing, helps to ensure his financial, social, and sexual triumphs. Emerging as a highly influential archetype for the modern urban hero (or anti-hero) in nineteenth-century literature, Balzac's Rastignac helped to embed haute couture into subsequent portrayals of masculinity both in the Parisian context and beyond it.

For *Père Goriot*'s well-heeled protagonist can also be viewed as a prototype for a related (typically) male literary figure, one that appeared with some frequency across nineteenth-century letters: the *flâneur*, or the urban stroller, who observed and chronicled modern life in the century's rapidly growing metropolitan centers. Perhaps the most well-known writings on the flâneur come from the French poet Charles Baudelaire (1821–67), whose essays "The Heroism of Modern Life" ("*De l'héroïsme de la vie moderne*") (1846) and "The Painter of Modern Life" ("*Le peintre de la vie moderne*") (1863) provide a description somewhat at odds with the conspicuously-dressed dandy. In these writings we find Baudelaire's own rendition of the flâneur who does not make a spectacle of himself but rather blends anonymously into crowded city streets clothed in a nondescript black suit, a garment that seemed, for him, to be worn identically by all men strolling the urban boulevards (Figure 9.7).[31] Likening this homogenizing outfit to the mournful uniform of an undertaker, Baudelaire referenced a decline in the vibrant colors and ornamentation in menswear that had once reigned in France prior to a rise in the mid-nineteenth century of the somber, middle-class black suit. Yet, even if he saw men's suits as representative of his era's dark sobriety, Baudelaire still imbued them with elegance through tailored cut and fit, which he related to democratic ideals and poetic aesthetics, arguing that "the dress-coat and the frock-coat not only possess their political beauty, which is an expression of universal equality, but also their poetic beauty, which is an expression of the public soul."[32] For Baudelaire, dark suits that facilitated the flâneur's anonymity in thronged urban thoroughfares conveyed their own kind of popular, refined grace.

FIGURE 9.7: *Paris Street; Rainy Day*, Gustave Caillebotte, 1877. Photo: Fine Art Images/ Heritage Images/Getty Images.

Balzac's Rastignac, more flamboyantly dressed and less democratically motivated, can still be considered an early incarnation of Baudelaire's flâneur, particularly for the way in which he constantly travels the avenues of Paris. Per Vautrin's instructions, for much of the narrative Rastignac is often suspended above the street in showy carriages, the period's equivalent to today's flashy sports cars. However, in the novel's final paragraph, Balzac suddenly foreshadows Baudelaire's pavement-hitting flâneur, writing that Rastignac "walked" ("*fit quelques pas*")[33] to the summit of Père Lachaise cemetery, a high vantage point from where he looks down upon the city teeming below and announces his desire to master it, famously asserting "Now it's just the two of us!—I'm ready!"[34] Like Rastignac's story, which seems not to end on the last page but rather to begin with his energetic declaration, *Père Goriot* marks an important start for literary flânerie, one that would resurface in the writings of many other eminent French writers from Émile Zola to Guy de Maupassant and Marcel Proust.

Common fashion-related tropes in literature—dandies and flâneurs—thus provide an aesthetic bridge between "east" and "west" as well as other corners of the world often erroneously considered totally separate from one another in the 1800s. Flânerie resonated also in Chinese urban fiction, for instance, through well-dressed fop characters walking about and observing their respectively modernizing cities. When Lu Shu from *Courtesans and Opium* dresses himself meticulously in his eye-catching bright red tasseled hat, luxuriously lined silk robe, and belt decorated with buttons of semi-precious stones and dangling ornamental items, not only does he turn his body into an aesthetic object like a dandy, he does so to circulate in the urban modernity of Yangzhou as a flâneur. Once Lu Shu is suitably adorned, the author of *Courtesans and Opium* proceeds to describe his peregrinations through the city's walkways. Sights, sounds, and smells are all documented while crowds, shops, and city-dwellers from the various social classes of Yangzhou that Lu Shu witnesses constitute the very same aspects of modern life that were catching the attention of literary flâneurs in Paris. Indeed, in her enumeration of quintessential male character traits in late-Qing courtesan novels, Zamperini specifically calls up the term "flâneur,"[35] suggesting connections between roving, fashion-conscious men in fiction from Chinese and French contexts alike. The concept of a Chinese flâneur seems also present in Patrick Hanan's description of *Courtesans and Opium* as "the first city novel"[36] and his observation that "a novelist, as distinct from a geographer, tends to give us a city in terms of his characters' observations and movements—a city of the eye and the foot,"[37] wherein visual engagement ("eye") and strolling ("foot") invoke the flâneur's essential activities: to walk and to observe. Dapper literary flâneurs thus evoke correspondences in novels from geographically disparate Paris and Yangzhou, but also, we will now see, in London at the turn of the century, a locale remote from Balzac's city not so much in space as in time, and in artistic concerns that were developing at the end of the 1800s in radical new directions.

The Picture of Dorian Gray (1890), the lone novel by Irish-born playwright Oscar Wilde (1854–1900), is an iconic example of late-century dandyism and flânerie, one that demonstrates an evolving set of social and aesthetic preoccupations. A novel at the crossroads of several fin de siècle literary currents, including realism, symbolism, and decadence, Wilde's is the story of a beautiful gentleman, the titular Dorian Gray, whose inner degradation is recorded not on his perennially handsome face but rather on a painting made in his likeness. In *Dorian Gray*, male attractiveness and navigation through urban locales are conjoined themes of the plot; these are also metaphors through which Wilde explores his philosophies on artistic expression, sexuality, and desire. However, notable for a text that is "about" male dandyism, the novel does not, in fact, include the same types of lavish descriptions of garments typical of realist authors such as Zola and Maupassant in the French tradition, or George Eliot and Charles Dickens in the English. Rather, fashion in *Dorian Gray* seems less to do with specific clothing items and more to do with how the deliberate aestheticization of the self, a quintessential activity of the dandy, relates to a new approach to daily living based on embracing art as well as forbidden pleasures.

Dorian's views on these matters crystallize in a passage outlining his thoughts on dandyism and his ambition to be more than simply a fashion trendsetter:

> Fashion, by which what is really fantastic becomes for a moment universal, and dandyism, which, in its own way, is an attempt to assert the absolute modernity of beauty, had, of course, their fascination for him. His mode of dressing, and the particular styles that from time to time he affected, had their marked influence on the young exquisites ... who copied him in everything that he did, and tried to reproduce the accidental charm of his graceful, though to him only half-serious, fopperies ... yet in his inmost heart he desired to be something more than a mere arbiter elegantiarum, to be consulted on the wearing of a jewel, or the knotting of a necktie, or the conduct of a cane. He sought to elaborate some new scheme of life that would have its reasoned philosophy and its ordered principles, and find in the spiritualizing of the senses its highest realization.[38]

Dorian, fascinated by dandyism, welcomes the chance to exert influence over the dressing habits of other young men "exquisites" and to dictate sartorial mannerisms. He also links elegant style in menswear to a manner of living aesthetically that privileges "the spiritualizing of the senses," those sometimes illicit pleasures of the body and mind that the protagonist enjoys throughout the novel. As Wilde takes pains to insist, though, the protagonist is not just interested in hedonistic, sensory gratifications, for the "new scheme of life" that he proposes is a "reasoned philosophy" having "ordered principles." Dorian's appreciation of fine fashion thereby relates to an elevated "philosophy" governed by reason rather than irrational reactions, sentiment or bodily sensations alone.

Dorian's "new scheme of life" is expressed in distinctive touches of dress, in subtle fashion gestures such as how he ties his cravats or holds a walking stick. For such relatively discrete sartorial (under)statements Dorian can be contrasted with his creator Wilde, who built for himself a scandalous reputation in part by clothing himself in opulent, attention-grabbing garments, an effete and ostentatious manner of dress that Talia Schaffer names "Aesthetic fashion" and which, she argues, "was the focus of late-Victorian attention because it so clearly displayed the anxieties, stresses, and formulations of the movement"[39] (Figure 9.8). Schaffer notes, for example, that Wilde was "condemned for effeminacy"[40] for wearing flowers, feathers, and "colors, styles, fabrics, and accessories from the women's sphere."[41] She perceptively reads Wilde's appropriation of dress elements associated with femininity as part of a strategy that he and other Aesthete men adopted in their attempts to infiltrate and simultaneously distinguish themselves as superior in realms of authorship that women dominated at the turn of the century, such as lighthearted novels and plays. At the same time, Wilde's affiliation with femininity through his tastes in fashion and literary genres was primarily for his own benefit (as opposed to that of women), and he aligned himself with an aristocratic mentality that interpreted his own aesthetic preferences as a sign of innate supremacy.[42] Wilde thereby shared traits with nineteenth-century

FIGURE 9.8: Oscar Wilde (1854–1900) in New York in January 1882. Wilde was known for enjoying a flamboyant style of dress. Photo: DEA Picture Library/Getty Images.

colonial imperialism, both being founded on assumed superiority over others—women and colonized subjects—who were placed in positions of inferiority to stunning male "genius" or the equally aristocratic assumptions of those claiming imperialist power.

In *Dorian Gray*, the central character, succumbing to dark impulses, becomes a murderer and then himself dies, killed when he slashes the painting that records his inner ugliness in a dramatic ending that rips Wilde's novel away from traditional realism and into the realms of psychological fiction and fantasy. In a parallel, real-life tragedy, the gems, pretty purple attire, and long curly locks of hair that Wilde adopted did much to render him the victim of homophobic British law, which outlawed homosexuality and condemned him to prison for practices that his detractors associated with, among other things, Wilde's penchant for flamboyant dress. These related cases of literal and literary criminalization, represented by the opulently-styled Wilde and his dandy protagonist, bring the focus to other commonly found meanings of fashion in literature during this period, namely those of transgression and danger, which were often perceived when limits once thought to be fixed —those of gender, class, and sexuality, for instance—were violated through clothing.

FASHION, GENDER, TRANSGRESSION

Wilde, demonized in part for what was perceived to be feminized attire, brings up a connection frequently made in this period between fashion and dangerous women. Garments and activities related to dress, such as shopping, were linked with female vice and misconduct, particularly in mid- and late-century realist novels, which sought to break from the heightened drama of the previous romantic period by showing the "realities" of life, often in lengthy descriptive passages. This technique of developing a scene in sometimes gritty detail demonstrated an attempt to show a scene "in its entirety," one of literary realism's main preoccupations. In France, prominent (male) realist writers such as Gustave Flaubert (1821–80) and Émile Zola (1840–1902), articulated their anxieties about dangerous women in several career-defining texts. For Flaubert, it was the novel *Madame Bovary* (1856), in which adulterous housewife Emma attempts to assuage the boredom of her dull provincial life by way of that period's version of retail therapy. Purchasing fine silks and other costly adornments, first to attract lovers and then to inject excitement into her affairs with "little coquettish refinements in her dress,"[43] her sartorial efforts instead lead Emma to insurmountable debt and wretched despair. Flaubert's story of perilous fashion consumption by a woman set the stage for Zola to take up the theme in his *Rougon-Maquart* series, twenty novels published from the 1870s through the 1890s in which the author strove to apply scientific methods to literature in order to understand what he thought of as the social ills and pathologies of modernity. Through this process Zola created an offshoot of realism known as "naturalism." In *The Kill* (*La Curée*) (1872), *Nana* (1880), *Pot Luck* (*Pot-Bouille*)(1882) and *The Ladies' Paradise* (*Au Bonheur des dames*) (1883), Zola linked women to what he considered "disorders"—incest, prostitution, infidelity, sexual insatiability, lesbianism, hysteria, and kleptomania—often connecting these "syndromes" to buying, wearing, or displaying articles of clothing.

The Ladies' Paradise, for instance, which is set in one of Paris's dazzling department stores (Figure 9.9), turns the novel's female clientele into lace thieves and incurable shopaholics, rendering them powerless against the lures of the clothing emporium. Through Zola's misogynist caricaturizing, most women, having weak minds and bodies, are eventually driven mad by fashion.

FIGURE 9.9: Women shopping at a Parisian *grand magasin* or department store. Lithograph, c. 1890. Bibliothèque Nationale de France.

Across the Atlantic, North American writers during these same years were also connecting femininity with crime and consumerism and, not unlike their French counterparts, using garments to do so. In 1900, Theodore Dreiser created a version of the woman consumer who is awed and led morally astray by big-city shopping, fashion, and glamour in his Chicago-based novel *Sister Carrie*. Earlier in the century, Nathaniel Hawthorne's historical fiction *The Scarlet Letter* (1850) literalized the period's symbolic associations between adornment and female depravity by way of the red "A" (for "adultery") that protagonist Hester Prynne wears as a sign of her sinful, extramarital past. Hawthorne's evocative description of the crimson "A" is less reminiscent of Puritan-era prison garb and more in line with Zola's meticulous renderings of stunning haute couture finery worn by chic Parisians:

On the breast of her gown, in fine red cloth, surrounded with an elaborate embroidery and fantastic flourishes of gold thread, appeared the letter A. It was so artistically done, and with so much fertility and gorgeous luxuriance of fancy, that it had all the effect of a last and fitting decoration to the apparel which she wore, and which was of a splendour in accordance with the taste of the age, but greatly beyond what was allowed by the sumptuary regulations of the colony.[44]

Underscoring the letter's high-quality fabric, sparkling gold thread, well-sewn embellishments, and splendid beauty, this passage communicates not penitence but luxurious stylishness, the titular "A" being "in accordance with the taste of the age." The scarlet letter, described as a fashion reporter might depict a gleaming decoration sewn onto the bodice of a gown, draws the eye and the reader's imagination to the body ("breast") of the woman who wears it. However, for Hawthorne, Hester's body is dangerous, and the A is a cipher not of modest beauty but of her role as lovely femme fatale, a role that Hester insinuates by revealing the letter "with a haughty smile."[45] In describing the A as an object of elegant style, Hawthorne uses the language of fashion to create a second coming of Eve—a woman with her own problematic associations to fig-leaf clothing—and ascribes Hester with imperfections recalling her Biblical model, such as a weakness in the face of temptation which proves fatal to men around her (and to herself).

Hawthorne's at times sympathetic but ultimately condemning view of Hester is expressed in reactions of the colony women, who witness the A's unveiling and praise Hester's skill at needlework but decry the inappropriateness of applying such sewing prowess to a showy embroidered trimming, by which the young lady transforms what is meant to be society's reprimand of her into an attractive accessory:

"She hath good skill at her needle, that's certain," remarked one of her female spectators; "but did ever a woman, before this brazen hussy, contrive such a way of showing it! Why, gossips, what is it but to laugh in the faces of our godly magistrates, and make a pride out of what they, worthy gentlemen, meant for a punishment?"

"It were well," muttered the most iron-visaged of the old dames, "if we stripped Madam Hester's rich gown off her dainty shoulders; and as for the red letter, which she hath stitched so curiously, I'll bestow a rag of mine own rheumatic flannel, to make a fitter one!"[46]

The dialog between Hester's neighbors articulates a difference between the verbs "to clothe" and "to fashion." The former, the Oxford English Dictionary explains, emphasizes the covering of the body (*clothe*, from Middle English, "To cover with a garment or with clothing") while the latter (*fashion*, from the French, "To make good-looking; to beautify") implies beautification for an audience, or "spectator," to use Hawthorne's term for the first woman speaker. Hester has not "clothed" herself, or hidden her body behind a "rag" of "rheumatic flannel" to symbolize her shame, as another observer had expected. Instead, she dons what is seen as a "rich gown" and fashions it with the elegant "A" trimming, inviting visual spectatorship, showing off her sensuality, and highlighting through adornment that she is "good-looking." For those who stand in judgment of her, Hester's crime of passion manifests materially as a crime of fashion.

Other chapters in this volume confirm that dress in the long nineteenth century could be exquisitely beautiful, a quality that even Hawthorne invokes despite the unlikely setting of luxury-averse Puritan New England (hardly anyone's idea of a high-fashion capital!). As suggested by what we have already observed, though, acclaimed works of fiction from this period tended to turn to dress not to articulate characteristics of fashion that might be worth celebrating, such as its ability to stimulate fantasy, its cultivation of artistic creativity, and its support of gender emancipation (for example, through the wearing of pants by suffragettes in the late 1800s). Instead, garments seemed often to express writers' concerns about destabilizing, alienating, or constricting experiences of modern life. To be sure, connections between dress and modernity are not surprising, since fashion, as Baudelaire and other writers intuited, is an excellent expression of the modern moment itself: both are characterized by the opposing forces of change and constancy, or, as Baudelaire famously put it, "the ephemeral" and "the eternal." Fashion was thereby an effective shorthand for modernity—a character's clothing choice could instantly transmit to readers whether s/he was "modern" or not—and also a way to frame how literature itself always will be in a constant state of transformation ("ephemeral") based, simultaneously, on the unchanging ("eternal") canonical works, authors, and methods of writing that come before it.

How, then, might we interpret tensions between the potentially positive associations between human existence and fashion and the ways in which dress was depicted in literature during this period? The title of the present volume provides a possible clue. That is to say, the fact that fashion, represented during the period by stunning haute-couture finery, skilled handiwork, human imagination, and artistic innovation, would be routinely condemned in fictional works, might well relate to the reality that the once stable colonization-based Age of Empire was itself in a state of crisis, as overseas lands, once seized for their peoples and commodities in the name of empire building and colonial supremacy, were becoming increasingly destabilized, many in violent contexts.[47] This phenomenon was likely troubling to those in traditional seats of power watching this collapse unfold, and to authors who may or may not have shared their points of view. Since literature is, among other things, a reflection of a larger cultural and social zeitgeist, and fashion was a common marker of modernity for writers in this period, it is perhaps logical that dress in texts would become a lightning rod for the expression of deeply held contemporary concerns.

FASHION, GENDER, POWER

A notable exception to the trend of authors depicting fashion in a damaging light could occur in situations where garments were politicized and used as instruments of empowerment or signs of resistance by those oppressed by various forces of imperialism. One example can be found in Juana Manuela Gorriti (1818–92), whom Francine Masiello has called "the most important woman writer in nineteenth-century Argentina."[48] Born in Argentina and exiled to Bolivia as a child, Gorriti then moved to Peru, where she founded a girls' school, cultivated a literary salon, and established herself as a prominent public figure. In 1885 she took up permanent residence in Buenos Aires, where she remained until her death.[49] A prolific novelist, essayist, and journalist, Gorriti inserted dress into her fiction in powerful and diverse ways. In her 1882 novel *The Oasis in Life* (*Oasis en la vida*), for instance, Gorriti incorporated garments into her depiction of Buenos Aires's urban modernity to illuminate, as Regina A. Root has shown, women's roles in a society enjoying post-colonial economic prosperity and modernization. "Turning to the rhetoric of fashion" in this novel, Root argues, Gorriti "discussed the prospects of female emancipation in a society wrought by change."[50]

FIGURE 9.10: *Portrait of Manuelita Rosas*, Prilidiano Pueyrredón, 1851. Manuela Rosas (1818–92) was the daughter of Federalist leader Juan Manuel de Rosas. Although the novella was not published until the 1860s, Gorriti probably wrote "The Black Glove" in the decade that Pueyrredón painted this 1851 portrait, which underscores Manuelita's stylishness as well as the color red, a hue associated with her father's military regime. Photo: DeAgostini/Getty Images.

However, depicting fashionable, cosmopolitan Buenos Aires was far from Gorriti's sole project. The daughter of a general who had fought for Argentina's independence from Spain, and a life-long activist herself, Gorriti produced fiction that reflected an engagement with political instability, paralleling the volatile struggles for autonomy from former European colonizers and from within that were taking place in the nineteenth-century Latin American countries through which she migrated. As Masiello observes of Gorriti's lifelong textual output, "politics was never far from her literary creations."[51] This political commitment is embedded in "The Black Glove" ("El guante negro") (1865), a dramatization of civil conflict in post-colonial Argentina that features the theme of violent intra-family murder and ends on a bloody battlefield strewn with corpses. Demonstrating Susan Hiner's point that "because of its trivialized status, the feminine fashion accessory could accomplish ideological work imperceptibly, both avowing and disavowing its connection to some of the most complex processes of modernity,"[52] "The Black Glove" uses a seemingly inconsequential fashion accessory as a potent symbol of gendered political critique. The novella, a love triangle drawing on real people and events from a newly independent and politically tense Argentina, involves fashionable Federalist Manuelita Rosas (Figure 9.10), beautiful Isabel from the rival Unitarian faction, and Wenceslao, the handsome Federalist soldier who loves Isabel to the point of deserting father and country for her. "The black, tulle glove embroidered with arabesques,"[53] an elegantly stitched accessory gifted to Wenceslao from stylish Manuelita in gratitude for defending her honor, serves first as a symbol of the sexually charged childhood friendship between the two characters and a sign of their shared allegiance to the Federalist camp. However, when Isabel finds the glove, which is inscribed with Manuelita's name, the accessory becomes a catalyst for her jealous ultimatum to Wenceslao: that he commit treason and take up arms for the Unitarians. Wenceslao's acquiescence triggers a string of murderous events, including his desperate mother killing his father to prevent filicide, and then Wenceslao's own death on the battlefield. The tale ends with Isabel singing mournfully over the mangled bodies of the deceased men from both armies, dressed in a "long, white robe"[54] that communicates her role as the phantom bride who will never be.

Gorriti relies on somewhat obvious symbolism for the colors of her garments: the black glove is an allegory for seduction, discord, and death, and the white gown represents ghostliness and virginal purity. But she also complicates things by ending the story with the image of "a strange-looking woman . . . in a long shroud"[55] who reappears at night to circle the city and sing mournfully "every time that the tyrant of Buenos Aires was about to decree . . .one of those horrible acts of butchery that have desolated the city."[56] With this feminine figure in the novella's coda, Gorriti, who was devoted to feminist causes and served as "a strong reminder of the role of women in public action,"[57] may have been inciting women to become the resistors to brutal conflicts perpetrated by men seeking power and land and instigating deadly wars in the name of nationalism. For white is also the color of peace,[58] the garment worn by Gorriti's recurring ghostly feminine presence representing, perhaps, a call for armistice coming not from military men, focused on conquest, but from women, who could remind society of the suffering that war inflicts on all.

PROUST'S FORTUNY GOWNS

We began with Goethe's *The Sorrows of Young Werther*, a text having a profound impact on literature in the emerging nineteenth century. Accordingly, we end here with Marcel

FIGURE 9.11: Evening dress. Mariano Fortuny (1871–1949). 1920s. Fortuny's evening gowns may have been inspired by robes from classical antiquity but their body-hugging pleats, glass bead decorations and bright jewel tones also perfectly expressed the daring sensibilities of the 1920s. © 2015. Image copyright The Metropolitan Museum of Art/Art Resource/Scala, Florence.

Proust (1871–1922), whose multi-volume tour de force novel *In Search of Lost Time* (*A la recherche du temps perdu*) (1913–27) bridged the nineteenth century with the twentieth, and whose influence on later authors, like Goethe's, would be deeply and widely felt. As Hiner notes, *In Search of Lost Time* is "a veritable fashion show of the Belle Epoque,"[59] partly because Proust provides lavish descriptions of his many characters' garments, but also because, in the final pages, he reveals that writing his magnum opus was akin to "patiently sewing together . . . little bits of paper . . . 'like a dress'."[60] This clothing metaphor evokes nostalgia—a main concept explored in the novel—in that the narrator imagines "sewing" his "bits of paper" with the assistance of Françoise, the maid he remembers from his childhood. For Proust, the writing process itself is thus steeped in memory, and indeed the narrative frequently takes him back to fashionable society of the late 1800s. At the same time, these remembrances are filtered through his observations of the early decades of the 1900s, in sudden recollections produced through what he terms "involuntary memory," such as when a madeleine cake dipped in a cup of tea triggers the flood of thoughts that end up forming the novel.

In Search of Lost Time is a watershed text of twentieth-century literary modernism. Like his Irish contemporary James Joyce, Proust recorded modern experience in ways that radically departed from the nineteenth-century realists, breaking down formal narrative structures through paragraph-long, near stream-of-conscious sentences, and rejecting linear time in favor of chronologies that mixed the past with the present to form new modes of representation. Fashions, typically with real-life referents, were cited prominently in Proust's resuscitation of lost time. The antiquity-inspired gowns by Venice-based *haute couturier* Mariano Fortuny (1871–1949) (Figure 9.11) that are worn by the narrator's love interest, Albertine, are one example:

> These Fortuny gowns, faithfully antique but markedly original, brought before the eye like a stage décor . . . that Venice saturated with Oriental splendour where they would have been worn and of which they constituted, even more than a relic in the shrine of St Mark, evocative as they were of the sunlight and the surrounding turbans, the fragmented, mysterious and complementary colour. Everything of those days had perished, but everything was being reborn, evoked and linked together by the splendour and swarming of life of the city.[61]

This description of the young woman's dress reveals what the narrator desires to understand: Venice and Albertine, or what they symbolize, which is that which is gone and that which cannot be known. Paradoxically he eventually "finds"[62] these things in a manner of speaking, both in the Fortuny gowns that "constitute" the ancient city and in the process of writing about them.

Through Proust's narrative searching through the modern by way of the past we have ourselves come, sartorially and literarily speaking, full circle, for also in this passage we discern traces of young Werther's romantic longings, Isabella Thorpe's stylish turban, a narrative construction of "oriental splendor," connections between eastern and western dandy-flâneurs in the "swarming life" of the city, and Albertine's embodiment of the fashionable, dangerously alluring woman. Proust struggled to come to terms with the end of his generation's Age of Empire, his narrator's nostalgia for a lost history of imperialist and aristocratic privilege expressing this dilemma. At the same time, it was this very anxiety-producing problem that catalyzed Proust as an author and also mobilized much fashion-conscious literature in this period, a corpus of texts that paved the way for the literary avant-garde of the unfolding twentieth century.

NOTES

Introduction

1. For the etymology of the term *modernité* as a nineteenth-century neologism, see Robert Kopp, "Baudelaire: Mode et modernité," *48/14: La revue du Musée d'Orsay* 4 (1997): 51.

2. "La modernité, c'est le transitoire, le fugitif, le contingent," Charles Baudelaire, *Curiosités esthétiques, L'Art romantiques, et autres Oeuvres critiques de Baudelaire* (Paris: Éditions Garnier Frères, 1962), 467. Translated by Jonathan Mayne in *The Painter of Modern Life and Other Essays by Charles Baudelaire* (London: Phaidon, 1964), 13.

3. "La haute spiritualité de la toilette" and "la majesté des formes artificielles," Baudelaire, *Curiosités esthétiques*, 491; *The Painter of Modern Life*, 32.

4. "La femme est bien dans son droit, et même elle accomplit une espèce de devoir en s'appliquant à paraître magique et surnaturelle; l faut qu'elle étonne, qu'elle charme; idole, elle doit se dorer pour être adorée. Elle doit donc emprunter à tous les arts les moyens de s'élever au-dessus de la nature pour mieux subjuguer les coeurs et frapper les esprits. Il importe fort peu que la ruse et l'artifice soient connus de tous, si le succès e nest certain et l'effet toujours irrésistible." *Éloge du maquillage* in *Le Peintre de la vie moderne*, Baudelaire, *Curiosités esthétiques*, 492; *The Painter of Modern Life*, 33.

5. "La morale et l'esthétique du temps," cited in *Achille Devéria: Temoin du romantisme parisien, 1800–1857* (Paris: Musée Renan-Scheffer, 1985), 43.

6. For a recent discussion of the fashionable progression from the cage crinoline to the bustle, see Lina Maria Paz, "Crinolines and Bustles: The Reign of Metallic Artifices," in the exquisite exhibition catalogue, *Fashioning the Body: An Intimate History of the Silhouette*, ed. Denis Bruna (New Haven and London: Yale University Press for the Bard Graduate Center, 2015), 176–97.

7. For an excellent investigation of the crinoline empire corresponding to France's Second Empire, see the Musée Galliera's publication to accompany its 2008–9 exhibition, *Sous l'empire des crinolines* (Paris: Paris musées, 2008).

8. F. Th. Vischer, *Mode und Cynismus* (Stuttgart, 1879), 6, cited in Walter Benjamin, *The Arcades Project*, trans. Howard Eiland and Kevin McLaughlin (Cambridge, MA and London: Belknap Press of Harvard University Press, 1999), 70.

9. Egon Friedell, *Kulturgeschichte der Neuzeit*, vol. 3 (Munich, 1931): 203 cited in Benjamin, 75.

10. For the resurgence of the rococo in the arts and culture of the Second Empire, the classic text is Carol Duncan, *The Pursuit of Pleasure: The Rococo Revival in French Romantic Art* (New York and London: Garland, 1976). See also the more recent, Allison Unruh, "Aspiring to La Vie Galante: Reincarnations of Rococo in Second Empire France," (Ph.D. diss.: Institute of Fine Arts at New York University, 2008).

11. Karl Marx, "The Fetishism of the Commodity," in *The Visual Culture Reader*, 2nd edition, ed. Nicholas Mirzoeff (London and New York: Routledge, 2002), 122.

12. Eric Hobsbawm, *The Age of Empire, 1875–1914* (New York: Pantheon, 1987); *The Age of Revolution, 1789–1848* (Cleveland: World Publishing Co., 1962); and *The Age of Capital, 1848–1875* (New York: Scribner, 1975).

13. Anne McClintock, *Imperial Leather: Race, Gender, and Sexuality in the Colonial Conquest* (New York: Routledge, 1995), 5.

14. Key texts that exemplify these new approaches include Kathleen Wilson (ed.), *A New Imperial History: Culture, Identity and Modernity in Britain and the Empire, 1660–1840* (Cambridge: Cambridge University Press, 2004) and Catherine Hall and Sonya O. Rose (eds), *At Home with the Empire: Metropolitan Culture and the Imperial World* (Cambridge: Cambridge University Press, 2006).

15. See, for instance, Auguste Racinet, *Le costume historique* (Paris: Firmin-Didot et Cie., 1888).

Chapter 1

1. Lesley Ellis Miller, "Perfect Harmony: Textile Manufacturers and Haute Couture 1947–57," in *The Golden Age of Couture: Paris and London 1947–57*, ed. Clare Wilcox (London: V&A Publishing), 116.

2. Isabella Ducrot, *Text on Textile* (Lewes: Sylph Editions, 2008), 25.

3. Jane Austen, "Letter from Jane Austen to Cassandra Elizabeth Austen, January 25, 1801," in *Jane Austen's Letters to Her Sister Cassandra and Others, Vol. 1: 1796–1809*, ed. R.W. Chapman (Oxford: Clarendon Press, [1801] 1932), 266.

4. Eric T. Svedenstierna, *Svedenstierna's Tour: Great Britain 1802–3: The Travel Diary of an Industrial Spy*, trans. E.L. Dellow (Newton Abbot: David & Charles, [1804] 1973), 174.

5. Wigan Heritage Service, Charles Hilton & Son Archive: B78.530 and B78.541.

6. Philipp Andreas Nemnich, *Beschreibung einer im Sommer 1799 von Hamburg nach und durch England geschehenen Reise* (Whitefish, MT: Kessinger Publishing Legacy Reprint, [1800] 2010).

7. Ibid., 302–3.

8. "Twist wird sowohl zum Einschlag, als zum Zettel genommen. Der Einschlag muss wenigstens zwey Numern höher zehn, als der Zettel; z. B. ist der Zettel No. 32, so ist der Einschlag No. 34. Alle Nankine werden im Garn gefärbt, und da die Farben nur gemein sind, so gehen sie beym Bleichen fast alle aus. Indessen bleicht die gewöhnliche Fleischfarbe (Buff, Chamois) der Nankine nich leicht aus; denn die Farbe wird aus dem sogenannten Iron-liquor bereitet. Iron-liquor ist Eisenrost mit Säure aufgelöset." Nemnich, *Beschreibung einer im Sommer 1799*, 298. Author's own translation.

9. Florence Montgomery, *Textiles in America 1650–1870* (New York: W.W. Norton), 308.

10. Anon., "Topographical and Commercial History of Manchester," *The Tradesman; or, Commercial Magazine*. 5, no. 26 (August 1810): 144.

11. Sonia Ashmore, *Muslin* (London: V&A Publishing, 2012).

12. Commissioners and Trustees for Fisheries, Manufactures and Improvements in Scotland, "Premiums, on Various Articles of Scotch Manufacture." *Caledonian Mercury* (May 7, 1794): 4.

13. William Watson, *Advanced Textile Design*, 2nd ed. (London: Longmans, Green and Co., 1925), 297.

14. Manchester Archives: Calico Printers' Association: M75/ Design Dept. 3.

15. Ducrot, *Text on Textile*, 26.

16. Linda Theophilus, *Peter Collingwood-Master Weaver* (Colchester: Firstsite, 1998), 11.

17. Rosemary Crill, "Mashru in India," in *Indian Ikat Textiles* (London: V&A Publications, 1998), 119–47.

18. Rudolph Ackermann, *The Repository of Arts, Literature, Commerce, Manufactures, Fashion, and Politics,* 1 (March 1809): 186.

19. P. Cusack, "Classified advertisement," *Norfolk Chronicle*, January 16, 1814: 1.

20. G.P. & J. Baker Archives: Inv.096: Order Book 1821–3.

21. No record of an actual patent has been found.

22. Fox and Co., "Classified advertisement," *Morning Post*, December 18, 1823: 1.

23. Gentleman's Magazine of Fashions, "A Riding Frock Coat," *Dublin Morning Register*, June 3, 1828: 3.

24. Gentleman's Magazine of Fashions, "Gentlemen's Fashions," *Morning Post*, September 30, 1831: 4.

25. Anon., *The Rhenish Album, or Scraps from the Rhine: The Journal of a Travelling Artist* . . . (London: Leigh & Son, 1836), 2.

26. Sylvanus Swanquill, (pseud.), "The First of September," *The New Monthly Magazine*, 39 (1833): 54.

27. Fox & Co., "Advertisement," in John Stephens, *The Land of Promise being an authentic and impartial history of the rise and progress of the new British province of South Australia* . . . (London: Smith, Elder & Co., 1839), n.p.

28. John James, *History of the Worsted Manufacture in England* (London: Frank Cass & Co., [1857] 1968), 445.

29. National Archives. Buckley: BT42/3. Ibotson & Walker: BT42/1–BT42/4. Harrison: BT42/1.

30. G.P. & J. Baker Archives: Inv. 077: Swaisland *Gambroons 1838–9*.

31. Charles Dickens (ed.), "A Manchester Warehouse," in *Household Words*, 9 (1854): 270.

32. Thomas E. Lightfoot, "History of Broad Oak," unpublished ms.: Accrington Library, 1926.

33. Charles Dickens (ed.), "The Great Yorkshire Llama," in *Household Words*, 6 (1852): 253.

34. William Walton, *A memoir addressed to proprietors of mountains and other waste lands, and agriculturalists of the United Kingdom, on the naturalization of the alpaca* (London: Smith, Elder & Co., 1841), 39.

35. Dickens (ed.), "The Great Yorkshire Llama": 253.

36. Anon., "The Llama or Paco," *The Treasury of Literature and The Ladies' Treasury*, April 1, 1869: 136.

37. H.B., "The Adulteration of Dress Materials," *The Ladies' Treasury*, April 1, 1881: 209–10.

38. Anon., "The Llama or Paco": 136.

39. Natalie Rothstein, "The Introduction of the Jacquard Loom to Great Britain," in *Studies in Textile History*, ed. Veronika Gervers (Toronto: Royal Ontario Museum, 1977), 281–304.

40. See Jacques Anquetil with Pascale Ballesteros, *Silk* (Paris: Flammarion, 1995); Chiara Buss (ed.), *Silk and Colour* (Como: Ratti, 1997); Musée Carnavalet, *L'Art de la Soie: Prelle 1752–2002* (Paris: Paris Musées, 2002); and Mary Schoeser, *Silk* (New Haven: Yale University Press, 2007).

41. Old Draper (pseud.), *Reminiscences of an Old Draper* (London: Sampson Low, Marston, Searle & Rivington, 1876), 102.

42. Edmund Potter, "Calico Printing as an Art Manufacture," *Manchester Guardian*, July 14, 1852: 3.

43. Anon., "Selected Patterns for Dress: Calico, Printed by Thomas Hoyle and Sons," *Journal of Design and Manufactures*, 2 (November 1849): 108.

44. Edmund Potter, *Calico Printing as an Art Manufacture: a lecture read before the Society of Arts, 22 April 1852* (London: John Chapman, 1852), 51.

45. Anon., "A Word for the Servant Girl," *The Cornishman*, November 1, 1883: 6, extracted from *The Queen*.

46. Joan L. Severa, *Dressed for the Photographer: Ordinary Americans and Fashion, 1840–1900* (Kent, OH: Kent State University Press, 1995), 204.

47. Adelheide Rasche and Gundula Wolter (eds), *Ridikül! Mode in der Karikatur 1600 bis 1900* (Berlin: SMB-DuMont, 2003), 308.

48. Société Industrielle de Mulhouse, *Histoire documentaire de l'Industrie de Mulhouse et de ses environs au XIXe siècle* (Mulhouse: Veuve Bader & Cie, 1902), 399.

49. Joanna Bourke, "The Great Male Renunciation: Men's dress reform in interwar Britain," *Journal of Design History* 9, no. 1 (1996): 23–33.

50. Entry for November 21, 1660 in *The Diary of Samuel Pepys: a new and complete transcription, vol. 1 (1660)*, eds, Robert Latham and William Matthews (London: G. Bell and Sons, 1970), 298.

51. James Trilling, *The Language of Ornament* (London: Thames & Hudson, 2001), 203.
52. L.C. Otway, L.C. "Report on the Commerce of Lombardy," in House of Commons [2757], *Further Correspondence relating to the Affairs of Italy*, LXIII (1861), 192.
53. Hon. Eleanor Eden, *False and True* (London: n.p., 1859), 153.
54. Harriet M. Carey, "Woman in Daily Life: or Shadows on Every Hill-Side," in *The Rose, the Shamrock, and the Thistle* 2 (November 1862): 81.
55. Miles Lambert, *Fashion in Photographs 1860–1880* (London: B.T. Batsford, 1991), 47.
56. Fabio Giusberti, "The Riddle of Secrecy," in *Les Archives de l'Invention: Écrits, Objects et Images de l'Activité Inventive*, eds, Marie-Sophie Corcy, Christiane Douyère-Demeulenaere, and Liliane Hilaire-Pérez (Toulouse: CNRS-Université de Toulouse-Le Mirail, 2006), 73–88.
57. Lou Taylor, *Mourning Dress: A Costume and Social History* (London: George Allen & Unwin, 1983), 216–17.
58. Ibid., 217–19.
59. Anon., "New Styles and Coming Fashions," *Western Daily Press*, June 20, 1870: 4.
60. *Journal des Modes*, "Fashions for December," in *Lincolnshire Chronicle*, December 9, 1870: 3.
61. Anon., "Ladies' Fashions," *Royal Cornwall Gazette*, May 7, 1872: 7.
62. D.C. Coleman, *Courtaulds: An Economic and Social History* (Oxford: Oxford University Press, 1969).
63. G.W. Armitage, "A History of Cockhedge Mill, Warrington," unpublished ms., Warrington Library Archive and Local Studies Collection, 1938.
64. Friedrich Carl Theis, *'Khaki' on cotton and other textile material*, trans. E.C. Kayser (London: Heywood & Co, 1903), 5.
65. Jane Tynan, *British Army Uniform and the First World War: Men in Khaki* (Basingstoke: Palgrave Macmillan, 2013).
66. Cecil Cowper (ed.), "Colour as an Influence," in *The Academy and Literature*, 2227, January 9, 1915: 23.
67. Thomas Burberry, "BP 17,928 Compound fabrics," in Patent Office, 1896, *Patents for Inventions: Abridgments of Specifications: Class 142, Weaving and Woven Fabrics, 1884–88* (London: HMSO, [1888] 1896), 266.
68. C. Willett Cunnington, *English Women's Clothing in the Nineteenth Century* (London: Faber & Faber, 1937), 431.
69. Thomas Burberry and Frederick D. Unwin, "BP 4065," in Patent Office, 1903, *Patents for Inventions: Abridgments of Specifications: Class 142, Weaving and Woven Fabrics, 1897–1900* (London: HMSO, [1897] 1903), 9.
70. Anon., *The Cornishman*, October 17, 1889: 4.
71. Cunnington, *English Women's Clothing in the Nineteenth Century*, 426.
72. Burberrys, *Burberry for Ladies*, XIX edition. (London, Paris, and Basingstoke: Burberrys, c. 1910): 5.
73. Ibid.: 13.
74. Victoria & Albert Museum: Furniture, Textiles and Dress. Joseph Lockett engraving book, 1806–8.
75. Rothschild Archive. 1/218/45, "Manchester Stock Price & Printing Book 1802/1807."
76. Milnrow (pseud.), "Coloured stripe designing.–II," *The Textile Manufacturer*, September 15, 1925: 296.
77. For example, in January 1767, Lady Mary Coke recalls Lady Suffolk setting her ruffle on fire "which immediately blazed up her arm . . ." See J.A. Home (ed.), *The Letters and Journals of Lady Mary Coke* (Bath: Kingsmead Reprints [1889] 1970), 107.
78. Anon., "Caution to Parents," *Lincolnshire Chronicle*, October 28, 1842: 3.
79. W.H. Perkin, "The Permanent Fireproofing of Cotton Goods," *Popular Science Monthly*, 81 (October 1912): 397–408.

80. See Nancy E. Rexford, *Women's Shoes in America, 1795–1930* (Kent, OH: Kent State University Press, 2000), 279–87 and Sarah Levitt, "Manchester Mackintoshes: A History of the Rubberized Garment Trade in Manchester" *Textile History* 17 (1986): 51–69.

81. Rexford, *Women's Shoes in America*, 285.

82. Robin W. Doughty, *Feather Fashions and Bird Preservation: A Study in Nature Protection* (Berkeley: University of California Press, 1975).

83. W.H. Flower and R. Lydekker, *An Introduction to the Study of Mammals Living and Extinct* (London: Adam & Charles Black, 1891), 237.

84. Anon., "Epitome of News—Foreign and Domestic," *Illustrated London News*, September 5, 1857: 254.

85. Anon., "Skeleton of the Greenland Whale in the Museum of the College of Surgeons," *Illustrated London News*, February 24, 1866: 176.

86. Priscilla Wakefield, *Mental Improvement: or, the Beauties and Wonders of Nature and Art* (Dublin: P. Wogan, 1800), 4–7.

87. Ibid., 4–7.

88. C.T. Hinckley, "Calico-Printing," *Godey's Magazine and Lady's Book* 45 (1852): 121.

89. Ducrot, *Text on Textile*, 26.

Chapter 2

1. Raymond Carré, "Les Couturières à La Recherche d'un Statut Social," *Gavroche: Revue d'Histoire Populaire* 36 (1987): 8.

2. Nancy L. Green, *Ready-to-Wear and Ready to Work: A Century of Industry and Immigrants in Paris and New York* (Durham: Duke University Press, 1997), 26–7.

3. Susan Kaiser, *Fashion and Cultural Studies* (New York: Berg, 2012), 14.

4. Ibid., 19.

5. Clare Haru Crowston, *Fabricating Women: The Seamstresses of Old Regime France 1675–1791* (Durham: Duke University Press, 2001), 49.

6. Regina Lee Blaszczyk, "The Hidden Spaces of Fashion Production," in *The Handbook of Fashion Studies*, eds Sandy Black, et al. (New York: Bloomsbury, 2013), 187.

7. See Heidi Brevik-Zender, "Interstitial Narratives: Rethinking Feminine Spaces of Modernity in Nineteenth-Century French Fashion Plates," *Nineteenth-Century Contexts* 36:2 (May 2014): 91–123; see also Margaret Beetham, *A Magazine of Her Own? Domesticity and Desire on the Woman's Magazine, 1800–1914* (New York: Routledge, 1996).

8. Valerie Steele, *Paris Fashion: A Cultural History* (New York: Berg, 1999), 3.

9. Gavin Waddell, *How Fashion Works: Couture, Ready-to-Wear, and Mass Production* (Oxford: Blackwell, 2004), xi.

10. Susan Hiner, *Accessories to Modernity: Fashion and the Feminine in Nineteenth-Century France* (Philadelphia: University of Pennsylvania Press, 2010).

11. Philippe Perrot, *Fashioning the Bourgeoisie: A History of Clothing in the Nineteenth Century*, trans. Richard Bienvenu (Princeton: Princeton University Press 1994) and Rosalind H. Williams, *Dream Worlds: Mass Consumption in Late Nineteenth-Century France* (Berkeley: University of California Press, 1982).

12. Piedade da Silveira, "Les magasins de nouveautés," in *Au Paradis des dames: nouveautés, modes et confections 1810–1870* (Paris: Paris-Musées, 1992), 23.

13. H. Hazel Hahn, *Scenes of Parisian Modernity: Culture and Consumption in the Nineteenth Century* (New York: Palgrave McMillan, 2009).

14. Jennifer Jones, *Sexing la Mode: Gender, Fashion, and Commercial Culture in Old Regime France* (New York: Berg, 2004).

15. Waddell, *How Fashion Works*, 71.

16. See Crowston, *Fabricating Women*.

17. Green, *Ready-to-Wear and Ready to Work*, 22, 31.

18. Ibid., 26. See also Perrot, *Fashioning the Bourgeoisie.*
19. Rebecca Arnold, *Fashion: A Very Short Introduction* (New York: Oxford, 2009), 14.
20. Françoise Tétart-Vittu, "Couture et nouveautés confectionnées," in *Au Paradis des dames: nouveautés, modes et confections 1810–1870* (Paris: Paris-Musées, 1992), 35.
21. See Yvonne Verdier, *Façons de dire, façons de faire: la laveuse, la couturière, la cuisinière* (Paris: Gallimard, 1979).
22. Perrot, *Fashioning the Bourgeoisie,* 40.
23. Ibid.
24. "The Tailor. He walks with an arched back, his shoulders like a coat-hanger and his elbows out. His clothes are of the latest cut, but often clashing with his boots and hat. He nearly always has a very melodious name such as Wahaterkermann or Pikprunman."
25. Christopher Breward, *Fashion* (Oxford: Oxford University Press, 2003), 32.
26. Theresa M. McBride, "A Woman's World: Department Stores and the Evolution of Women's Employment, 1870–1920," *French Historical Studies* 10, no. 4 (Autumn, 1978): 668.
27. Crowston, *Fabricating Women,* 66.
28. Ibid., 67.
29. Arnold, *Fashion: A Very Short Introduction,* 13.
30. Jones, *Sexing la Mode,* 95.
31. See Hollis Clayson, *Painted Love: Prostitution in French Art of the Impressionist Era* (New Haven: Yale University Press, 1991) and Anne Higonnet, "Real Fashion: Clothes Unmake the Working Woman," in *Spectacles of Realism: Gender, Body, Genre,* eds Margaret Cohen and Christopher Prendergast (Minneapolis: University of Minnesota Press, 1995), 137–62.
32. Daniel Roche, *The Culture of Clothing: Dress and Fashion in the "ancien régime",* trans. Jean Birrell (Cambridge: Cambridge University Press, 1994 (Fayard, 1989)), 309.
33. See Clayson, *Painted Love,* and Judith Coffin, *The Politics of Women's Work: The Paris Garment Trades, 1750–1915* (Princeton: Princeton University Press, 1996).
34. Perrot, *Fashioning the Bourgeoisie,* 36; Verdier, *Façons de dire, façons de faire,* 254.
35. Susan Hiner, "Monsieur Calicot: French Masculinity between Commerce and Honor," *West 86th: A Journal of Decorative Arts, Design, and Material Culture* 19, no. 1 (2012): 46.
36. See Michael Miller, *The Bon Marché: Bourgeois Culture and the Department Store, 1869–1920* (Princeton: Princeton University Press, 1981) and Williams, *Dream Worlds.*
37. Elizabeth Ann Coleman, *The Opulent Era: Fashions of Worth, Doucet, and Pingat,* exhibition catalog, December 1, 1989–February 26, 1990 (Brooklyn: The Brooklyn Museum, 1990), 39.
38. Anne Hollander, "When Worth was King," in *The Fashion Reader,* eds Linda Welters and Abby Lillethun (New York: Berg, 2007), 314.
39. Hollander, "When Worth was King," 315.
40. For an original and nuanced reading of the haptic in Winterhalter's painting and the gendered pleasures of the crinoline, see Lynda Nead, "The Layering of Pleasure: Women, Fashionable Dress, and Visual Culture in the mid-Nineteenth Century," *Nineteenth-Century Contexts* 35, no. 5 (2013): 489–509.
41. Susan North, "From Neoclassicism to the Industrial Revolution 1790–1860" in *The Fashion Reader,* eds Linda Welters and Abby Lillethun (New York: Berg, 2007), 31.
42. For a fascinating look at the cultural significance of the omnibus in nineteenth-century Paris, see Masha Belenky, "Transitory Tales: Omnibus in Nineteenth-Century Paris," *Dix-Neuf* 16, no. 3 (November 2012): 283–303. I am grateful to Professor Belenky for generously sharing this image, which she discovered at the Musée Carnavalet, with me.
43. Alison Matthews David, *Fashion Victims: The Pleasures and Perils of Dress in the Nineteenth Century,* exhibition catalog (Toronto: The Bata Shoe Museum, 2014), 26.
44. Kevin Seligman, *Cutting for All: The Sartorial Arts, Related Crafts, and the Commercial Paper Pattern* (Carbondale: Southern Illinois University Press, 1996), 22. See also Joy Spanabel Emery, *A History of the Paper Pattern Industry: The Home Dressmaking Fashion Revolution* (London: Bloomsbury, 2014).

45. Perrot, *Fashioning the Bourgeoisie*, 54.

46. See Rosalind Williams, *Dream Worlds*.

47. Walter Benjamin, "Paris: Capital of the Nineteenth Century," *Perspecta* 12 (1969): 165.

48. Perrot, *Fashioning the Bourgeoisie*, 51.

49. Green, *Ready-to-Wear and Ready to Work*, 77.

50. Waddell, *How Fashion Works*, 23.

51. Ibid., 26.

52. Perrot, *Fashioning the Bourgeoisie*, 52.

53. Ibid., 58.

54. See Susan Hiner, "Becoming (M)other: Reflectivity in *Le Journal des Demoiselles*," *Romance Studies* 31, no. 2, (2013): 84–100.

55. See Rhonda K. Garelick. *Mademoiselle: Coco Chanel and the Pulse of History* (New York: Random House, 2014).

56. On the subject of contemporary sweatshops, see in particular the 2005 documentary film by Micha X. Peled, *China Blue*. Available on line: http://www.argotpictures.com/ChinaBlue.html

Chapter 3

1. George Ellington, *The Women of New York, or the Under-World of the Great City* (New York City: The New York Book Company, 1869), 82.

2. Ibid., 90.

3. Ibid., 89.

4. Joanne B. Entwistle, *The Fashioned Body: Dress, Fashion, and Modern Social Theory* (Cambridge, MA: Polity, 2000).

5. Anne Hollander, *Seeing Through Clothes* (New York: Viking Press, 1978).

6. Charles Baudelaire, *The Painter of Modern Life and Other Essays*, trans and ed. Jonathan Mayne (London: Phaidon Press, 1964), 32–3.

7. Ibid.

8. A distinction between empire and Empire styles should be mentioned here, as empire carries with it connotations of colonialism and the political expansion of European countries, while Empire refers to contemporary styles in fashion and decorative arts. This style—which is described in several of the following paragraphs—is alternatively referred to as *Directoire*, Regency or Georgian dress, depending on the country in which it was worn.

9. Aileen Ribeiro, *Fashion in the French Revolution* (New York: Holmes & Meier Publishers, Inc., 1988), 53, 58.

10. Valerie Steele, *The Corset: A Cultural History* (New Haven and London: Yale University Press, 2001), 28–31.

11. Hollander, *Seeing Through Clothes*, 122.

12. Aileen Ribeiro, *Ingres in Fashion: Representations of Dress and Appearance in Ingres's Images of Women* (New Haven and London: Yale University Press, 1999), 36.

13. Susan Hiner, "'Cashmere Fever': Virtue and the Domestication of the Exotic," in *Accessories to Modernity: Fashion and the Feminine in Nineteenth-Century France* (Philadelphia: University of Pennsylvania Press, 2010), 83.

14. Daniel Delis Hill, *American Menswear: From the Civil War to the Twenty-First Century* (Lubbock: Texas Tech University Press, 2011), 40.

15. Ribeiro, *Ingres in Fashion*, 15.

16. See Carl Flügel, *Psychology of Clothes* (London: Hogarth Press, 1930).

17. See further Ann Hollander, *Sex and Suits* (New York: Alfred A. Knopf, 1994).

18. While many scholars, commencing with Carl Flügel, discuss the "Great Renunciation" of men's fashion after the early nineteenth century, this has been challenged, importantly:

Christopher Breward, *The Hidden Consumer: Masculinities, Fashion and City Life 1860–1914* (Manchester: Manchester University Press, 1999); Brent Shannon, *The Cut of His Coat: Men, Dress, and Consumer Culture in Britain, 1860–1914* (Athens, Ohio: Ohio University Press, 2006); Christopher Breward, "The Politics of Fashion and the Pleasures of Youth: Young Men and Their Clothes, 1814–1914" in *Artist/Rebel/Dandy: Men of Fashion*, eds Kate Irvin and Laurie Anne Brewer (New Haven: Yale University Press, 2013), 72–87.

19. Hollander, *Seeing Through Clothes*, 130.

20. Thorstein Veblen, *Theory of the Leisure Class: An Economic Study of Institutions* (New York: Macmillan, 1899).

21. Ibid., 179.

22. For further: Ludmilla Jordanova, *Sexual Visions: Images of Gender in Science and Medicine between the Eighteenth and Twentieth Centuries* (Madison: University of Wisconsin Press, 1989).

23. Mary S. Gove Nichols, "The New Costume, and Some Other Matters," *The Water-Cure Journal* (August 1851): 30.

24. Harold Koda, *Extreme Beauty: The Body Transformed* (New York: Metropolitan Museum of Art, 2001), 11.

25. D.C. Bloomer, *Life and Writings of Amelia Bloomer* (Boston: Arena Publishing Company, 1895), 72.

26. Aileen Ribeiro, "Fashion and Whistler," in *Whistler, Women and Fashion*, ed. Margaret F. MacDonald (New York: Frick Collection; New Haven, Connecticut: in association with Yale University Press, 2003), 25.

27. Susan Vincent, *The Anatomy of Fashion: Dressing the Body from the Renaissance to Today* (London: Berg, 2010).

28. Mrs. M.S. Gove Nichols, "A Lecture on Woman's Dress," *The Water-Cure Journal* (August 1851): 35.

29. For further: Patricia Cunningham, *Reforming Women's Fashion, 1850–1920* (Kent, Ohio: Kent State University Press, 2003).

30. Mary B. Williams, "The Bloomer and Weber Dresses: A Glance at their Respective Merits and Advantage," *The Water-Cure Journal* (August 1851): 33.

31. Text originally published in *The Lily* in February 1851. Reprinted in *Hear Me Patiently: The Reform Speeches of Amelia Jenks Bloomer*, ed. Anne C. Coon (Westport, CT: Greenwood Press, 1994), 10.

32. Bloomer's relationship to, and opinions of, reform dress varied greatly over her lifetime. For a thorough discussion refer to Bloomer, *Life and Writings of Amelia Bloomer*.

33. "Hasbrouck, Lydia Sayer," *Notable American Women, 1607–1950*, ed. Edward T. James (Cambridge, MA: Belknap Press of Harvard University Press, 1971), 151. This quotation was originally published in *Sybil*, December 1875.

34. James Whorton, *Crusaders for Fitness: The History of American Health Reformers* (Princeton, NJ: Princeton University Press, 2014).

35. "Springfield Bloomer Celebration by a Patient of the Water-Cure," *The Water-Cure Journal* (October 1851): 83–4.

36. Dress reformers, with their varying ways of approaching their clothing and their bodies, employed a wide range of rhetorical approaches in justifying their unconventional clothing. For more: Carol Mattingly, *Appropriate[ing] Dress: Women's Rhetorical Style in Nineteenth-Century America* (Carbondale, IL: Southern Illinois University Press, 2002); Gayle Fischer, *Power and Pantaloons: A Nineteenth-Century Dress Reform in the United States* (Kent, OH: Kent State University Press, 2001); and Catherine Smith and Cynthia Greig, *Women in Pants: Manly Maidens, Cowgirls, and Other Renegades* (New York City: Harry N. Abrams, Inc., 2003).

37. Examples of these paired images of fashionable and reform bodies—both men and women—can be found in the October 1851, November 1853, and October 1854 issues of *The Water-Cure Journal*.

38. See Alison Mathews David, *Fashion Victims: The Dangers of Dress Past and Present* (New York and London: Bloomsbury, 2015). I am grateful to Dr Matthews David in generously allowing me pre-publication access to her research.

39. Hollander, *Seeing Through Clothes*, 364.

40. Leigh Summers, *Bound to Please* (Oxford: Berg, 2001) and Steele, *The Corset*.

41. For an illustrated guide to nineteenth-century waistlines, refer to Richard Martin and Harold Koda, *Waist Not: The Migration of the Waist, 1800–1960* (New York: Metropolitan Museum of Art, 1994).

42. Summers, *Bound to Please*, 27.

43. *Lady's Gazette of Fashion* (July 1879).

44. Summers, *Bound to Please*, 66.

45. Ibid.

46. Kimberly Wahl, *Dressed as in a Painting: Women and British Aestheticism in an Age of Reform* (Durham, NH: University of New Hampshire Press, 2013), 10.

47. Mary Eliza Haweis, *The Art of Beauty* (New York: Harper & Brothers, 1878), 40.

48. Ibid., 31.

49. Wahl, *Dressed as in a Painting*, p. 11.

50. Ibid., p. 143.

51. Diana Crane, "Clothing behaviour as non-verbal resistance: Marginal women and alternative dress in the nineteenth century," in *The Fashion History Reader: Global Perspectives*, eds Giorgio Riello and Peter McNeil (London: Routledge, 2010), 339.

52. Frances Mary Steele and Elizabeth Livingston Steele Adams, *Beauty of Form and Grace of Vesture* (New York: Dodd, Mead, and Company, 1892), 78–9.

53. Ibid., 80.

54. Patricia Campbell Warner, *When the Girls Came Out to Play* (Amherst, MA: University of Massachusetts Press, 2006).

55. Ibid., 109–10, 137.

Chapter 4

1. See, in particular, the edited volumes of Linda B. Arthur, *Religion, Dress, and the Body* (Oxford and New York: Berg, 1999) and *Undressing Religion: Commitment and Conversion from a Cross-Cultural Perspective* (Oxford and New York: Berg, 2000), as well as Lynne Hume, *The Religious Life of Dress: Global Fashion and Faith* (London: Bloomsbury, 2013).

2. For a nineteenth-century historiography, see Robert Alexander Stewart Macalister, *Ecclesiastical Vestments: Their Development and History* (London: E. Stock, 1896). For a more contemporary consideration, see Janet Mayo, *A History of Ecclesiastical Dress* (London: Batsford, 1984).

3. Sally Dwyer-McNulty, *Common Threads: A Cultural History of Clothing in American Catholicism* (Chapel Hill: University of North Carolina Press, 2014), 8.

4. For this history, see Ralph Gibson, *A Social History of French Catholicism, 1789–1914* (London: Routledge, 1989).

5. The most significant of these French Marian apparitions include those to Catherine Labouré in Paris in 1830, Mélanie Calvat at La Salette in 1842 and Bernadette Soubirous in Lourdes in 1858.

6. Henry Rousseau, *William Joseph Chaminade, Founder of the Society of Mary*, trans. J.E. Garvin (Dayton: Brothers of Mary, 1914), 294.

7. William J.F. Keenan, "Clothed with Authority: The Rationalization of Marist Dress-Culture," in Linda B. Arthur, *Undressing Religion*, 88.

8. Elizabeth Kuhns, *The Habit: A History of the Clothing of Catholic Nuns* (New York: Doubleday, 2003), 17.

9. "There is a sect called Roman Catholics—a sect, that in my young days I was taught to look upon as monsters, capable of any crime in the calendar of human frailties, who have hospitals under their own charge, attended by? Sisters of Charity . . . If a soldier is dangerously sick, you will see . . . one of these heaven-born angels, ministering to his every want." "Hospital Scenes—Heartrending Sights," *Advocate*, January 23, 1863, cited in Katherine E. Coon, "The Sisters of Charity in Nineteenth-Century America: Civil War Nurses and Philanthropic Pioneers" (MA thesis: Indiana University, 2010), 131–2.

10. Ruth Vickers Clayton, "Clothing and the Temporal Kingdom: Mormon Clothing Practices, 1847–1887," (Ph.D. diss.: Purdue University, 1987), 40 and Gayle Veronica Fischer, "The Obedient and Disobedient Daughters of the Church: Strangite Mormon Dress as a Mode of Control," in *Religion, Dress, and the Body*, ed. Linda B. Arthur, 75.

11. This is true in both the case of the established Mormon community in Utah as well as the splinter Strangite Mormons in Michigan. For the former, see Clayton, "Clothing and the Temporal Kingdom" and for the latter, Fischer, "The Obedient and Disobedient Daughters of the Church."

12. Gayle V. Fischer, *Pantaloons and Power: A Nineteenth-Century Dress Reform in the United States* (Kent, OH: Kent State University Press, 2001), 75–6.

13. For an account of how this controversy played out in the courts, see Sarah Barringer Gordon, "The Mormon Question: Polygamy and Constitutional Conflict in Nineteenth-Century America," *Journal of Supreme Court History* 28, no. 1 (March 2003): 14–29.

14. Philippe Perrot, *Fashioning the Bourgeoisie: A History of Clothing in the Nineteenth Century*, trans. Richard Bienvenu (Princeton: Princeton University Press, 1994), 20.

15. *Cris*, such as the *Cris de Paris*, refer to both the calls of various merchants and the prints that depicted them in their specificity of dress. For a nineteenth-century compilation of *cris de Paris*, see Victor Fournel, *Le cris de Paris: Types et physiognomies d'autrefois* (Paris: Firmin-Didot, 1888).

16. Perrot, *Fashioning the Bourgeoisie*, 81–2.

17. For the extent of these editions, see Graeme Tytler, *Physiognomy in the European Novel: Faces and Fortunes* (Princeton: Princeton University Press, 1982); Melissa Percival and Graeme Tytler (eds), *Physiognomy in Profile: Lavater's Effect on European Culture* (Newark, DE: University of Delaware Press, 2005); and Sharrona Pearl, *About Faces: Physiognomy in Nineteenth-Century Britain* (Cambridge, MA: Harvard University Press, 2010).

18. For the relationship between Lavater's goals, connoisseurship, and artistic and art historical practice, see Joan K. Stemmler, "The Physiognomical Portraits of Johann Caspar Lavater," *The Art Bulletin* 75, no. 1 (March 1993): 151–68; Melissa Percival, *The Appearance of Character: Physiognomy and Facial Expression in Eighteenth-Century France* (Leeds: Modern Humanities Research Association, 1999); and Melissa Percival, "Johann Caspar Lavater: Physiognomy and Connoisseurship," *British Journal for Eighteenth-Century Studies* 26, no. 1 (March 2003): 77–90.

19. [Johann Caspar Lavater], *The Pocket Lavater, or, The Science of Physiognomy*, Second edition (New York: C. Wiley & Co., 1818), n.p.

20. Joan K. Stemmler, "The Physiognomical Portraits of Johann Caspar Lavater," 153.

21. Louis-Sébastien Mercier, *Tableau de Paris*, Nouv. éd., corr. & augm. (Amsterdam, 1782).

22. Ernest Desprez, *Paris, Ou Le Livre Des Cent-Et-Un* (Paris: Librairie Ladvocat, 1832); Jules Janin, *Les français peints par eux-mêmes: Encyclopédie morale du dix-neuvième siècle* (Paris: L. Curmer, [1840] 1862); and Louis Huart, *Physiologie de la grisette* (Paris: Aubert, 1841). For a sampling critical engagements with these texts and images as classificatory strategies, see Courtney Ann Sullivan, "Classification, Containment, Contamination, and the Courtesan: The Grisette, Lorette, and Demi-Mondaine in Nineteenth-Century French Fiction," (Ph.D. diss.: University of Texas at Austin, 2003); Denise Z. Davidson, "Making Society 'Legible': People-Watching in Paris after the Revolution," *French Historical Studies* 28, no. 2 (Spring 2005): 265–96; Jillian Taylor Lerner, "The French Profiled by Themselves: Social Typologies,

Advertising Posters, and the Illustrations of Consumer Lifestyles," *Grey Room* 27 (Spring 2007): 6–35; and Denise Amy Baxter "*Grisettes, Cocottes,* and *Bohèmes:* Fashion and Fiction in the 1820s," in *Fashion in Fiction: Text and Clothing in Literature, Film, and Television*, eds Peter NcNeil, Vicki Karaminas, and Catherine Cole (Oxford: Berg, 2009), 23–33.

23. John Conolly's "The Physiology of Insanity," originally published in *The Medical Times and Gazette* (1858), is reproduced in Sander L. Gilman (ed.), *The Face of Madness: Hugh W. Diamond and the Origin of Psychiatric Photography* (Secaucus, NJ: Citadel Press, 1976). For more on the photographs of Hugh Welch Diamond and the subsequent use to which the prints after them by John Conolly were used, see Adrienne Burrows and Iwan Schumacher, *Portraits of the Insane: The Case of Dr. Diamond* (London and New York: Quarto Books, [1979] 1990); and Andrée Leigh Flagollé, "The Demystification of Dr. Hugh Welch Diamond," (Ph.D. diss: University of New Mexico, 1994).

24. For an initial study of the power of dress within the nineteenth-century asylum context, see Jane Hamlett and Lesley Hoskins, "Comfort in Small Things? Clothing, Control, and Agency in County Lunatic Asylums in Nineteenth- and Early Twentieth-Century England," *Journal of Victorian Culture* 18, no. 1 (2013): 93–114.

25. For more on the photographic element of Dr. Barnardo's project see Valerie Lloyd, *The Camera and Dr. Barnardo* (London: National Portrait Gallery, 1974) and, more recently, the work of Susan Ash, such as "Heroin Baby: Barnardo's, Benevolence, and Shame," *Journal of Communication Inquiry* 32, no. 2 (2008): 179–200.

26. Similar texts circulated widely throughout Western Europe and the United States, with frequent translations and reprints. For an exploration of the profusion of etiquette guides within the French context during the Second Empire, see Perrot, *Fashioning the Bourgeoisie*, 88, 91.

27. Philip Nicholas Furbank and Alex M. Cain (eds), *Mallarmé on Fashion: A Translation of the Fashion Magazine, La Dernière Mode, with Commentary*, trans. Philip Nicholas Furbank and Alex M. Cain (Oxford and New York: Berg, 2004), 2016.

28. Explorations of the history of the wedding dress include Shelley Tobin, Sarah Pepper, and Margaret Willes, *Marriage à la Mode: Three Centuries of Wedding Dress* (London: The National Trust, 2003) and exhibition catalogs Edwina Erhman, *The Wedding Dress: 300 Years of Bridal Fashion* (London: V&A Publishing, 2014) and, for the American context, *American Brides: Inspiration and Ingenuity* (Denton, TX: Greater Denton Arts Council, 2014).

29. For details on the dress, see Kay Staniland and Santina M. Levey, "Queen Victoria's Wedding Dress and Lace," *Costume: The Journal of the Costume Society* 17 (1983): 1–32 and Jane Roberts, *Five Gold Rings: A Royal Wedding Souvenir Album from Queen Victoria to Queen Elizabeth II* (London: Royal Collection Publications, 2010). For the influence of the wedding of Queen Victoria and Prince Albert more generally, see Jennifer Phegley, *Courtship and Marriage in Victorian England* (Santa Barbara, CA: Praeger, 2012).

30. For an account of Queen Victoria and the media, see John Plunkett, *Queen Victoria: First Media Monarch* (Oxford: Oxford University Press, 2003).

31. The subsequent collaboration between Fenton and watercolorist Edward Henry Corbould in hand-coloring the albumen silver print rendered the scene even more nuptial, with the photographed pedestal now readable as an altar. Anne M. Lyden, *A Royal Passion, Queen Victoria and Photography* (J. Paul Getty Museum, 2014). For details of when Queen Victoria wore which parts of her bridal lace and when she allowed others to wear it, see Kay Staniland and Santina M. Levey, "Queen Victoria's Wedding Dress and Lace."

32. Eric Hobsbawm, "Introduction: Inventing Traditions," in *The Invention of Tradition*, eds Eric Hobsbawm and Terence Ranger (Cambridge: Cambridge University Press, 1983), 1.

33. *The Etiquette of Courtship and Matrimony: With a Complete Guide to the Forms of a Wedding* (London: David Bogue, 1852), 62; *The Mystery of Love, Courtship, and Marriage Explained* (New York: Wehman Bros., 1890).

34. For international reinterpretations of French fashion plates, see Karin J. Bohleke, "Americanizing French Fashion Plates: *Godey's* and *Peterson's* Cultural and Socio-Economic Translation of *Les Modes Parisiennes*," *American Periodicals: A Journal of History, Criticism, and Bibliography* 20, no. 2 (2010): 120–55. For specifically British commercial tie-ins, see Phegley, *Courtship and Marriage in Victorian England*, 108. For the rise of the wedding industry within the American context, see Vicki Jo Howard, "American Weddings: Gender, Consumption, and the Business of Brides" (Ph.D. diss., University of Texas, 2000) and Barbara Penner, "A Vision of Love and Luxury, the Commercialization of Nineteenth-Century American Weddings" *Winterthur Portfolio* 39, no. 1 (Spring 2004): 1–20.

35. For a survey of dress for these rites of passage, see Phillis Cunnington and Catherine Lucas, *Costumes for Births, Marriages, and Deaths* (London: A.&C. Black, 1972). For the relationships between invented traditions and commercial culture within the American context, see Leigh Eric Schmidt, *Consumer Rites: The Buying & Selling of American Holidays* (Princeton: Princeton University Press, 1995).

36. The key text for understanding mourning dress is Lou Taylor, *Mourning Dress: A Costume and Social History* (New York: Routledge, [1983] 2010). See also Anne Buck, "The Trap Re-Baited: Mourning Dress 1860–1890," *Costume* 2, no. 1 (March 1968): 32–7 and, for mourning jewelry, Patricia Campbell Warner, "Mourning and Memorial Jewelry of the Victorian Age," *Dress* 12 (1986), 55–60.

37. To take as a single example, what was printed as a letter from Mme L . . . ., TOULOUSE to *La Dernière mode*, published in the October 4, 1874 issue in which the author—Mallarmé—replies, "For you will be glad to question me on the strict etiquette of mourning: black cashmere and crêpe during the first six months, black silk and smooth black crêpe during the six which follow; finally, grey, violet or black during the last six weeks. Yes, one wears mourning for a father-in-law just as for a father." Philip Nicholas Furbank and Alex M. Cain, eds, *Mallarmé on Fashion*, 86–7.

38. Annette Becker, "Walker's Mourning Ensemble: Mourning Practices and Local Culture in Late Nineteenth-Century Aberdeen, Mississippi," unpublished ms., 2013.

39. In "The Trap Re-Baited," Anne Buck claims that "Letters to women's journals reveal that the etiquette of mourning was a matter of concern to many who, not accustomed to its rules and restrictions, were anxious not to transgress them," 32–7. Yet, as mourning was a consistently repeating occurrence, the anxiety appears generated rather than relieved by women's journals. Buck also points to the formation in England in 1875 of The National Funeral Mourning Reform Association to address issues of "excessive mourning" becoming conventionalized to the financial detriment of the populace—save the funeral industry, 37.

40. Lou Taylor, *Mourning Dress*, 188.

41. See James Steven Curl, "Funerals, Ephemera, and Mourning," in *The Victorian Celebration of Death* (Thrupp: Sutton, 2000), 194–221. For mourning culture and the technological transformations—such as embalming—that came about in order to deal with the deaths of 620,000 American soldiers, see Mark S. Schantz, *Awaiting the Heavenly Country: The Civil War and America's Culture of Death* (Ithaca and London: Cornell University Press, 2008).

42. Lou Taylor, *Mourning Dress*, 136.

43. J.C. Flügel, *The Psychology of Clothes* (London: Hogarth Press and the Institute of Psycho-analysis, [1930] 1950), 111.

44. Flügel, *The Psychology of Clothes*, 110–11.

45. For an exploration of the relatively hushed manifestation of masculine sartorial display in the era, see Christopher Breward, "Renouncing Consumption: Men, Fashion, and Luxury, 1870–1914," in *Defining Dress: Dress as Object, Meaning, and Identity*, eds Amy de la Haye and Elizabeth Wilson (Manchester and New York: Manchester University Press, 1999), 48–62.

46. Perrot, *Fashioning the Bourgeoisie*, 127.

47. Deborah Cherry and Griselda Pollock, "Woman as Sign in Pre-Raphaelite Literature: The Representations of Elizabeth Siddal," in *Vision and Difference: Femininity, Feminism, and the Histories of Art*, ed. Griselda Pollock (London and New York: Routledge, 1988), 113.

48. Abigail Solomon-Godeau, "The Other Side of Venus: The Visual Economy of Feminine Display," in *The Sex of Things: Gender and Consumption in Historical Perspective*, ed. Victoria de Grazia (Berkeley: University of California Press, 1996), 113–50.

49. See also Kaja Silverman, "Fragments of a Fashionable Discourse," in *Studies in Entertainment: Critical Approaches to Mass Culture*, ed. Tania Modleski (Bloomington: Indiana University Press, 1986), 139–52.

50. Veblen explicitly points to the display aspect of the wife, describing her "vicarious leisure and consumption." Thorstein Veblen, *The Theory of the Leisure Class* (Oxford and New York: Oxford University Press, [1899] 2007), 57.

51. For other analyses of the corset, see the contributions of both Annette Becker and Ariel Beaujot in this volume.

52. Veblen, *The Theory of the Leisure Class*, 58 and Helene E. Roberts, "The Exquisite Slave: The Role of Clothes in the Making of the Victorian Woman," *Signs* 2, no. 3 (Spring 1977): 554–69.

53. William Tait, *Magdalenism: An Inquiry into its Extent, Causes, and Consequences of Prostitution in Edinburgh* (Edinburgh: P. Rickard, 1840), 63.

54. Susan Buck-Morss, "The Flâneur, the Sandwichman, and the Whore: The Politics of Loitering," *New German Critique* 13, no. 39 (Fall 1986): 120.

55. Legally regulated *maisons de tolerance* began in France around 1810. Women twice caught soliciting were obliged to register as prostitutes and take up residence in one of these establishments. For the French context, see Alain Corbin, *Women for Hire: Prostitution and Sexuality in France after 1850*, trans. Alan Sheridan (Cambridge, MA: Harvard University Press, [1978] 1990); Alexandre Parent-Duchâtelet, *La Prostitution à Paris au XIXe siècle*, ed. Alain Corbin (Paris: Éditions du Seuil, 1981); and Jill Harsin, *Policing Prostitution in Paris in the 19th Century* (Princeton: Princeton University Press, 1985). For the British context, see Judith R. Walkowitz, *Prostitution and Victorian Society: Women, Class, and the State* (Cambridge: Cambridge University Press, 1979).

56. Lynda Nead, *Myths of Sexuality: Representations of Women in Victorian Britain* (Oxford: Basil Blackwell, 1988), 92. See also Nead's later work, *Victorian Babylon: People, Streets and Images in Nineteenth-Century London* (New Haven and London: Yale University Press, 2000).

57. Hollis Clayson, *Painted Love: Prostitution in French Art of the Impressionist Era* (New Haven and London: Yale University Press, 1991), 58.

58. William Acton, *Prostitution Considered in its Moral, Social and Sanitary Aspects in London and Other Large Cities and Garrison Towns with Proposals for the Control and Prevention of its Attendant Evils* (London: John Churchill and Sons, 1857), 56.

59. "Quelle difference y-a-t-il à première vue, entre une grande dame et une petite dame? Leur costume est le même, ells vont au bois à la même heure, ells reçoivent les mêmes Messieurs . . ." Lithograph reproduced in Charles Bernheimer, *Figures of Ill Repute: Representing Prostitution in Nineteenth-Century France* (Cambridge, MA: Harvard University Press, 1989), 91.

60. "Peut-on et doit-on obliger les prostituées à porter un costume particulier?" Alexandre-Jean-Baptiste Parent-Duchâtelet, *De la prostitution dans la ville de Paris*, 3rd ed. (Paris: J.-B. Ballière et fils, 1857), 338.

61. Clayson, *Painted Love*, 56.

62. Tait, *Magdalenism*, 87.

63. Henry Mayhew, *London Labour and the London Poor*, vol. 4 (London: Griffin, Bohn & Co., 1862), 214.

64. Theodore Dreiser, *Sister Carrie* (New York: Doubleday, 1900). For a classic study of the manifestations of consumer culture in contemporary literature, see Rachel Bowlby, *Just*

Looking: Consumer Culture in Dreiser, Gissing, and Zola (New York: Methuen, 1985). For British representations of the "fallen woman," see Linda Nochlin, "Lost and Found: Once More the Fallen Woman," *Art Bulletin* 60, no. 1 (March 1978): 139–53. For an exploration of medical and political discourses framing the construction of a "love of finery" as causal to prostitution, see Mariana Valverde, "The Love of Finery: Fashion and the Fallen Woman in Nineteenth-Century Social Discourse," *Victorian Studies* 32, no. 2 (1989): 168–88.

65. Émile Zola, *The Ladies' Paradise: A Realistic Novel* (London: Vizetelly & Co., [1883] 1886), 8.

66. Peter Stallybrass, "Marx's Coat," in *Border Fetishisms: Material Objects in Unstable Spaces*, ed. Patricia Spyer (London: Routledge, 1998), 183–207.

67. For more on the second-hand circulation of clothes in the British context, see Vivienne Richmond, *Clothing the Poor in Nineteenth-Century England* (Cambridge: Cambridge University Press, 2013), as well as her chapter in this volume.

68. For an exploration of middle class women who did not "fall" into prostitution, but shoplifting instead, see Elaine S. Abelson, *When Ladies Go a-Thieving: Middle-Class Shoplifters in the Victorian Department Store* (New York and Oxford: Oxford University Press, 1989).

69. Michael B. Miller, *The Bon Marché: Bourgeois Culture and the Department Store, 1869–1920* (Princeton: Princeton University Press, 1981), 3.

70. See Louisa Iarocci, "Dressing Rooms: Women, Fashion, and the Department Store," in *The Places and Spaces of Fashion, 1800–2007*, ed. John Potvin (New York and London: Routledge, 2009), 169–85 and Christopher Breward, "Images of Desire: The Construction of the Feminine Consumer in Women's Fashion Journals, 1875–1890" (MA thesis: Royal College of Art, 1992).

71. Erika Diane Rappaport, *Shopping for Pleasure: Women in the Making of London's West End* (Princeton: Princeton University Press, 2000).

Chapter 5

1. Anne Oakley, *Sex, Gender, and Society* (London: Temple Smith, 1979); Sherry B. Ortner, *Making Gender: The Politics and Erotics of Culture* (Boston: Beacon Press, 1996); Robert Stoller, *Sex and Gender: On the Development of Masculinity and Femininity* (London: Hogarth Press Institute of Psychoanalysis, 1968). Many second wave feminist thinkers have made the argument that sex and gender are different phenomenon. Sex is defined by them as the biological difference between men and women in terms of genitalia and reproductive functions. Gender is defined as the cultural construction of masculinity and femininity. More recently it has been shown by scholars such as Judith Butler and Thomas Laqueur that sex has been culturally constructed. For Butler this has been done through the creation of the heterosexual normativity and Laqueur has made the argument for sex as a cultural construction by historicizing the one- and two-sex models. Thomas Walter Laqueur, *Making Sex: Body and Gender from the Greeks to Freud* (Cambridge: Harvard University Press, 2003); Judith Butler, *Gender Trouble: Feminism and the Subversion of Identity* (New York: Routledge, 1990).

2. Butler, *Gender Trouble*, viii.

3. Ibid., viii.

4. Ibid., viii–ix.

5. Joanne Entwistle, *The Fashioned Body: Fashion, Dress and Modern Social Theory* (Cambridge: Polity Press, 2000), 152.

6. Anne Hollander, *Sex and Suits* (New York: Alfred A. Knopf, 1994), 66.

7. For an overview about the ways in which finery and fashion were depicted as vices and attached to women through Christian texts and interpretations see: Efrat Tseëlon, *The Masque of Femininity: The Presentation of Woman in Everyday Life* (London: Sage, 1997), 12–16.

8. Laqueur, *Making Sex*.
9. Leonore Davidoff and Catherine Hall, *Family Fortunes: Men and Women of the English Middle Classes* (London: Hutchinson, 1987).
10. Thorstein Veblen, *The Theory of the Leisure Class: An Economic Study of Institutions* (New York: Macmillan, 1953); J.C. Flügel, *The Psychology of Clothes* (London: Hogarth Press, 1930).
11. Valerie Steele, *Fetish: Fashion, Sex, and Power* (Oxford: Oxford University Press, 1996), 22.
12. Entwistle, *The Fashioned Body*, 183.
13. Steele, *Fetish*, 9.
14. Sigmund Freud, *Three Contributions to the Theory of Sex*, trans. Abraham Brill (Auckland: The Floating Press, 2003), 45.
15. Ibid., 27–8.
16. Sigmund Freud, "Fetishism," trans. J. Strachey, in *The Complete Psychological Works of Sigmund Freud* XXI (London: Hogarth and the Institute of Psychoanalysis), 153–4.
17. Michel Foucault, *The History of Sexuality Volume I: An Introduction*, trans. Robert Hurley (New York: Vintage Books, 1990), 127–8.
18. Foucault, *The History of Sexuality Volume I*, 154.
19. Butler, *Gender Trouble*, 11. Butler criticizes feminists for essentializing womanhood, or thinking of women as having particular traits she calls maternal. For Butler, this understanding of womanhood is false because sex/gender is an illusion. The maternal feminist position has become powerful and hegemonic, according to Butler, and the framework reinforces the idea of masculinity and femininity as real positions rather than cultural constructs. See Butler, 84.
20. Ibid., 180.
21. Ibid., 67.
22. Ibid., 58.
23. Ibid., 90.
24. Ibid., 172–3.
25. Ibid., 187.
26. Ibid., 179.
27. Matt Houlbrook, "'The Man with the Powder Puff' in Interwar London," *The Historical Journal* 50, no. 1 (March, 2007): 147–71.
28. Flügel, *The Psychology of Clothes*, 111.
29. Ibid., 113.
30. This argument is also made by American sociologist Thorstein Veblen. Veblen, *The Theory of the Leisure Class*.
31. Flügel, *The Psychology of Clothes*, 118.
32. Hollander, *Sex and Suits*, 65–6, 79.
33. Hardy Amies, *The Englishman's Suit* (London: Quartet Books, 1994), 2–3.
34. David Kuchta, "The Making of the Self-Made Man: Class, Clothing and English Masculinity, 1688–1832," in *The Sex of Things: Gender and Consumption in Historical Perspective*, eds Victoria de Grazia and Hellen Furlough (Berkeley: University of California Press, 1996), 55–62. See also David Kuchta, *The Three-Piece Suit and Modern Masculinity England, 1550–1850* (Berkley: University of California Press, 2002).
35. Christopher Breward, *The Hidden Consumer: Masculinities, Fashion, and City Life 1860–1914* (Manchester: Manchester University Press, 1999); Brent Shannon, *The Cut of His Coat: Men, Dress, and Consumer Culture in Britain, 1860–1914* (Athens: Ohio University Press, 2006); Brent Shannon, "Refashioning Men: Fashion, Masculinity, and the Cultivation of the Male Consumer in Britain, 1860–1914," *Victorian Studies* 46, no. 4 (Summer, 2004): 596–630.
36. Ariel Beaujot, "If you want to get ahead, get a hat: Manliness, power, and politics via the top hat," forthcoming.

37. For a discussion of dandies in real life and fiction see Rhonda K. Garelick, *Rising Star: Dandyism, Gender, and Performance in the Fin De Siècle* (Princeton: Princeton University Press, 1998), 6–10. The first dandy is said to have been Coke of Norfolk, a British landowner who rode to London in the 1760s and had a meeting with King George wearing his riding clothes. Riding clothes, according to Amies, was the origin of the three-piece suit, the future dandy uniform. Amies, *The Englishman's Suit;* Susan Fillin-Yeh, "Introduction: New Strategies for a Theory of Dandies" in *Dandies: Fashion and Fineness in Art and Culture* (New York: New York University Press, 2001), 8.

38. Shannon, *The Cut of his Coat*, 130. For information on how clothes were made so that men appeared like Greek athletes see Hollander, *Sex and Suits*, 90–1.

39. Shannon, *The Cut of his Coat*, 130.

40. Garelick, *Rising Star*, 3; Christopher Breward, "The Dandy Laid Bare: Embodying practices and fashion for men," in *Fashion Cultures: Theories, Explorations, and Analysis,* eds Stella Bruzzi and Pamela Church Gibson (London: Routledge, 2000), 223.

41. Garelick, *Rising Star*, 3.

42. Susan Fillin-Yeh, *Dandies: Fashion and Finesse in Art and Culture* (New York: New York University Press, 2001), 4.

43. Garelick, *Rising Star*, 5.

44. Shannon, *The Cut of his Coat*, 131; for a discussion of types of ideal masculinity see Christopher Breward, "Renouncing consumption: Men, fashion and luxury, 1870–1914," in *Defining Dress: Dress as Object, Meaning, and Identity,* eds Amy de la Haye and Elizabeth Wilson (Manchester: Manchester University Press, 1999), 53.

45. Ellen Moers, *The Dandy: Brummel to Beerbohm* (London: Secker and Warburg, 1960), 229.

46. James Eli Adams, "Dandyism and late Victorian masculinity," in *Oscar Wilde in Context,* eds Kerry Powell and Peter Raby (Cambridge: Cambridge University Press, 2013), 223–4.

47. "Mr. Oscar Wilde," *Freeman's Journal and Daily Commercial Advertiser* (Dublin, Ireland), Tuesday, February 21, 1882: 7.

48. "Mr. Oscar Wilde," *Freeman's Journal and Daily Commercial Advertiser* (Dublin, Ireland), Tuesday, February 21, 1882: 7. See also David Friedman, *Wilde in America: Oscar Wilde and the Invention of Modern Celebrity* (New York: W.W Norton & Co., 2014).

49. Sean Nixon, "Exhibiting Masculinity," in *Representation: Cultural Representations and Signifying Practices*, ed. Stuart Hall (Thousand Oaks: Sage, 1997), 297; Jon Stratton, *The Desirable Body* (Manchester: Manchester University Press, 1996), 120–1, 182.

50. Shannon, *The Cut of his Coat*, 158.

51. Breward, "The Dandy Laid Bare," 231.

52. Ibid., 232.

53. Shannon, *The Cut of his Coat*, 132–46.

54. Steele, *The Corset*, 33.

55. Ibid., 44, 52. For more details about the size of Victorian waists see Christine Bayles Kortsch, *Dress Culture in Late Victorian Women's Fiction: Literacy, Textiles, and Activism* (Surrey: Ashgate, 2009), 75.

56. Entwistle, *The Fashioned Body*, 196.

57. Steele, *The Corset*, 26–7, 36.

58. Ibid., 15–16. While the French called their corsets "corps" early English corsets were similarly called "whalebone bodies."

59. Ibid., 60; Jill Fields, *An Intimate Affair: Women, Lingerie, and Sexuality* (Berkeley: University of California Press, 2007), 62.

60. Steele, *The Corset*, 6.

61. Ibid., 12.

62. Hollander, *Sex and Suits*, 139.

63. Steele, *The Corset*, 13.

64. Hollander, *Sex and Suits*, 138–40.

65. Steele, *The Corset*, 28, 36.

66. Leigh Summers, *Bound to Please: A History of the Victorian Corset* (Oxford: Berg, 2001); Lois Banner, *American Beauty* (New York: Knopf, 1983), 48–9.

67. Veblen, *The Theory of the Leisure Class*, 172.

68. Hélène Roberts, "The Exquisite Slave: The Role of Clothes in the Making of the Victorian Woman," *Signs* 2, no. 3 (Spring 1977): 557.

69. David Kunzle, *Fashion and Fetishism: Corsets, Tight Lacing, and other Forms of Body Sculpture* (New York: Rowman and Littlefield, 1982), 2.

70. David Kunzle, "Dress Reform as Antifeminism: A Response to Hélène E. Roberts's 'The Exquisite Slave: The Role of Clothes in the Making of Victorian Women,'" *Signs* 2, no. 3 (Spring, 1977): 570–9.

71. Hollander, *Sex and Suits*, 140–1.

72. Steele, *The Corset*, 50–1.

73. Michel Foucault, *Discipline and Punish: The Birth of the Prison*, trans. Alan Sheridan (New York: Vintage Books, 1979), 25–6.

74. Fields, *An Intimate Affair*, 48.

75. Havelock Ellis, "An Anatomical Vindication of the Straight Front Corset," *Current Literature*, 48 (February, 1910): 172–4.

76. Ellis, "An Anatomical Vindication of the Straight Front Corset."

77. Valerie Steele, *Fashion and Eroticism: Ideals of Feminine Beauty from the Victorian Era to the Jazz Age* (New York: Oxford University Press, 1985), 169.

78. Mme. Roxey A. Caplin, *Health and Beauty; or corsets and clothing constructed in accordance with the physiological laws of the human body* (London: Darton & Co., 1854) as quoted in Steele, *The Corset*, 41.

79. Patricia Anderson, *When Passion Reigned: Sex and the Victorians* (New York: BasicBooks, 1995), 31.

80. Steele, *Fashion and Eroticism*, 161, 176.

81. Ibid., 176.

82. Ibid., p. 176; Steele, *The Corset*, 45–6; Anderson, *When Passion Reigned*, 32.

83. Entwistle, *The Fashioned Body*, 196.

84. Elizabeth Wilson, *Adorned in Dreams: Fashion and Modernity* (Berkeley: University of California Press, 1987), 97.

85. Steele, *Fetish*, 58. Hollander also views tight lacing as uncommon, Hollander, *Sex and Suits*, 141.

86. Steele, *Fetish*, 59.

87. A Male Wasp Waist, *The Family Doctor* (June 26, 1886), 263, as quoted in Valerie Steele, *Fashion and Eroticism*, 180.

Chapter 6

1. Wilkie Collins, *The Moonstone* (London: Penguin, [1868] 1994), 198.

2. Beverly Lemire, *The Business of Everyday Life: Gender, Practice, and Social Politics in England, c. 1600–1900* (Manchester: Manchester University Press, 2005), 110.

3. John Styles, *The Dress of the People: Everyday Fashion in Eighteenth-Century England* (New Haven and London: Yale University Press, 2007), 109.

4. Beverly Lemire, *Cotton* (Oxford: Berg, 2011), 126.

5. Robert Woods, *The Population of Britain in the Nineteenth Century* (Cambridge: Cambridge University Press, 1995), 10, 15.

6. Mark Blaug, "The Myth of the Old Poor Law and the Making of the New," *The Journal of Economic History* 23, no. 2 (June 1963): 151–84; Jose Harris, *Private Lives, Public Spirit: Britain 1870–1914* (London: Penguin, 1994), 41–3, 127; Woods, *Population of Britain*, 14.

7. Dudley Pope, *Life in Nelson's Navy* (London: Allen and Unwin, 1981), 163; Diana de Marly, *Working Dress: A History of Occupational Costume* (London: Batsford, 1986), 7; Vanda Foster, *A Visual History of Costume: The Nineteenth Century* (London: Batsford, 1992), 15.

8. Brian Maidment, "101 Things to do with a Fantail Hat: Dustmen, Dirt, and Dandyism, 1820–1860," *Textile History* 33, no. 1 (May 2002): 86.

9. Vivienne Richmond, *Clothing the Poor in Nineteenth-Century England* (Cambridge: Cambridge University Press, 2013), 123–4. See also Angela V. John, *By the Sweat of Their Brow: Women Workers at the Victorian Coal Mines* (London: Croom Helm, 1980).

10. Styles, *The Dress of the People*, 31–45.

11. For the growing working-class use of cotton fabrics in the eighteenth century, see Styles, *Dress of the People*, Chapter 7 and Beverly Lemire, *Fashion's Favourite: The Cotton Trade and the Consumer in Britain, 1660–1800* (Oxford: Pasold Research Fund and Oxford University Press, 1991), 96–108.

12. Edward Boys Ellman, *Recollections of a Sussex Parson* (London: Skeffington & Son, 1912), 21, 23.

13. Lemire, *Cotton*, 26.

14. Ibid., 58–60.

15. Jan de Vries, *The Industrious Revolution: Consumer Behavior and the Household Economy, 1650 to the Present* (Cambridge: Cambridge University Press, 2008), 137.

16. Friedrich Engels, *The Condition of the Working Class in England* (London: Penguin, [1845] 1987), 102.

17. Before decimalization in 1971, Britain used a monetary system of pounds (£), shillings (s), and pence (d). There were twelve pence/12d to one shilling/1s, and twenty shillings/20s to one pound/£1. Decimalization replaced this with a system of new pence and pounds (no shillings), in which one hundred new pence (100p) equals one pound (£1); 2½d were worth approximately 1p.

18. Engels, *The Condition of the Working Class*, 103.

19. Mary Thale (ed.), *The Autobiography of Francis Place* (Cambridge: Cambridge University Press, 1972), 51–2. Linsey woolsey was a flax and wool mix fabric, subsequently cotton and wool, often home-woven and coarse.

20. Engels, *The Condition of the Working Class*, 102.

21. Sarah Levitt, "Cheap Mass-produced Men's Clothing in the Nineteenth and Early Twentieth Centuries," *Textile History* 22, no. 2 (January 1991): 179–80.

22. See, for example, *The Family Economist* 1 (1854): 22.

23. Engels, *The Condition of the Working Class*, 102–3.

24. For an introduction to the 1832 Reform Act, see Eric J. Evans, *The Great Reform Act of 1832* (London: Methuen, 1983).

25. For an introduction to the Poor Law, see Anne Digby, *The Poor Law in Nineteenth-century England and Wales* (London: The Historical Association, 1982). For an introduction to Chartism, see Malcolm Chase, *Chartism: A New History* (Manchester: Manchester University Press, 2007).

26. Paul Pickering, "Class Without Words: Symbolic Communication in the Chartist movement," *Past and Present* 112 (August 1986): 144–62. The Chartists had six aims, contained in the People's Charter from which the movement's name derived: universal male suffrage, equal-sized electoral districts, vote by secret ballot, payment for MPs, no property qualification to stand as an MP. The sixth, annual Parliaments, has never been introduced.

27. John Belchem, *Popular Radicalism in Nineteenth-Century Britain* (Basingstoke: Macmillan, 1996), 93–4. See also Lemire, *Business of Everyday Life*, 132–3.

28. Lemire, *Cotton*, 126–7.

29. A Journeyman Engineer, *Some Habits and Customs of the Working Classes* (London: Tinsley Brothers, 1867), 188–9.

30. F.K. Prochaska, "Philanthropy," in *The Cambridge Social History of Britain 1750–1950*, vol. 3., ed. F.M.L. Thompson (Cambridge: Cambridge University Press, 1990), 357.

31. Steven King and Christiana Payne, "The Dress of the Poor," *Textile History* 33, no. 1 (May 2002): 3.

32. Richmond, *Clothing the Poor*, 134–5; Laura Ugolini, *Men and Menswear: Sartorial Consumption in Britain 1880–1939* (Aldershot: Ashgate, 2007), 29.

33. Steven King, *Poverty and Welfare in England 1700–1850* (Manchester University Press, 2000), 158; Eric J. Evans, *The Forging of the Modern State: Early Industrial Britain 1783–1870* (Harlow: Longman, 1983), 402.

34. Richmond, *Clothing the Poor*, 189–93.

35. Ibid., 272–8.

36. Boyd Hilton, *The Age of Atonement: The Influence of Evangelicalism on Social and Economic Thought, 1795–1865* (Oxford: Clarendon, 1988).

37. Samuel Smiles, *Self-Help; With Illustrations of Character and Conduct* (Boston: Tickner & Fields [1859] 1861), 285.

38. F.K. Prochaska, *Women and Philanthropy in 19th Century England* (Oxford: Clarendon Press, 1980).

39. F.K. Prochaska, "A Mother's Country: Mothers' Meetings and Family Welfare in Britain, 1850–1950," *History* 74, no. 242 (1989): 390.

40. Collins, *The Moonstone*, 198–9.

41. Richmond, *Clothing the Poor*, Ch. 8.

42. Prochaska, "A mother's country."

43. Richmond, *Clothing the Poor*, 193–211.

44. A Lady, *The Workwoman's Guide Containing Instructions to the Inexperienced in Cutting out and Completing Those Articles of Wearing Apparel, &c, Which are Usually Made at Home* (London: Simpkin, Marshall and Co.; Birmingham: Thomas Evans, 1838), 16, 29.

45. *Rules for the Clothing Club at Stutton* (Ipswich, 1833).

46. Ibid.

47. *The Fifth Annual Report of the Ladies' Benevolent Society, Liverpool* (Liverpool, 1815), 9; *St. Jude's, S. Kensington Parish Magazine* 11, no. 1 (1894). Linsey was a shortened form of linsey-woolsey. Grogram was a coarse fabric of silk, or silk mixed with wool and mohair.

48. It must be acknowledged that sincere evangelicals decried the wearing of finery by all classes, but not all evangelicals were sincere.

49. Jennifer Craik, *Uniforms Exposed: From Conformity to Transgression* (Oxford: Berg, 2005), 4.

50. Except when parents (or other close relatives) and children were employed in the same factories. See Jan Lambertz, "Sexual Harassment in the Nineteenth Century English Cotton Industry," *History Workshop Journal* 19 (1985), 29–61.

51. Richmond, *Clothing the Poor*, 144–5, 148–9.

52. *Census of Great Britain, 1851. Population Tables. II. Ages, Civil Condition, Occupations, and Birth-place of the People: With the Numbers and Ages of the Blind, the Deaf-and-Dumb, and the Inmates of Workhouses, Prisons, Lunatic Asylums, and Hospitals, Vol. I*, (London: HMSO, 1854), cxxii, cxxvi.

53. *Census of England and Wales. 1901. General Report with Appendices* (London: HMSO, 1904), 272, 278.

54. Edward Higgs, "Domestic Service and Household production," in *Unequal Opportunities: Women's Employment in England 1800–1918*, ed. Angela V. John (Oxford: Basil Blackwell, 1986), 125–50; Theresa M. McBride, *The Domestic Revolution: The Modernisation of Household Service in England and France, 1820–1920* (London: Croom Helm, 1976), 20. For an excellent general introduction to nineteenth-century domestic service see also *Useful Toil: Autobiographies of Working People From the 1820s to the 1920s*, ed. John Burnett (London: Routledge, 1994), 127–71.

55. Lemire, *Fashion's Favourite*, 96.

56. Burnett, *Useful Toil*, 144–5.

57. Emma Leslie, *Myra's Pink Dress* (London: Sunday School Union, 1873).

58. John Trusler, *Trusler's Domestic Management, or the Art of Conducting a Family, with Economy, Frugality & Method* (Bath: 1819), 41, 56.

59. Anon. [The Brothers Mayhew], *The Greatest Plague of Life: or The Adventures of a Lady in Search of a Good Servant* (Philadelphia: Carey and Hart, 1847), 55–6, 124.

60. Anon., *The New Female Instructor. Or, Young Woman's Guide to Domestic Happiness; Being an Epitome of all the Acquirements Necessary to Form the Female Character, in Every Class of Life: With Examples of Illustrious Women, etc.* (London: Thomas Kelly, 1824), 373; Anon., *The Management of Servants. A Practical Guide to the Routine of Domestic Service* (London: Warne and Co., 1880), 79.

61. Alison Adburgham, *Shops and Shopping 1800–1914: Where and in What Manner the Well-dressed Englishwoman Bought Her Clothes*, 2nd ed. (London: Allen & Unwin, 1981), 195.

62. Anon., *Every Woman's Encyclopaedia* (London: Amalgamated Press, 1910–11), 14.

63. John Burnett (ed.), *Destiny Obscure: Autobiographies of Childhood, Education and Family from the 1820s to the 1920s* (London: Routledge, 1994), 308.

64. William Lanceley, *From Hall-Boy to House Steward* (London: E. Arnold, 1925), 190.

65. *Daily News*, 9 September 1897: 6.

66. For a discussion of these challenges, and for examples of wealthier people adopting working-class dress styles, see Richmond, *Clothing the Poor*, 42–50. Philippe Perrot also points out men's exchange of breeches for trousers as an example of the upward spread of a plebeian dress style. Philippe Perrot, *Fashioning the Bourgeoisie: A History of Clothing in the Nineteenth Century* (Princeton: Princeton University Press, 1994), 31.

67. Richmond, *Clothing the Poor*, 220.

68. Prochaska, "Philanthropy," 366.

69. Anna Davin, *Growing Up Poor: Home, School and Street in London 1870–1914* (London: Rivers Oram, 1996), 69–74; Ellen Ross, *Love and Toil: Motherhood in Outcast London, 1870–1918* (Oxford: Oxford University Press, 1993), 12.

70. Richmond, *Clothing the Poor*, 130–4.

71. *Census of Great Britain, 1851. Population Tables. II*, cxxii, cxxvi.

72. Herbert P. Miller, *The Scarcity of Domestic Servants; The Cause and Remedy. With a Short Outline of the Law Relating to Master and Domestic Servant* (London, 1876), 16–17.

73. Richmond, *Clothing the Poor*, 223–41.

Chapter 7

1. Mary Ellen Roach-Higgins and Joanne B. Eicher, "Dress and Identity," *Clothing and Textiles Research Journal* 10, no. 4 (1992): 2.

2. Joanne B. Eicher and Barbara Sumberg, "World Fashion, Ethnic and National Dress," in *Dress and Ethnicity: Change Across Space and Time*, ed. Joanne B. Eicher (Oxford: Berg, 1995), 299.

3. See Elizabeth Wilson, *Adorned in Dreams: Fashion and Modernity* (Berkeley: University of California Press, 1987); Fred Davis, *Fashion, Culture, and Identity* (Chicago: University of Chicago Press, 1992); and Diana Crane, *Fashion and Its Social Agendas* (Chicago: University of Chicago Press, 2000).

4. See Leslie W. Rabine, *The Global Circulation of African Fashion* (Oxford: Berg, 2002); Jennifer Craik, *The Face of Fashion: Cultural Studies in Fashion* (London: Routledge, 1993); and Suzane Baizerman, Joanne B. Eicher, and Catherine Cerny, "Eurocentrism in the Study of Ethnic Dress," in *The Visible Self: Global Perspectives on Dress, Culture, and Society*, eds, Joanne B. Eicher, Sandra Lee Evenson, and Hazel A. Lutz (New York: Fairchild, 2008).

5. Jan Morris, *Pax Britannica: The Climax of Empire* (London: Penguin, 1979), 46.

6. Eric J. Hobsbawm, *The Age of Empire: 1875–1914* (New York: Vintage, 1989), 14.

7. Stephen E. Cornell and Douglas Hartmann, *Ethnicity and Race: Making Identities in a Changing World* (Thousand Oaks, CA: Sage, 2007), 20.

8. See Christopher Breward, *The Culture of Fashion* (Manchester: Manchester University Press, 1995), 8–40 and Wilson, *Adorned in Dreams*, 16–26.

9. Ruth Benedict, "Dress," in *Fashion Foundations: Early Writings on Fashion and Dress*, eds, Kim K.P. Johnson, Susan J. Torntore, and Joanne B. Eicher (Oxford: Berg, 2003), 29–34.

10. See Baizerman, Eicher, and Cerny, "Eurocentrism in the Study of Ethnic Dress."

11. See Michael Banton, *Racial Theories* (Cambridge: Cambridge University Press, 1998) and Richard Jenkins, *Rethinking Ethnicity* (London: Sage, 2008).

12. See Christine Bolt, *Victorian Attitudes to Race* (London: Routledge and Kegan Paul, 1971) and Stephen Jay Gould, *The Mismeasure of Man* (London: Penguin Books, 1997).

13. Charles Darwin, *The Descent of Man* (London: John Murray, 1871).

14. Sophie White, *Wild Frenchmen and Frenchified Indians: Material Culture and Race in Colonial Louisiana* (Philadelphia: University of Pennsylvania Press, 2012), 1.

15. Helen Bradley Foster, *"New Raiments of Self": African American Clothing in the Antebellum South* (Oxford: Berg, 1997), 134.

16. Jenkins, *Rethinking Ethnicity*, 111–27.

17. Foster, *"New Raiments of Self,"* 1–4.

18. Sarah Cheang, "Roots: Hair and Race," in *Hair: Styling, Culture, and Fashion*, eds, Geraldine Biddle-Perry and Sarah Cheang (Oxford: Berg, 2008), 31–2.

19. See Shane White and Graham White, *Stylin': African American Expressive Culture from Its Beginnings to the Zoot Suit* (Ithaca, NY: Cornell University Press, 1998).

20. Foster, *"New Raiments of Self,"* 136–7.

21. Ibid., 139.

22. Ibid.

23. Ibid., 78.

24. See White and White, *Stylin'*, and Monica L. Miller, *Slaves to Fashion: Black Dandyism and the Styling of Black Diasporic Identity* (Durham: Duke University Press, 2009).

25. Miller, *Slaves to Fashion*, 85–7.

26. Ibid., 90.

27. White and White, *Stylin'*, 85–124.

28. Cited in White and White, *Stylin'*, 94.

29. Susan Kaiser, Leslie Rabine, Carol Hall, and Karyl Ketchum, "Beyond Binaries: Respecting the Improvisation in African-American Style," in *Black Style*, ed. Carol Tulloch (London: V&A Publications, 2007), 51. See also Carol Tulloch, *The Birth of Cool: Style Narratives of the African Diaspora* (London: Bloomsbury, 2016).

30. See Martin W. Lewis and Kären E. Wigen, *The Myth of Continents: A Critique of Metageography* (Berkeley: University of California Press, 1997), 104–23.

31. See Sylvia H. Bliss, "The Significance of Clothes," in *Fashion Foundations: Early Writings on Fashion and Dress*, eds, Kim K.P. Johnson, Susan J. Torntore, and Joanne B. Eicher (Oxford: Berg, 2003), 19.

32. See Foster, *"New Raiments of Self,"* 61–4 and Pedro Machado, "Awash in a Sea of Cloth: Gujarat, Africa, and the Western Indian Ocean, 1300–1800," in *The Spinning World: A Global History of Cotton Textiles, 1200–1850*, eds, Giorgio Riello and Prasannan Parthasarathi (Oxford: Oxford University Press, 2009), 161–80.

33. See Ruth Nielsen, "The History and Development of Wax-Printed Textiles Intended for West Africa and Zaire," in *The Fabrics of Culture: The Anthropology of Clothing and Adornment*, eds, Justine M. Cordwell and Ronald A. Schwartz (The Hague: Mouton Publishers, 1979), 467–98, and Nina Sylvanus, "The Fabric of Africanity: Tracing the Global Threads of Authenticity," *Anthropological Theory* 7, no. 2 (2007): 201–16.

34. See Rabine, *The Global Circulation of African Fashion*, 135–68, and Jean Allman, "Fashioning Africa: Power and the Politics of Dress" in *Fashioning Africa: Power and the Politics of Dress*, ed. Jean Allman (Bloomington, IN: Indiana University Press, 2004).

35. See Ulf Hannerz, *Transnational Connections: Culture, People, Places* (London: Routledge, 1996).

36. See Christian Karner, *Ethnicity and Everyday Life* (London: Routledge, 2007), 21–3 and Jenkins, *Rethinking Ethnicity*, 93.

37. See Emma Tarlo, *Clothing Matters: Dress and Identity in India* (London: Hurst, 1996), 23–61.

38. Tarlo, *Clothing Matters*, 52.

39. See Homi Bhabha, *The Location of Culture* (London: Routledge, 1994).

40. John Forbes Watson, *Textile Manufactures and the Costumes of the People of India* (London: George Edward Eyre & William Spottiswoode for the India Office, 1866).

41. See Felix Driver and Sonia Ashmore, "The Mobile Museum: Collecting and Circulating Indian Textiles in Victorian Britain," *Victorian Studies* 52, no. 3 (Spring 2010): 353–85.

42. John Forbes Watson and John William Kaye, *The People of India: A Series of Photographic Illustrations with Descriptive Letterpress, of the Races and Tribes of Hindustan* (London: C. Whiting, 1868–75). See also Christopher Pinney, *Camera Indica: The Social Life of Photographs* (London: Reaktion Books, 1997), 16–71.

43. Bernard S. Cohn, "Representing Authority in Victorian India," in *The Invention of Tradition*, eds, Eric Hobsbawm and Terence Ranger (Cambridge: Cambridge University Press, 1983), 183.

44. Jane Tynan, *British Army Uniform and the First World War: Men in Khaki* (Basingstoke: Palgrave Macmillan, 2013), 131–42.

45. See Cohn, "Representing Authority in Victorian India," 176–7.

46. Ibid., 106–62, Donald Clay Johnson, "Clothes Make the Empire: British Dress in India," in *Dress Sense: Emotional and Sensory Experiences of the Body and Clothes*, eds Donald Clay Johnson and Helen Bradley Foster (Oxford: Berg, 2007), xx.

47. Nupur Chaudhuri, "Shawls, Jewelry, Curry, and Rice in Victorian Britain," in *Western Women and Imperialism: Complicity and Resistance*, eds, Nupur Chaudhuri and Margaret Strobel (Bloomingon: Indiana University Press, 1992), 231–46.

48. See Nandi Bhatia, "Fashioning Women in Colonial India: The Political Utility of Clothes in Colonial India," *Fashion Theory* 7 no. 3/4 (September 2003): 327–44.

49. See Helen Calloway, "Dressing for Dinner in the Bush: Rituals of Self-Definition and British Imperial Authority," in *Dress and Gender: Making and Meaning in Cultural Contexts*, eds, Ruth Barnes and Joanne B. Eicher (Oxford: Berg, 1992), 232–47.

50. Chitralekha Zutshi, "'Designed for Eternity': Kashmiri Shawls, Empire, and Cultures of Production and Consumption in Mid-Victorian Britain," *Journal of British Studies* 48, no. 2 (April 2009): 422.

51. Michelle Maskiell, "Consuming Kashmir: Shawls and Empires, 1500–2000," *Journal of World History* 13, no. 1 (Spring 2002): 33–4.

52. See Rosemary Crill, "Embroidery in Kashmir Shawls," in *Kashmir Shawls: The Tapi Collection*, eds, Steven Cohen, Rosemary Crill, Monique Lévi-Strauss, and Jeffrey B. Spurr (Mumbai: The Shoestring Publisher, 2012).

53. See Maskiell, "Consuming Kashmir."

54. Steven Cohen, "What is a Kashmir Shawl?" in *Kashmir Shawls*.

55. See Chaudhuri, "Shawls, Jewelry, Curry, and Rice in Victorian Britain."

56. Zutshi, "Designed for Eternity," 421.

57. See Lara Kriegel, "Narrating the subcontinent in 1851: India at the Crystal Palace," in *The Great Exhibition of 1851: New Interdisciplinary Essays*, ed. Louise Purbrick (Manchester: Manchester University Press, 2001), 146–78.

58. "A Chapter on Shawls," *Harper's New Monthly Magazine* 2, no. 7 (1850): 40–1.

59. Zutshi, "Designed for Eternity," 430.

60. Ibid., 440.

61. Chaudhuri, "Shawls, Jewelry, Curry, and Rice in Victorian Britain," 231–6.

62. See Jeffrey B. Spurr, "The Kashmir Shawl: Style and Markets," in *Kashmir Shawls,* 54–63.

63. Jenkins, *Rethinking Ethnicity*, 149.

64. Craik, *The Face of Fashion*, 177–203.

65. See Christopher Breward, *The Hidden Consumer: Masculinities, Fashion, and City Life 1860–1914* (Manchester: Manchester University Press, 1999).

66. See Regina Root, "Fashioning Independence: Gender, Dress and Social Space in Postcolonial Argentina," *The Latin American Fashion Reader*, ed. Regina Root (Oxford: Berg, 2005), 31–44.

67. See Elizabeth Kramer, "'Not So Japan-Easy': The British Reception of Japanese Dress in the Late Nineteenth Century," *Textile History* 44, no. 1 (May 2013), 3–24, and Penelope Francks, "Was Fashion a European Invention? The Kimono and Economic Development in Japan," *Fashion Theory* 19, no. 3 (June 2015), 331–62.

68. Toby Slade, *Japanese Fashion: A Cultural History* (Oxford: Berg, 2009), 41–9.

69. Kramer, "'Not So Japan-Easy' The British Reception of Japanese Dress in the Late Nineteenth Century," 9–10.

70. Francks, "Was Fashion a European Invention?" 337.

71. See Verity Wilson, *Chinese Dress* (London: V&A Publishing, 1986).

72. See Antonia Finnane, *Changing Clothes in China: Fashion, History, Nation* (London: Hurst, 2007), 139–67.

73. See Dorothy Ko, "Jazzing into Modernity: High Heels, Platforms and Lotus Shoes," in *China Chic: East Meets West*, eds Valerie Steele and John S. Major (New Haven: Yale University Press, 1999): 141–54.

74. Wessie Ling, *Fusionable Cheongsam* (Hong Kong: Hong Kong Arts Centre, 2007), 21.

75. Benedict, "Dress," 32.

Chapter 8

1. "Poiret, Creator of Fashions, Here," *The New York Times*, September 21, 1913.

2. Charles Baudelaire, "Salon of 1846," in *The Mirror of Art: Critical Studies by Charles Baudelaire*, ed. Jonathan Mayne (New York: Doubleday Anchor Books, 1956), 92.

3. Ibid., 88.

4. For a list, see Raymond Gaudriault, *La gravure de mode féminine en France* (Paris: Éditions de l'Amateur, 1983), 193–6.

5. As translated in Alice Mackrell, *An Illustrated History of Fashion: 500 Years of Fashion Illustration* (London: Batsford, 1997), 85.

6. Alison Adburgham, *Women in Print: Writing Women and Women's Magazines from the Restoration to the Accession of Victoria* (London: Allen and Unwin, 1972), 208.

7. The title is misleading as the original *merveilleuses* (like Mme Récamier) and *incroyables* were associated with the Directory and Vernet's father, Carle, had caricatured them, but these plates describe a new set of fashionable men and women at the end of the First Empire (c. 1810–14).

8. Alison Adburgham, *Women in Print,* 226.

9. Hazel Hahn, "Fashion Discourses in Fashion Magazines and Madame de Girardin's *Lettres parisiennes* in July-Monarchy France (1830–48)," *Fashion Theory* 9, no. 2 (June 2005): 211–12.

10. Annemarie Kleinert, *Le "Journal des dames et des modes": ou la conquête de l'Europe féminin (1797--1839)*, Beihefte zu Francia, Bd. 46 (Stuttgart: J. Thorbecke, 2001), 286.

11. For more on this, see Catherine Flood and Sarah Grant, *Style and Satire: Fashion in Print, 1777–1927* (London: V&A Publishing, 2014).

12. Gaudriault, *La gravure de mode féminine en France*, 70.

13. Peter McNeil, "Caricature and Fashion," in *The Berg Companion to Fashion*, ed. Valerie Steele (New York: Berg, 2010), 121.

14. Elizabeth Anne McCauley, "The Carte de Visite and Portrait Painting during the Second Empire," in *A.A.E. Disdéri and the Carte de Visite Portrait Photograph* (New Haven: Yale University Press, 1985), 149.

15. Nadar, "Salon de 1855. IV. M. Ingres," *Le Figaro*, no. 77 (September 16, 1855), 5. As translated in Heather McPherson, *The Modern Portrait in Nineteenth-Century France* (Cambridge: Cambridge University Press, 2001), 4.

16. Pierre Apraxine et al., *"La Divine Comtesse": Photographs of the Countess de Castiglione* (New Haven: Yale University Press, 2000).

17. Elizabeth Anne McCauley, "Photography, Fashion, and the Cult of Appearances," in *Impressionism, Fashion & Modernity*, ed. Gloria Groom (New Haven: Yale University Press, 2012).

18. For more on the advent of photography in fashion magazines, see Gaudriault, *La gravure de mode féminine en France*, 31–3, 101.

19. For more, see Gloria Groom, *Impressionism, Fashion & Modernity* (New Haven: Yale University Press, 2012).

20. Justine De Young, "Fashion and Intimate Portraits," in *Impressionism, Fashion & Modernity*, ed. Gloria Groom (New Haven: Yale University Press, 2012).

21. As translated in McCauley, "Photography, Fashion, and the Cult of Appearances," 206.

22. Harold Hutchison, *The Poster: An Illustrated History from 1860* (New York: Viking Press, 1968), 11.

23. H. Hazel Hahn, *Scenes of Parisian Modernity: Culture and Consumption in the Nineteenth Century* (New York: Palgrave Macmillan, 2009), 158.

24. Ibid., 155.

25. Ruth Iskin, *Modern Women and Parisian Consumer Culture in Impressionist Painting* (Cambridge: Cambridge University Press, 2007), 17.

26. Robert Herbert, "Seurat and Jules Chéret," *The Art Bulletin* 40, no. 2 (June 1958): 156–8.

27. Iskin, *Modern Women and Parisian Consumer Culture in Impressionist Painting*, 123. Iskin discusses the image in comparison to Caillebotte's 1877 *Paris Street: Rainy Day*.

28. Daniel Imbert, "Le monument des frères Morice, place de la République," in *Quand Paris dansait avec Marianne, 1879–1889* (Paris: Musée du Petit Palais, 1989), 32.

29. Paul Greenhalgh, *Art Nouveau, 1890–1914* (New York: Harry N. Abrams, 2000), 37.

30. Iskin, *Modern Women and Parisian Consumer Culture in Impressionist Painting*, 217. That said, I've been unable to find any period sources that confirm this idea commonly repeated by scholars.

31. Maurice Rheims, *19th Century Sculpture*, trans. Robert E. Wolf (New York: H.N. Abrams, 1977), 249.

32. James Holderbaum, "Portrait Sculpture," in *The Romantics to Rodin: French Nineteenth-Century Sculpture from North American Collections*, eds Peter Fusco and H. W. Janson (Los Angeles: Los Angeles County Museum of Art, 1980), 43.

33. Michelle Tolini Finamore, *Hollywood Before Glamour: Fashion in American Silent Film* (New York: Palgrave Macmillan, 2013), 80.

34. Caroline Evans, *The Mechanical Smile: Modernism and the First Fashion Shows in France and America, 1900–1929* (New Haven: Yale University Press, 2013), 32.

35. Ibid., 30.

36. Caroline Evans, "The Walkies: Early French Fashion Shows as a Cinema of Attractions," in *Fashion in Film*, ed. Adrienne Munich (Bloomington: Indiana University Press, 2011), 113.

37. Finamore, *Hollywood Before Glamour*, 77.

38. Ibid., 79.

39. Evans, *The Mechanical Smile*, 66.

40. Finamore, *Hollywood Before Glamour*, 77.

41. Nancy Hall-Duncan, *The History of Fashion Photography* (New York: Alpine Book Co., 1979), 26.

42. Mackrell, *An Illustrated History of Fashion*, 158.
43. Ibid., 158–9.
44. Ibid., 155.
45. Henry Bidou, "Le Bon ton," *Gazette du Bon Ton* 1, no. 1 (November 1912): 4.
46. Evans, "The Walkies: Early French Fashion Shows as a Cinema of Attractions," 110.
47. Ibid., 112.
48. Finamore, *Hollywood Before Glamour*, 36.
49. "Dress and the Picture," *Moving Picture World* 7, no. 2 (July 9, 1910): 74.
50. William Lord Wright, "Dame Fashion and the Movies," *Motion Picture Magazine* (September 1914): 107, 108.
51. Finamore, *Hollywood Before Glamour*, 46.
52. Ibid., 63.
53. Ibid., 62.
54. Randy Bryan Bigham, *Lucile, Her Life by Design: Sex, Style, and the Fusion of Theatre and Couture* (San Francisco: MacEvie Press Group, 2012), 177–85.
55. "A Model of the 'Movies'," *Cosmopolitan* LVII, no. 2 (July 1914): 262–3.
56. Finamore, *Hollywood Before Glamour*, 93–4.
57. "The Perils of Pauline," *Motography* XI, no. 7 (April 4, 1914): 6.
58. Wright, "Dame Fashion and the Movies," 110.

Chapter 9

1. Johann Wolfgang von Goethe, *The Sorrows of Young Werther and Novella*, trans. Elizabeth Mayer and Louise Brogan (New York: The Modern Library, 1993), 106.
2. David P. Phillips, "The Influence of Suggestion on Suicide: Substantive and Theoretical Implications of the Werther Effect," *American Sociological Review* 39, no. 3 (1974): 340–54.
3. Bruce Duncan, *Goethe's* Werther *and the Critics* (Rochester: Camden House, 2005), 1.
4. Martin Puchner et al, *The Norton Anthology of World Literature, Volume E* (New York: Norton, 2012), 99.
5. Catriona MacLeod, introduction to *The Sorrows of Young Werther*, by Johann Wolfgang von Goethe (New York: Barnes and Noble Classics, 2005), NOOK edition.
6. Ibid.
7. Jane Austen, *Northanger Abbey*, eds Barbara M. Benedict and Deirdre Le Faye (Cambridge: Cambridge University Press, 2006), 12.
8. Ibid., 13.
9. Ibid., 36–7.
10. Ibid., 222.
11. Charlotte Brontë, *Jane Eyre*, ed. Margaret Smith (Oxford: Oxford University Press, 2000), 268.
12. Catherine A. Milton, "A Heterogeneous Thing: Transvestism and Hybridity in *Jane Eyre*," in *Styling Texts: Dress and Fashion in Literature*, eds Cynthia Kuhn et. al. (Youngstown: Cambria, 2007), 198.
13. Brontë, *Jane Eyre*, 269.
14. In his discussion of "conspicuous consumption" Thorstein Veblen posited that one function of luxurious dress on a wife was to signal her husband's wealth and power. See Thorstein Veblen, *The Theory of the Leisure Class: An Economic Study of Institutions* (New York: The Macmillan Co., 1953).
15. See Edward W. Saïd's critique of nineteenth-century Western appropriations and constructions of the "Orient," in *Orientalism* (New York: Pantheon Books, 1978).
16. Bertha is the character to which Sandra M. Gilbert and Susan Gubar refer in the title of *The Madwoman in the Attic*, their pioneering feminist reading of women writers and Victorian

literature. See *The Madwoman in the Attic: The Woman Writer and the Nineteenth-Century Literary Imagination* (New Haven: Yale University Press, 1979).

17. Milton, "A Heterogeneous Thing," 202.
18. Antonia Finnane, "Yangzhou's 'Mondernity': Fashion and Consumption in the Early Nineteenth Century," *positions* 11, no. 2 (2003): 414.
19. Several English versions for this title exist. Finnane uses the literal translation "*Dreams of Wind and Moon.*" Purely for convenience I adopt here the title of the most recent full translation of the text: Patrick Hanan (trans.), *Courtesans and Opium: Romantic Illusions of the Fool of Yangzhou* (New York: Columbia University Press, 2009).
20. Finnane, "Yangzhou's 'Mondernity'," 412.
21. Hanan, *Courtesans*, 2.
22. Ibid., 72–3.
23. Ibid., 2.
24. Finnane, "Yangzhou's 'Mondernity'," 416. See also William T. Rowe, *China's Last Empire: The Great Qing* (Cambridge, MA: Harvard University Press, 2010), 84.
25. See Kristina Kleutghen, "Chinese Occidenterie: The Diversity of 'Western' Objects in Eighteenth-Century China," *Eighteenth-Century Studies* 47, no. 2 (2014): 118.
26. Cited in Finnane, "Yangzhou's 'Mondernity'," 412.
27. Finnane, "Yangzhou's 'Mondernity'," 413; Rowe, *China's Last Empire*, 84.
28. Paola Zamperini, "Clothes that Matter: Fashioning Modernity in Late Qing Novels," *Fashion Theory* 5, no. 2 (2001): 201.
29. Honoré de Balzac, *Père Goriot*, trans. Burton Raffel, ed. Peter Brooks (New York: Norton, 1994), 118.
30. Ibid., 91.
31. See Ulrich Lehmann, *Tigersprung: Fashion in Modernity* (Cambridge: MIT Press, 2000) and Valerie Steele, *Paris Fashion: A Cultural History* (Oxford: Berg, 1998).
32. Jonathan Mayne (ed.), *Art in Paris 1845–1862: Salons and Other Exhibitions Reviewed by Charles Baudelaire*, trans. Jonathan Mayne (New York: Phaidon, 1965), 118.
33. Balzac, *Père Goriot*, 389.
34. Ibid., 217.
35. Lest the case for similarities be overstated, it is important to note that Zamperini is also somewhat reluctant to ascribe the term "flâneur" to nineteenth-century China because, she persuasively submits, the French word might be "too site-specific, and does not include all the nuances" of Qing fictional masculinities. Zamperini, "Clothes that Matter," 210, n. 27.
36. Patrick Hanan, "Fengyue Meng and the Courtesan Novel," *Harvard Journal of Asiatic Studies* 58, no. 2 (1998): 349.
37. Ibid.
38. Ibid., 110.
39. Talia Schaffer, "Fashioning Aestheticism by Aestheticizing Fashion: Wilde, Beerbohm, and The Male Aesthetes' Sartorial Codes," *Victorian Literature and Culture* 28, no. 1 (2000): 39.
40. Ibid.
41. Ibid.: 42.
42. Ibid.
43. Gustave Flaubert, *Madame Bovary*, trans. Eleanor Marx Aveling and Paul de Man, ed. Margaret Cohen (New York: Norton, 2005), 223.
44. Nathaniel Hawthorne, *The Scarlet Letter*, ed. Brian Harding (Oxford: Oxford University Press, 2007), 43–4.
45. Ibid., 43.
46. Ibid., 44–5.
47. The subject of empires failing by way of social and political revolutions and instances of decolonization in this period is too vast a topic to be discussed here meaningfully. We will

simply note that such global instabilities were great in number, variety and impact during the long nineteenth century.

48. Francine Masiello, introduction to *Dreams and Realities: Selected Fiction of Juana Manuela Gorriti*, trans. Sergio Wiseman (Oxford: Oxford University Press, 2003), xv.

49. Mary G. Berg, "Juana Manuela Gorriti," in *Spanish American Women Writers: A Bio-Bibliographic Sourcebook*, ed. Diane E. Marting (Westport: Greenwood Press, 1990), 226–7.

50. Regina A. Root, "Searching for the *Oasis in Life*: Fashion and the Question of Female Emancipation in Late Nineteenth-Century Argentina," *The Americas* 60, no. 3 (2004), 384.

51. Masiello, *Dreams and Realities*, xxiii.

52. Susan Hiner, *Accessories to Modernity: Fashion and the Feminine in Nineteenth-Century France* (Philadelphia: University of Pennsylvania Press, 2010), 1.

53. Juana Manuela Gorriti, "The Black Glove," in *Dreams and Realities: Selected Fiction of Juana Manuela Gorriti*, trans. Sergio Wiseman (Oxford: Oxford University Press, 2003), 107.

54. Ibid., 125.

55. Ibid., 127.

56. Ibid.

57. Masiello, *Dreams and Realities*, xxxiii.

58. White was adopted by the Unitarians while the Federalists were associated with the color red. Gorriti would have been aware of the famous book *Facundo* (1845) by Domingo Sarmiento, future president of Argentina, in which Sarmiento writes that the white stripes of the Argentine flag symbolize peace. I am grateful to Ana Sabau Fernandez for these references.

59. Hiner, *Accessories to Modernity*, 173.

60. Hiner, *Accessories to Modernity*, 244, n. 67. Also see Mary Lydon, "Pli Selon Pli: Proust and Fortuny," *Romanic Review* 82, no. 4 (1990): 438–9.

61. Cited in Adam Geczy, *Fashion and Orientalism: Dress, Textiles, and Culture from the 17th to the 21st Century* (London: Bloomsbury, 2013), 150.

62. The last word of the title in Proust's final volume, *Le Temps Retrouvé*, means "rediscovered" or "regained."

BIBLIOGRAPHY

Abelson, E. (1989), *When Ladies Go A-Thieving: Middle-Class Shoplifters in the Victorian Department Store*, New York and Oxford: Oxford University Press.

Achille Devéria: Temoin du romantisme parisien, 1800–1857 (1985), Paris: Musée Renan-Scheffer.

Ackermann, R. (March 1809), *The Repository of Arts, Literature, Commerce, Manufactures, Fashion and Politics* 1.

Acton, W. (1857), *Prostitution Considered in its Moral, Social and Sanitary Aspects in London and Other Large Cities and Garrison Towns with Proposals for the Control and Prevention of its Attendant Evils*, London: John Churchill & Sons.

Adams, J. (2013), "Dandyism and late Victorian masculinity," in K. Powell and P. Raby (eds), *Oscar Wilde in Context,* Cambridge: Cambridge University Press.

Adburgham, A. (1972), *Women in Print: Writing Women and Women's Magazines from the Restoration to the Accession of Victoria*. London: Allen & Unwin.

—— (1981), *Shops and Shopping 1800–1914: Where and in What Manner the Well-Dressed Englishwoman Bought Her Clothes*, London: Allen & Unwin.

Allman, J. (2004), "Fashioning Africa: Power and the Politics of Dress," in J. Allman (ed.), *Fashioning Africa: Power and the Politics of Dress*, Bloomington: Indiana University Press.

Amann, E. (2015), *Dandyism in the Age of Revolution: The Art of the Cut*, Chicago and London: University of Chicago Press.

American Brides: Inspiration and Ingenuity (2014), exhibition, Denton, TX: Greater Denton Arts Council.

Amies, H. (1994), *The Englishman's Suit*, London: Quartet Books.

Anderson, P. (1996), *When Passion Reigned: Sex and the Victorians*, New York: Basic Books.

Anquetil, J., and P. Ballesteros (1995), *Silk*. Paris: Flammarion.

Apraxine, P., X. Demange, F. Heilbrun, and M. Falzone del Barbarò (2000), *"La Divine Comtesse": Photographs of the Countess de Castiglione*, New Haven: Yale University Press.

Armitage, G. (1938), "A History of Cockhedge Mill, Warrington," unpublished ms., Warrington Library Archive and Local Studies Collection.

Arnold, R. (2009), *Fashion: A Very Short Introduction*, New York: Oxford.

Arthur, L. (1999), *Religion, Dress, and the Body*, Oxford and New York: Berg.

—— (2000), *Undressing Religion: Commitment and Conversion from a Cross-Cultural Perspective*, Oxford and New York: Berg.

Ash, S. (2008), "Heroin Baby: Barnardo's, Benevolence, and Shame," *Journal of Communication Inquiry* 32, no. 2: 179–200.

Ashmore, S. (2012), *Muslin*, London: V&A Publishing.

Austen, J. (1932), "Letter from Jane Austen to Cassandra Elizabeth Austen, January 25, 1801," in R. Chapman (ed.), *Jane Austen's Letters to Her Sister Cassandra and Others, Vol. 1: 1796–1809*, Oxford: Clarendon Press.

—— (2006), *Northanger Abbey*, B. Benedict and D. le Faye (eds), Cambridge: Cambridge University Press.

Baizerman, S., J. Eicher, and C. Cerny (2008), "Eurocentrism in the Study of Ethnic Dress," in J. Eicher, S. Evenson, and H. Lutz (eds), *The Visible Self: Global Perspectives on Dress, Culture, and Society*, New York: Fairchild.

Balzac, H. (1994), *Père Goriot*, trans. B. Raffel and ed. P. Brooks, New York: Norton.

Banner, L. (1983), *American Beauty*, New York: Knopf, 1983.

Banton, M. (1998), *Racial Theories*, Cambridge: Cambridge University Press.

Baudelaire, C. (1956), "Salon of 1846," in J. Mayne (ed.), *The Mirror of Art: Critical Studies by Charles Baudelaire*, New York: Doubleday Anchor Books.

—— (1962), *Curiosités esthétiques, L'Art romantiques, et autres Oeuvres critiques de Baudelaire*, Paris: Éditions Garnier Frères.

—— (1964), *The Painter of Modern Life and Other Essays*, trans. and ed. J. Mayne, London: Phaidon Press.

Baxter, D. (2009), "*Grisettes, Cocottes,* and *Bohèmes:* Fashion and Fiction in the 1820s," in P. McNeil, V. Karaminas, and C. Cole (eds), *Fashion in Fiction: Text and Clothing in Literature, Film, and Television*, Oxford: Berg.

Becker, A. (2013), "Walker's Mourning Ensemble: Mourning Practices and Local Culture in Late Nineteenth-Century Aberdeen, Mississippi," unpublished ms.

Beetham, M. (1996), *A Magazine of Her Own? Domesticity and Desire on the Woman's Magazine, 1800–1914*, New York: Routledge.

Belchem, J. (1996), *Popular Radicalism in Nineteenth-Century Britain*, Basingstoke: Macmillan.

Belenky, M. (November 2012), "Transitory Tales: Omnibus in Nineteenth-Century Paris," *Dix-Neuf* 16, no. 3: 283–303.

Benedict, R. (2003), "Dress," in K. Johnson, S. Torntore, and J. Eicher (eds), *Fashion Foundations: Early Writings on Fashion and Dress*, Oxford: Berg.

Benjamin, W. (1999), *The Arcades Project*, trans. Howard Eiland and Kevin McLaughlin, Cambridge, MA and London: Belknap Press of Harvard University Press.

Berg, M. (1990), "Juana Manuela Gorriti," in D. Marting (ed.), *Spanish American Women Writers: A Bio-Bibliographic Sourcebook*, Westport: Greenwood Press.

Bernheimer, C. (1989), *Figures of Ill Repute: Representing Prostitution in Nineteenth-Century France*, Cambridge, MA: Harvard University Press.

Bhabha, H. (1994), *The Location of Culture*, London: Routledge.

Bhatia, N. (September 2003), "Fashioning Women in Colonial India: The Political Utility of Clothes in Colonial India," *Fashion Theory* 7, no. 3–4: 327–44.

Bidou, H. (November 1912), "Le Bon ton," *Gazette du Bon Ton* 1, no. 1: 4.

Bigham, R. (2012), *Lucile, Her Life by Design: Sex, Style, and the Fusion of Theatre and Couture*, San Francisco: MacEvie Press Group.

Blaszczyk, R. (2013), "The Hidden Spaces of Fashion Production," in S. Black, A. de la Haye, A. Rocamora, R. Root, and H. Thomas (eds), *The Handbook of Fashion Studies*, New York: Bloomsbury.

Blaug, M. (June 1963), "The Myth of the Old Poor Law and the Making of the New," *The Journal of Economic History* 23, no. 2: 151–84.

Bliss, S. (2003), "The Significance of Clothes," in K. Johnson, S. Torntore, and J. Eicher (eds), *Fashion Foundations: Early Writings on Fashion and Dress*, Oxford: Berg.

Bloomer, A.J. (1994), *Hear Me Patiently: The Reform Speeches of Amelia Jenks Bloomer*, ed. A. Coon, Westport, CT: Greenwood Press.

Bloomer, D. (1895), *Life and Writings of Amelia Bloomer*, Boston: Arena Publishing Company.

Bohleke, K. (2010), "Americanizing French Fashion Plates: *Godey's* and *Peterson's* Cultural and Socio-Economic Translation of *Les Modes Parisiennes*," *American Periodicals: A Journey of History, Criticism, and Bibliography* 20, no. 2: 120–55.

Bolt, C. (1971), *Victorian Attitudes to Race*, London: Routledge & Kegan Paul.

Bourke, J. (1996), "The Great Male Renunciation: Men's dress reform in interwar Britain," *Journal of Design History* 9, no. 1: 23–33.

Bowlby, R. (1985), *Just Looking: Consumer Culture in Dreiser, Gissing, and Zola*, New York: Methuen.

Brevik-Zender, H. (May 2014), "Interstitial Narratives: Rethinking Feminine Spaces of Modernity in Nineteenth-Century French Fashion Plates," *Nineteenth-Century Contexts* 36, no. 2: 91–123.

Breward, C. (1992), "Images of Desire: The Construction of the Feminine Consumer in Women's Fashion Journals, 1875–1890," Master's thesis: Royal College of Art.

—— (1995), *The Culture of Fashion*, Manchester: Manchester University Press.

—— (1999a) *The Hidden Consumer: Masculinities, Fashion, and City Life, 1860–1914*, Manchester: Manchester University Press.

—— (1999b), "Renouncing consumption: Men, fashion and luxury, 1870–1914," in A. de la Haye and E. Wilson (eds), *Defining Dress: Dress as Object, Meaning, and Identity*, Manchester: Manchester University Press.

—— (2000), "The Dandy Laid Bare: Embodying practices and fashion for men," in S. Bruzzi and P. Gibson (eds), *Fashion Cultures: Theories, Explorations, and Analysis*, London: Routledge.

—— (2003), *Fashion*, Oxford: Oxford University Press.

Brontë, C. (2000), *Jane Eyre*, ed. M. Smith, Oxford: Oxford University Press.

Bruna, D. (2015), *Fashioning the Body: An Intimate History of the Silhouette*, New Haven and London: Yale University Press for the Bard Graduate Center.

Buck, A. (March 1968), "The Trap Re-Baited: Mourning Dress 1860–1890," *Costume* 2, no. 1: 32–7.

Buck-Morss, S. (Fall 1986), "The Flâneur, the Sandwichman, and the Whore: The Politics of Loitering," *New German Critique* 13, no. 39: 99–139.

Burberry, T. (1888), "BP 17,928 Compound fabrics." In Patent Office. 1896. *Patents for Inventions: Abridgments of Specifications: Class 142, Weaving and Woven Fabrics, 1884–88*, London: HMSO.

Burberry, T. and F. Unwin (1897), "BP 4065." In Patent Office. 1903. *Patents for Inventions: Abridgments of Specifications: Class 142, Weaving and Woven Fabrics, 1897–1900*, London: HMSO.

Burberrys (1910), *Burberry for Ladies*, London, Paris, and Basingstoke: Burberrys.

Burnett, J. (1994a), *Destiny Obscure: Autobiographies of Childhood, Education, and Family from the 1820s to the 1920s*, London: Routledge.

—— (1994b), *Useful Toil: Autobiographies of Working People from the 1820s to the 1920s*, London: Routledge.

Burrows, A., and I. Schumacher ([1979] 1990), *Portraits of the Insane: The Case of Dr. Diamond*, London and New York: Quarto Books.

Buss, C. (1997), *Silk and Colour*, Como: Ratti.

Butler, J. (1990), *Gender Trouble: Feminism and the Subversion of Identity*, New York: Routledge.

Calloway, H. (1992), "Dressing for Dinner in the Bush: Rituals of Self-Definition and British Imperial Authority," in R. Barnes and J. Eicher (eds), *Dress and Gender: Making and Meaning in Cultural Contexts*, Oxford: Berg.

Carey, H. (November 1862), "Woman in Daily Life: or Shadows on Every Hill-Side," *The Rose, the Shamrock, and the Thistle* 2: 81.

Carré, R. (1987), "Les Couturières à La Recherche d'un Statut Social," *Gavroche: Revue d'Histoire Populaire* 36: 5–8.

"Caution to Parents," (October 28, 1842), *Lincolnshire Chronicle*: 3.

Census of England and Wales, 1901. General Report with Appendices, London: HMSO, 1904.

Census of Great Britain, 1851. Population Tables. II. Ages, Civil Condition, Occupations, and Birth-place of the People: With the Numbers and Ages of the Blind, the Deaf-and-Dumb, and the Inmates of Workhouses, Prisons, Lunatic Asylums, and Hospitals, Vol. I, London: HMSO, 1854.

"A Chapter on Shawls," (1850), *Harper's New Monthly Magazine* 2, no. 7: 39–41.

Chase, M. (2007), *Chartism: A New History*, Manchester: Manchester University Press.

Chaudhuri, N. (1992), "Shawls, Jewelry, Curry, and Rice in Victorian Britain," in N. Chaudhuri and M. Strobel (eds), *Western Women and Imperialism: Complicity and Resistance*, Bloomington: Indiana University Press.

Cheang, S. (2008), "Roots: Hair and Race," in G. Biddle-Perry and S. Cheang (eds), *Hair: Styling, Culture, and Fashion*, Oxford: Berg.

Cherry, D., and G. Pollock. (1988), "Woman as Sign in Pre-Raphaelite Literature: The Representations of Elizabeth Siddal," in G. Pollock (ed.), *Vision and Difference: Femininity, Feminism, and the Histories of Art*, London and New York: Routledge.

Clayson, H. (1991), *Painted Love: Prostitution in French Art of the Impressionist Era*, New Haven and London: Yale University Press.

Clayton, V. (1987), "Clothing and the Temporal Kingdom: Mormon Clothing Practices, 1847–1887," Ph.D. diss.: Purdue University.

Coffin, J. (1996), *The Politics of Women's Work: The Paris Garment Trades, 1750–1915*, Princeton: Princeton University Press.

Cohen, S. (2012), "What is a Kashmir Shawl?" in S. Cohen, R. Crill, M. Lévi-Strauss, and J. Spurr (eds), *Kashmir Shawls: The Tapi Collection*, Mumbai: The Shoestring Publisher.

Cohn, B. (1983), "Representing Authority in Victorian India," in E. Hobsbawm and T. Ranger (eds), *The Invention of Tradition*, Cambridge: Cambridge University Press.

—— (1996), *Colonialism and Its Forms of Knowledge: The British in India*, Princeton: Princeton University Press.

Coleman, D. (1969), *Courtaulds: An Economic and Social History*, Oxford: Oxford University Press.

Coleman, E. (1989), *The Opulent Era: Fashions of Worth, Doucet, and Pingat*, Brooklyn: The Brooklyn Museum.

Collins, W. (1994), *The Moonstone*, London: Penguin.

Commissioners and Trustees for Fisheries, Manufactures, and Improvements in Scotland (May 7, 1794), "Premiums, on Various Articles of Scotch Manufacture," *Caledonian Mercury*: 4.

Coon, K. (2010), "The Sisters of Charity in Nineteenth-Century America: Civil War Nurses and Philanthropic Pioneers," Master's thesis: Indiana University.

Corbin, A. ([1978] (1990), *Women for Hire: Prostitution and Sexuality in France after 1850*, trans. A. Sheridan, Cambridge, MA: Harvard University Press.

Cornell, S., and D. Hartmann (2007), *Ethnicity and Race: Making Identities in a Changing World*, Thousand Oaks, CA: Sage.

The Cornishman (October 17, 1889).

Courtesans and Opium: Romantic Illusions of the Fool of Yangzhou (2009), trans. P. Hanan, New York: Columbia University Press.

Cowper, C. (January 9, 1915), "Colour as an Influence," *The Academy and Literature*: 23–4.

Craik, J. (1993), *The Face of Fashion: Cultural Studies in Fashion*, London: Routledge.

—— (2005), *Uniforms Exposed: From Conformity to Transgression*, Oxford: Berg.

Crane, D. (2000), *Fashion and Its Social Agendas*, Chicago: University of Chicago Press.

Crill, R. (1998), "Mashru in India," in *Indian Ikat Textiles*, London: V&A Publications.

—— (2010), "The Golden Age of the Indian Textile Trade," in C. Breward, P. Crang, and R. Crill (eds), *British Asian Style: Fashion and Textiles/Past and Present*, London: V&A Publishing.

—— (2012), "Embroidery in Kashmir Shawls," in S. Cohen, R. Krill, M. Lévi-Strauss, and J. Spurr (eds), *Kashmir Shawls: The Tapi Collection*, Mumbai: The Shoestring Publisher.

Crowston, C. (2001), *Fabricating Women: The Seamstresses of Old Regime France, 1675–1791*, Durham, NC: Duke University Press.

Cunningham, P. (2003), *Reforming Women's Fashion, 1850–1920*, Kent, OH: Kent State University Press.

Cunnington, C. (1937), *English Women's Clothing in the Nineteenth Century*, London: Faber & Faber.

Cunnington, P. and C. Lucas (1972), *Costumes for Births, Marriages, and Deaths*, London: A.&C. Black.

Curl, J. (2000), "Funerals, Ephemera, and Mourning," in *The Victorian Celebration of Death*, Thrupp: Sutton.

Cusack, P. (January 16, 1813), Classified advertisement, *Norfolk Chronicle*: 1.

Darwin, C. (1871), *The Descent of Man*, London: John Murray.

David, A. (2014), *Fashion Victims: The Pleasures and Perils of Dress in the Nineteenth Century*, Toronto: The Bata Shoe Museum.

—— (2015), *Fashion Victims: The Dangers of Dress Past and Present*, New York: Bloomsbury Publishing.

Davidoff, L. and C. Hall (1987), *Family Fortunes: Men and Women of the English Middle Classes*, London: Hutchinson.

Davidson, D. (Spring 2005), "Making Society 'Legible': People-Watching in Paris after the Revolution," *French Historical Studies* 28, no. 2: 265–96.

Davin, A. (1996), *Growing Up Poor: Home, School, and Street in London, 1870–1914*, London: Rivers Oram.

Davis, F. (1992), *Fashion, Culture, and Identity*, Chicago: University of Chicago Press.

Desprez, E. (1832), *Paris, Ou Le Livre Des Cent-Et-Un*, Paris: Librairie Ladvocat.

Dickens, C. (1852), "The Great Yorkshire Llama," *Household Words* 6: 250–3.

—— (1854), "A Manchester Warehouse," *Household Words* 9: 268–72.

Digby, A. (1982), *The Poor Law in Nineteenth-Century England and Wales*, London: The Historical Association.

Doughty, R. (1975), *Feather Fashions and Bird Preservation: A Study in Nature Protection*, Berkeley: University of California Press.

"Dress and the Picture," (July 9, 1910), *Moving Picture World* 7, no. 2: 74.

Driver, F., and S. Ashmore (2010), "The Mobile Museum: Collecting and Circulating Indian Textiles in Victorian Britain," *Victorian Studies* 52, no. 3: 353–85.

Ducrot, I. (2008), *Text on Textile*, Lewes: Sylph Editions.

Duncan, B. (2005), *Goethe's* Werther *and the Critics*, Rochester, NY: Camden House.

Duncan, C. (1976), *The Pursuit of Pleasure: The Rococo Revival in French Romantic Art*, New York and London: Garland.

Dwyer-McNulty, S. (2014), *Common Threads: A Cultural History of Clothing in American Catholicism*, Chapel Hill: University of North Carolina Press.

Eden, E. (1859), *False and True*, London.

Ehrman, E. (2014), *The Wedding Dress: 300 Years of Bridal Fashion*, London: V&A Publishing.

Eicher, J., and B. Sumberg (1995), "World Fashion, Ethnic and National Dress," in J. Eicher (ed.), *Dress and Ethnicity: Change Across Space and Time*, Oxford: Berg.

Ellington, G. (1869), *The Women of New York, or the Under-World of the Great City*, New York: The New York Book Company.

Ellis, H. (February 1910), "An Anatomical Vindication of the Straight Front Corset," *Current Literature* 48: 172–4.

Ellman, E. (1912), *Recollections of a Sussex Parson*, London: Skeffington & Son.

Emery, J. (2014), *A History of the Paper Pattern Industry: The Home Dressmaking Fashion Revolution*, London: Bloomsbury.

Engels, F. ([1845] 1987), *The Condition of the Working Class In England*, London: Penguin].

Entwistle, J. (2000), *The Fashioned Body: Fashion, Dress, and Modern Social Theory*, Cambridge: Polity Press.

"Epitome of News—Foreign and Domestic," (September 5, 1857), *Illustrated London News*: 254.

The Etiquette of Courtship and Matrimony: With a Complete Guide to the Forms of a Wedding (1852), London: David Bogue.

Evans, C. (2011), "The Walkies: Early French Fashion Shows as a Cinema of Attractions," in A. Munich (ed.), *Fashion in Film*, Bloomington: Indiana University Press.

—— (2013), *The Mechanical Smile: Modernism and the First Fashion Shows in France and America, 1900–1929*, New Haven: Yale University Press.

Evans, E. (1983a), *The Forging of the Modern State: Early Industrial Britain 1783–1870*, London: Longman Press.

—— (1983b), *The Great Reform Act of 1832*, London: Methuen.

Every Woman's Encyclopaedia (1910–11), London: Amalgamated Press.

Fields, J. (2007), *An Intimate Affair: Women, Lingerie, and Sexuality*, Berkeley: University of California Press.

The Fifth Annual Report of the Ladies' Benevolent Society, Liverpool (1815), Liverpool.

Fillin-Yeh, S. (2001), "Introduction: New Strategies for a Theory of Dandies," in *Dandies: Fashion and Fineness in Art and Culture*, New York: New York University Press.

Finamore, M. (2013), *Hollywood Before Glamour: Fashion in American Silent Film*, New York: Palgrave Macmillan.

Finnane, A. (April 1996), "What Should Chinese Women Wear? A National Problem," *Modern China* 22, no. 2: 99–131.

—— (2003), "Yangzhou's 'Mondernity': Fashion and Consumption in the Early Nineteenth Century." *Positions* 11, no. 2: 395–425.

—— (2007), *Changing Clothes in China: Fashion, History, Nation*, London: Hurst.

Fischer, G. (1999), "The Obedient and Disobedient Daughters of the Church: Strangite Mormon Dress as a Mode of Control," in L. Arthur and G. Lazaridis (eds), *Religion, Dress, and the Body*, Oxford: Berg.

—— (2001), *Power and Pantaloons: A Nineteenth-Century Dress Reform in the United States*, Kent, OH: Kent State University Press.

Flagollé, A. (1994), "The Demystification of Dr. Hugh Welch Diamond," Ph.D. diss.: University of New Mexico.

Flood, C., and S. Grant (2014), *Style and Satire: Fashion in Print, 1777–1927*, London: V&A Publishing.

Flower, W., and R. Lydekker (1891), *An introduction to the study of mammals living and extinct*, London: A.&C. Black.

Flügel, J. (1930), *The Psychology of Clothes*, London: Hogarth Press.

Foster, H. (1997), *New Raiments of Self: African American Clothing in the Antebellum South*, Oxford: Berg.

Foster, V. (1992), *A Visual History of Costume: The Nineteenth Century*, London: Batsford.

Foster and Co. (June 13, 1811), "Presents from India," *Morning Chronicle*: 1.

Fournel, V. (1888), *Le cris de Paris: Types et physiognomies d'autrefois*, Paris: Firmin-Didot.

Fox and Co. (August 26, 1812), Classified advertisement, *Morning Chronicle*: 1.

—— (December 18, 1823), Classified advertisement, *Morning Post*: 1.

—— (1839), Advertisement, in J. Stephens, *The Land of Promise being an authentic and impartial history of the rise and progress of the new British province of South Australia . . .*, London: Smith, Elder & Co.

Foucault, M. (1979), *Discipline and Punish: The Birth of the Prison*, trans. A. Sheridan, New York: Vintage Books.

—— (1990), *The History of Sexuality Volume I: An Introduction*, trans. R. Hurley, New York: Vintage Books.

Francks, P. (June 2015), "Was Fashion a European Invention? The Kimono and Economic Development in Japan," *Fashion Theory* 19, no. 3: 331–62.

Freud, S. (1961), "Fetishism," in *The Complete Psychological Works of Sigmund Freud XXI*, trans. J. Strachey, London: Hogarth and the Institute of Psychoanalysis.

—— (2003), *Three Contributions to the Theory of Sex*, trans. A. Brill, Auckland: The Floating Press.

Friedman, D. (2014), *Wilde in America: Oscar Wilde and the Invention of Modern Celebrity*, New York: W.W. Norton.

Furbank, P. and A. Cain (eds), (2004), *Mallarmé on Fashion: A Translation of the Fashion Magazine, La Dernière Mode, with Commentary*, trans. P. Furbank and A. Cain, Oxford and New York: Berg.

Garelick, R. (1998), *Rising Star: Dandyism, Gender, and Performance in the Fin De Siècle*, Princeton: Princeton University Press.

—— (2014), *Mademoiselle: Coco Chanel and the Pulse of History*, New York: Random House.

Gaudriault, R. (1983), *La gravure de mode féminine en France*, Paris: Éditions de l'Amateur.

Geczy, A. (2013), *Fashion and Orientalism: Dress, Textiles, and Culture from the Seventeenth to the Twenty-First Century*, London: Bloomsbury.

Gentleman's Magazine of Fashions (June 3, 1828), "A Riding Frock Coat," *Dublin Morning Register*: 3.

—— (September 30, 1831), "Gentlemen's Fashions," *Morning Post*: 4.

Gibson, R. (1989), *A Social History of French Catholicism, 1789–1914*, London: Routledge.

Gilbert S., and S. Gubar (1979), *The Madwoman in the Attic: The Woman Writer and the Nineteenth-Century Literary Imagination*, New Haven: Yale University Press.

Gilchrist and Co. (March 18, 1799), "Elegant Furniture, Calicoes, and Carpets," *Caledonian Mercury*: 1.

Gilman, S. (ed.) (1976), *The Face of Madness: Hugh W. Diamond and the Origin of Psychiatric Photography*, Seacaucus, NJ: Citadel Press.

Giusberti, F. (2006), "The Riddle of Secrecy," in M. Corcy, C. Douyère-Demeulenaere, and L. Hilaire-Pérez (eds), *Les Archives de l'Invention: Écrits, Objects et Images de l'Activité Inventive*, Toulouse: CNRS-Université de Toulouse-Le Mirail.

Goethe, J. (1993), *The Sorrows of Young Werther and Novella*, trans. E. Mayer and L. Brogan, New York: The Modern Library, 1993.

Gordon, S. (March 2003), "The Mormon Question: Polygamy and Constitutional Conflict in Nineteenth-Century America," *Journal of Supreme Court History* 28, no. 1: 14–29.

Gorriti, J. (2003), "The Black Glove," in *Dreams and Realities: Selected Fiction of Juana Manuela Gorriti*, trans. S. Wiseman, Oxford: Oxford University Press.

Gould, S. (1997), *The Mismeasure of Man*, London: Penguin Books.

Green, N. (1997), *Ready-to-Wear and Ready to Work: A Century of Industry and Immigrants in Paris and New York*, Durham, NC: Duke University Press.

Groom, G. (2012), *Impressionism, Fashion, and Modernity*, New Haven: Yale University Press.

Hahn, H. (June 2005), "Fashion Discourses in Fashion Magazines and Madame de Girardin's *Lettres parisiennes* in July-Monarchy France (1830–48)," *Fashion Theory* 9, no. 2: 205–27.

—— (2009), *Scenes of Parisian Modernity: Culture and Consumption in the Nineteenth Century*, New York: Palgrave MacMillan.

Hall, C. and S.O. Rose. (2006), *At Home with the Empire: Metropolitan Culture and the Imperial World*, Cambridge: Cambridge University Press.

Hall-Duncan, N. (1979), *The History of Fashion Photography*, New York: Alpine Book Co.

Hamlett, J., and L. Hoskins (2013), "Comfort in Small Things? Clothing, Control, and Agency in County Lunatic Asylums in Nineteenth- and Early Twentieth-Century England," *Journal of Victorian Culture* 18, no. 1: 93–114.

Hanan, P. (1998), "Fengyue Meng and the Courtesan Novel," *Harvard Journal of Asiatic Studies* 58, no. 2: 345–72.

Hannerz, U. (1996), *Transnational Connections: Culture, People, Places,* London: Routledge.

Harris, J. (1994), *Private Lives, Public Spirit: Britain 1870–1914*, London: Penguin.

Harsin, J. (1985), *Policing Prostitution in Paris in the Nineteenth Century*, Princeton: Princeton University Press.

"Hasbrouck, Lydia Sayer," (1971), in E. James (ed.), *Notable American Women, 1607–1950*, Cambridge, MA: Belknap Press of Harvard University Press.

Haweis, M. (1878), *The Art of Beauty*, New York: Harper and Brothers.

Hawthorne, N. (2007), *The Scarlet Letter*, ed. B. Harding, Oxford: Oxford University Press.

H.B. (April 1, 1881), "The Adulteration of Dress Materials," *The Ladies' Treasury*: 209–10.

Herbert, R. (June 1958), "Seurat and Jules Chéret," *The Art Bulletin* 40, no. 2: 156–8.

Higgs, E. (1986), "Domestic Service and Household production," in A. John (ed.), *Unequal Opportunities: Women's Employment in England, 1800–1918*, Oxford: Basil Blackwell.

Higonnet, A. (1995), "Real Fashion: Clothes Unmake the Working Woman," in M. Cohen and C. Prendergast (eds), *Spectacles of Realism: Gender, Body, Genre*, Minneapolis: University of Minnesota Press.

Hill, D. (2011), *American Menswear: From the Civil War to the Twenty-First Century*, Lubbock: Texas Tech University Press.

Hill, G. (February 16, 1802), "Cheap Days Commence this and Eight following Days, at George Hill's, No. 82 Oxford-Street," *Morning Post*: 1.

Hilton, B. (1988), *The Age of Atonement: The Influence of Evangelicalism on Social and Economic Thought, 1795–1865*, Oxford: Clarendon.

Hinckley, C. (1852), "Calico-Printin," *Godey's Magazine and Lady's Book* 45: 121.

Hiner, S. (2010), *Accessories to Modernity: Fashion and the Feminine in Nineteenth-Century France*, Philadelphia: University of Pennsylvania Press.

—— (2012), "Monsieur Calicot: French Masculinity between Commerce and Honor," *West 86th: A Journal of Decorative Arts, Design, and Material Culture* 19, no. 1: 32–60.

—— (2013), "Becoming (M)other: Reflectivity in *Le Journal des Demoiselles*," *Romance Studies* 31, no. 2: 84–100.

Hobsbawm, E. (1962), *The Age of Revolution, 1789–1848*, Cleveland: World Publishing Co.

—— (1975), *The Age of Capital, 1848–1875*, New York: Scribner.

—— (1983), "Introduction: Inventing Traditions," in E. Hobsbawm and T. Ranger (eds), *The Invention of Tradition*, Cambridge: Cambridge University Press.

—— (1989), *Age of Empire: 1875–1914*, New York: Vintage.

Holderbaum, J. (1980), "Portrait Sculpture," in P. Fusco and H. Janson (eds), *The Romantics to Rodin: French Nineteenth-Century Sculpture from North American Collections*, Los Angeles: Los Angeles County Museum of Art.

Hollander, A. (1978), *Seeing Through Clothes*. New York: Viking Press.

—— (1994), *Sex and Suits*. New York: Alfred A. Knopf.

—— (2007), "When Worth was King," in L. Welters and A. Lillethun (eds), *The Fashion Reader*, New York: Berg.

Home, J. (ed.) ([1889] 1970), *The Letters and Journals of Lady Mary Coke*, Bath: Kingsmead Reprints.

"Hospital Scenes—Heartrending Sights," (January 23, 1863), *Advocate*.

Houlbrook, M. (March 2007), " 'The Man with the Powder Puff' in Interwar London," *The Historical Journal* 50, no. 1: 147–71.

Howard, V. (2000), "American Weddings: Gender, Consumption, and the Business of Brides," Ph.D. diss.: University of Texas.

Huart, L. (1841), *Physiologie de la grisette*, Paris: Aubert.

Hume, L. (2013), *The Religious Life of Dress: Global Fashion and Faith*, London: Bloomsbury.

Hutchison, H. (1968), *The Poster: An Illustrated History from 1860*, New York: Viking Press.

Iarocci, L. (2009), "Dressing Rooms: Women, Fashion, and the Department Store," in J. Potvin (ed.), *The Places and Spaces of Fashion, 1800–2007*, New York and London: Routledge.

Imbert, D. (1989), "Le monument des frères Morice, place de la République," in *Quand Paris dansait avec Marianne, 1879–1889*, Paris: Musée du Petit Palais.

Iskin, R. (2007), *Modern Women and Parisian Consumer Culture in Impressionist Painting*, Cambridge: Cambridge University Press.

Janin, J. ([1840] [1862), *Les français peints par eux-mêmes: Encyclopédie morale du dix-neuvième siècle*, Paris: L. Curmer.

Jenkins, R. (2008), *Rethinking Ethnicity*. London: Sage.

Jenness-Miller, A. (May 1887), "The Reason Why," *Dress* 1: 7.

—— (1894), "Dress Improvement," in M. Eagle (ed.), *The Congress of Women, Held in the Woman's Building, World's Columbian Exposition, Chicago, USA, 1893*, Chicago: Monarch Book Company.

John, A. (1980), *By the Sweat of Their Brow: Women Workers at the Victorian Coal Mines*, London: Croom Helm.

Johnson, D. (2007), "Clothes Make the Empire: British Dress in India," in D. Johnson and H. Foster (eds), *Dress Sense: Emotional and Sensory Experiences of the Body and Clothes*, Oxford: Berg.

Jones, J. (2004), *Sexing la Mode: Gender, Fashion, and Commercial Culture in Old Regime France*, New York: Berg.

Jordanova, L. (1989), *Sexual Visions: Images of Gender in Science and Medicine between the Eighteenth and Twentieth Centuries*, Madison: University of Wisconsin Press.

Journal des Modes (December 9, 1870), "Fashions for December," *Lincolnshire Chronicle*: 3.

A Journeyman Engineer (1867), *Some Habits and Customs of the Working Classes*, London: Tinsley Brothers.

Kaiser, S. (2012), *Fashion and Cultural Studies*, New York: Berg.

Karner, C. (2007), *Ethnicity and Everyday Life,* London: Routledge.

Keenan, W. (2000), "Clothed with Authority: The Rationalization of Marist Dress-Culture," in L. Arthur (ed.), *Undressing Religion*, Oxford and New York: Berg.

Kellogg, J. (1876), *The Evils of Fashionable Dress, and How to Dress Healthfully*, Battle Creek, MI: Office of the Health Reformer.

—— (1891), *The Influence of Dress in Producing the Physical Decadence of American Women, Annual Address Upon Obstetrics and Gynecology*, Battle Creek, MI: Michigan State Medical Society.

King, S. (2000), *Poverty and Welfare in England, 1700–1850*, Manchester: Manchester University Press.

King, S., and C. Payne (May 2002), "The Dress of the Poor," *Textile History* 33, no. 1: 1–8.

Kleinert, A. (2001), *Le "Journal des dames et des modes": ou la conquête de l'Europe féminin, 1797–1839,* Stuttgart: J. Thorbecke.

Kleutghen, K. (2014), "Chinese Occidenterie: The Diversity of 'Western' Objects in Eighteenth-Century China," *Eighteenth-Century Studies* 47, no. 2: 117–35.

Ko, D. (1999), "Jazzing into Modernity: High Heels, Platforms, and Lotus Shoes," in V. Steele and J. Major (eds), *China Chic: East Meets West*, New Haven: Yale University Press.

Koda, H. (2001), *Extreme Beauty: The Body Transformed*, New York: Metropolitan Museum of Art.

Kopp, R. (1997), "Baudelaire: Mode et modernité." *48/14: La revue de Musée d'Orsay* 4: 50–5.

Kortsch, C. (2009), *Dress Culture in Late Victorian Women's Fiction: Literacy, Textiles, and Activism*, Surrey: Ashgate.

Kramer, E. (2013), " 'Not So Japan-Easy' The British Reception of Japanese Dress in the Late Nineteenth Century," *Textile History* 44, no. 1: 3–24.

Kriegel, L. (2001), "Narrating the subcontinent in 1851: India at the Crystal Palace," in L. Purbrick (ed.), *The Great Exhibition of 1851: New Interdisciplinary Essays*, Manchester: Manchester University Press.

Kuchta, D. (1996), "The Making of the Self-Made Man: Class, Clothing, and English Masculinity, 1688–1832," in V. de Grazia and H. Furlough (eds), *The Sex of Things: Gender and Consumption in Historical Perspective*, Berkeley: University of California Press.

—— (2002), *The Three-Piece Suit and Modern Masculinity England, 1550–1850*, Berkeley: University of California Press.

Kuhns, E. (2003), *The Habit: A History of the Clothing of Catholic Nuns*, New York: Doubleday.

Kunzle, D. (Spring 1977), "Dress Reform as Antifeminism: A Response to Helene E. Roberts's 'The Exquisite Slave: The Role of Clothes in the Making of Victorian Women'," *Signs* 2, no. 3: 570–9.

—— (1982), *Fashion and Fetishism: Corsets, Tight Lacing, and other Forms of Body Sculpture*, New York: Rowman and Littlefield.

"Ladies' Fashions," (May 7, 1872), *Royal Cornwall Gazette*: 7.

Lady's Gazette of Fashion (July 1879).

Lambert, M. (1991), *Fashion in Photographs, 1860–1880*, London: Batsford.

Lambertz, J. (1985), "Sexual Harassment in the Nineteenth Century English Cotton Industry," *History Workshop Journal* 19: 29–61.

Lanceley, W. (1925), *From Hall-Boy to House Steward*, London: E. Arnold.

Laqueur, T. (2003), *Making Sex: Body and Gender from the Greeks to Freud*, Cambridge: Harvard University Press.

Lavater, J., and G. della Porta (1818), *The Pocket Lavater, or, The Science of Physiognomy*, New York: C. Wiley & Co.

Lehmann, U. (2000), *Tigersprung: Fashion in Modernity*, Cambridge, MA and London: The MIT Press.

Lemire, B. (1991), *Fashion's Favourite: The Cotton Trade and the Consumer in Britain, 1660–1800*, Oxford: Pasold Research Fund and Oxford University Press.

—— (2005), *The Business of Everyday Life: Gender, Practice, and Social Politics in England, c. 1600–1900*, Manchester: Manchester University Press.

—— (2011), *Cotton*, Oxford: Berg.

Lerner, J. (Spring 2007), "The French Profiled by Themselves: Social Typologies, Advertising Posters, and the Illustrations of Consumer Lifestyles," *Grey Room* 27: 6–35.

Leslie, E. (1873), *Myra's Pink Dress*. London: Sunday School Union.

Levitt, S. (1986), "Manchester Mackintoshes: A History of the Rubberized Garment Trade in Manchester," *Textile History* 17: 51–69.

—— (January 1991), "Cheap Mass-produced Men's Clothing in the Nineteenth and Early Twentieth Centuries," *Textile History* 22, no. 2: 179–92.

Lewis, M., and K. Wigen (1997), *The Myth of Continents: A Critique of Metageography*, Berkeley: University of California Press.

Lightfoot, T. (1926), "History of Broad Oak," unpublished ms.: Accrington Library.

Ling, W. (2007), *Fusionable Cheongsam*, Hong Kong: Hong Kong Arts Centre.

"The Llama or Paco," (April 1, 1869), *The Treasury of Literature and The Ladies' Treasury*: 136–8.

Lloyd, V. (1974), *The Camera and Dr. Barnardo*, London: National Portrait Gallery.

Lyden, A. (2014), *A Royal Passion, Queen Victoria and Photography*, J. Paul Getty Museum.

Lydon, M. (November 1990), "Pli Selon Pli: Proust and Fortuny," *Romanic Review* 82, no. 4: 438–54.

Macalister, R. (1896), *Ecclesiastical Vestments: Their Development and History*, London: E. Stock.

Machado, P. (2009), "Awash in a Sea of Cloth: Gujarat, Africa, and the Western Indian Ocean, 1300–1800," in G. Riello and P. Parthasarathi (eds), *The Spinning World: A Global History of Cotton Textiles, 1200–1850*, Oxford: Oxford University Press.

Mackrell, A. (1997), *An Illustrated History of Fashion: 500 Years of Fashion Illustration*, London: Batsford.

MacLeod, C. (2005), "Introduction," in J. Goethe, *The Sorrows of Young Werther*, New York: Barnes & Noble Classics.

Maidment, B. (May 2002), "101 Things to do with a Fantail Hat: Dustmen, Dirt, and Dandyism, 1820–1860," *Textile History* 33, no. 1: 79–97.

The Management of Servants. A Practical Guide to the Routine of Domestic Service (1880), London: Warne and Co.

de Marly, D. (1986), *Working Dress: A History of Occupational Costume*, London: Batsford.

Martin, R., and H. Koda (1994), *Waist Not: The Migration of the Waist, 1800–1960*, New York: Metropolitan Museum of Art.

Marx, K. (2002), "The Fetishism of the Commodity," in Nicholas Mirzoeff (ed.), *The Visual Culture Reader*, London and New York: Routledge.

Masiello, F. (2003), "Introduction," in *Dreams and Realities: Selected Fiction of Juana Manuela Gorriti*, trans. S. Wiseman, Oxford: Oxford University Press.

Maskiell, M. (Spring 2002), "Consuming Kashmir: Shawls and Empires, 1500–2000," *Journal of World History* 13, no. 1: 27–65.

Mattingly, C. (2002), *Appropriate[ing] Dress: Women's Rhetorical Style in Nineteenth-Century America*, Carbondale: Southern Illinois University Press.

Mayhew, A., and H. Mayhew (1847), *The Greatest Plague of Life: or The Adventures of a Lady in Search of a Good Servant*, Philadelphia: Carey & Hart.

Mayhew, H. (1862), *London Labour and the London Poor, vol. 4, Those Who Will Not Work*, London: Griffin, Bohn & Co.

Mayo, J. (1984), *A History of Ecclesiastical Dress*, London: Batsford.

McBride, T. (1976), *The Domestic Revolution: The Modernisation of Household Service in England and France, 1820–1920*, London: Croom Helm.

—— (Autumn 1978), "A Woman's World: Department Stores and the Evolution of Women's Employment, 1870–1920," *French Historical Studies* 10, no. 4: 664–83.

McCauley, E. (1985), "The Carte de Visite and Portrait Painting during the Second Empire," in *A.A.E. Disdéri and the Carte de Visite Portrait Photograph*, New Haven: Yale University Press.

McCauley, E. (2012), "Photography, Fashion, and the Cult of Appearances," in G. Groom (ed.), *Impressionism, Fashion, and Modernity*, New Haven: Yale University Press.

McClintock, A. (1995), *Imperial Leather: Race, Gender, and Sexuality in the Colonial Conquest*, New York: Routledge.

McNeil, P. (2010), "Caricature and Fashion," in V. Steele (ed.), *The Berg Companion to Fashion*, edited by. New York: Berg.

McPherson, H. (2001), *The Modern Portrait in Nineteenth-Century France*, Cambridge: Cambridge University Press.

Mercier, L. (1782), *Tableau de Paris*, Nouv. éd., corr. & augm. Amsterdam.

Miller, H. (1876), *The Scarcity of Domestic Servants; The Cause and Remedy. With a Short Outline of the Law Relating to Master and Domestic Servant*, London.

Miller, L. (2007), "Perfect Harmony: Textile Manufacturers and Haute Couture, 1947–57," in C. Wilcox (ed.), *The Golden Age of Couture: Paris and London, 1947–1957*, London: V&A Publishing.

Miller, M. (1981), *The Bon Marché: Bourgeois Culture and the Department Store, 1869–1920*, Princeton: Princeton University Press.

Miller, M. (2009), *Slaves to Fashion: Black Dandyism and the Styling of Black Diasporic Identity*, Durham, NC: Duke University Press.

Milnrow (pseud.) (September 15, 1925), "Coloured stripe designing–II," *The Textile Manufacturer*: 295–6.

Milton, C. (2007), "A Heterogeneous Thing: Transvestism and Hybridity in *Jane Eyre*," in C. Kuhn and C. Carlson (eds), *Styling Texts: Dress and Fashion in Literature*, Youngstown: Cambria.

"A Model of the 'Movies'," (July 1914), *Cosmopolitan* LVII, no. 2: 262–3.

Moers, E. (1960), *The Dandy: Brummell to Beerbohm*, London: Secker & Warburg.

Montgomery, F. (1984), *Textiles in America 1650–1870*, New York: W.W. Norton.

Morris, J. (1979), *Pax Britannica: The Climax of Empire*, London: Penguin.

Musée Carnavalet (2002), *L'Art de la Soie: Prelle, 1752–2002*, Paris: Paris Musées.

The Mystery of Love, Courtship, and Marriage Explained (1890), New York: Wehman Bros.

Nadar (September 16, 1855), "Salon de 1855. IV. M. Ingres," *Le Figaro* 77: 5.

Nead, L. (1988), *Myths of Sexuality: Representations of Women in Victorian Britain*, Oxford: Basil Blackwell.

—— (2000), *Victorian Babylon: People, Streets, and Images in Nineteenth-Century London*, New Haven and London: Yale University Press.

—— (2013), "The Layering of Pleasure: Women, Fashionable Dress, and Visual Culture in the mid-Nineteenth Century," *Nineteenth-Century Contexts* 35, no. 5: 489–509.

Nemnich, P. ([1800] (2010), *Beschreibung einer in Sommer 1799 von Hamburg nach und durch England geschehenen Reise*, Whitefish, MT: Kessinger Publishing LLC.

The New Female Instructor. Or, Young Woman's Guide to Domestic Happiness; Being an Epitome of all the Acquirements Necessary to Form the Female Character, in Every Class of Life: With Examples of Illustrious Women, etc. (1824), London: Thomas Kelly.

"New Styles and Coming Fashions," (June 20, 1870), *Western Daily Press*: 4.

Nichols, M. (August 1851a), "A Lecture on Woman's Dress," *The Water-Cure Journal*: 35.

—— (August 1851b), "The New Costume, and Some Other Matters." *The Water-Cure Journal*: 30.

Nielsen, R. (1979), "The History and Development of Wax-Printed Textiles Intended for West Africa and Zaire," in J. Cordwell and R. Schwartz (eds), *The Fabrics of Culture: The Anthropology of Clothing and Adornment*, The Hague: Mouton Publishers.

Nixon, S. (1997), "Exhibiting Masculinity," in S. Hall (ed.), *Representation: Cultural Representations and Signifying Practices*, Thousand Oaks: Sage.

Nochlin, L. (March 1978), "Lost and Found: Once More the Fallen Woman," *The Art Bulletin* 60, no. 1: 139–53.

North, S. (2007), "From Neoclassicism to the Industrial Revolution 1790–1860," in L. Welters and A. Lillethun (eds), *The Fashion Reader*, New York: Berg.

Oakley, A. (1979), *Sex, Gender, and Society*, London: Temple Smith.

Old Draper (1876), *Reminiscences of an Old Draper*, London: Sampson Low, Marston, Searle & Rivington.

Ortner, S. (1996), *Making Gender: The Politics and Erotics of Culture*, Boston: Beacon Press.

Otway, L. (1861), "Report on the Commerce of Lombardy," in *House of Commons (2757) Further Correspondence relating to the Affairs of Italy* LXIII: 189–96.

Parent-Duchâtelet, A. (1857), *De la prostitution dans la ville de Paris*, Paris: J.-B. Ballière et fils.

—— (1981), *La Prostitution à Paris au XIXe siècle*, ed. A. Corbin, Paris: Éditions du Seuil.

Pearl, S. (2010), *About Faces: Physiognomy in Nineteenth-Century Britain*, Cambridge, MA: Harvard University Press.

Peled, M. (2005), *China Blue*, documentary film. 2005, available online: http://www. argotpictures.com/ChinaBlue.html

Penner, B. (Spring 2004), "A Vision of Love and Luxury, the Commercialization of Nineteenth-Century American Weddings," *Winterthur Portfolio* 39, no. 1: 1–20.

Pepys, S. (1970–83), *The Diary of Samuel Pepys: A New and Complete Transcription*, eds R. Latham and W. Matthews, London: G. Bell.

Percival, M. (1999), *The Appearance of Character: Physiognomy and Facial Expression in Eighteenth-Century France*, Leeds, Modern Humanities Research Association.

—— (March 2003), "Johann Caspar Lavater: Physiognomy and Connoisseurship," *British Journal for Eighteenth-Century Studies* 26, no. 1: 77–90.

Percival M. and G. Tytler (eds) (2005), *Physiognomy in Profile: Lavater's Effect on European Culture*, Newark, DE: University of Delaware Press.

"The Perils of Pauline," (April 4, 1914), *Motography* 11, no. 7: 6.

Perkin, W. (October 1912), "The Permanent Fireproofing of Cotton Goods," *Popular Science Monthly* 81: 397–408.

Perrot, P. (1994), *Fashioning the Bourgeoisie: A History of Clothing in the Nineteenth Century*, trans. R. Bienvenu, Princeton: Princeton University Press.

Phegley, J. (2012), *Courtship and Marriage in Victorian England*, Santa Barbara, CA: Praeger.

Phillips, D. (1974), "The Influence of Suggestion on Suicide: Substantive and Theoretical Implications of the Werther Effect," *American Sociological Review* 39, no. 3: 340–54.

Pickering, P. (August 1986), "Class Without Words: Symbolic Communication in the Chartist Movement," *Past and Present* 112: 144–162.

Picton, J. (2004), "What to Wear in West Africa: Textile Design, Dress and Self-Representation," in C. Tulloch (ed.), *Black Style*, London: V&A Publishing.

Pinney, C. (1997), *Camera Indica: The Social Life of Photographs*, London: Reaktion Books.

Place, F. (1972), *The Autobiography of Francis Place (1771–1854)*, ed. M. Thale, Cambridge: Cambridge University Press.

Plunkett, J. (2003), *Queen Victoria: First Media Monarch*, Oxford: Oxford University Press.

"Poiret, Creator of Fashions, Here," (September 21, 1913), *The New York Times*.

Pope, D. (1981), *Life in Nelson's Navy,* London: Allen & Unwin.

Potter, E. (July 14, 1852), "Calico Printing as an Art Manufacture," *Manchester Guardian*: 3.

—— (1852), *Calico Printing as an Art Manufacture: a lecture read before the Society of Arts, 22 April 1852*, London: John Chapman.

Prochaska, F. (1980), *Women and Philanthropy in Nineteenth-Century England*, Oxford: Clarendon Press.

—— (1989), "A Mother's Country: Mothers' Meetings and Family Welfare in Britain, 1850–1950," *History* 74, no. 242: 379–99.

—— (1990), "Philanthropy," in F. Thompson (ed.), *The Cambridge Social History of Britain, 1750–1950, Volume III: Social Agencies and Institutions*, Cambridge: Cambridge University Press.

Puchner, M., et al. (2012), *The Norton Anthology of World Literature, Volume E*, New York: Norton.

Rabine, L. (2002), *The Global Circulation of African Fashion*, Oxford: Berg.

Racinet, A. (1888), *Le costume historique*, Paris: Firmin-Didot et Cie.

Rappaport, E. (2000), *Shopping for Pleasure: Women in the Making of London's West End*, Princeton: Princeton University Press.

Rasche, A. and G. Wolter (eds), *Ridikül! Mode in der Karikatur 1600 bis 1900*, Berlin: SMB-DuMont.

Rexford, N. (2000), *Women's Shoes in America, 1795–1930*. Kent, OH: Kent State University Press, 2000.

Rheims, M. (1977), *Nineteenth-Century Sculpture*, trans. R. Wolf, New York: H.N. Abrams.

Ribeiro, A. (1988), *Fashion in the French Revolution*, New York: Holmes & Meier Publishers, Inc.

—— (1999), *Ingres in Fashion: Representations of Dress and Appearance in Ingres's Images of Women*, New Haven and London: Yale University Press.

—— (2003), "Fashion and Whistler," in M. MacDonald (ed.), *Whistler, Women, and Fashion*, New York: Frick Collection; New Haven: in association with Yale University Press, 2003.

Richmond, R. (2013), *Clothing the Poor in Nineteenth-Century England*, Cambridge: Cambridge University Press.

Roach-Higgins, M., and J. Eicher (1992), "Dress and Identity," *Clothing and Textiles Research Journal* 10, no. 4: 1–8.

Roberts, H. (Spring 1977), "The Exquisite Slave: The Role of Clothes in the Making of the Victorian Woman," *Signs* 2, no. 3: 554–69.

Roberts, J. (2010), *Five Gold Rings: A Royal Wedding Souvenir Album from Queen Victoria to Queen Elizabeth II*, London: Royal Collection Publications.

Root, R. (2004), "Searching for the *Oasis in Life*: Fashion and the Question of Female Emancipation in Late Nineteenth-Century Argentina," *The Americas* 60, no. 3: 369–90.

—— (2005), "Fashioning Independence: Gender, Dress, and Social Space in Postcolonial Argentina," in R. Root (ed.), *The Latin American Fashion Reader*, Oxford: Berg.

Ross, E. (1993), *Love and Toil: Motherhood in Outcast London, 1870–1918*, Oxford: Oxford University Press.

Rothstein, N. (1977), "The Introduction of the Jacquard Loom to Great Britain," in V. Gervers (ed.), *Studies in Textile History*, Toronto: Royal Ontario Museum.

Rousseau, H. (1914), *William Joseph Chaminade, Founder of the Society of Mary*, trans. J. Garvin, Dayton: Brothers of Mary.

Rowe, W. (2010), *China's Last Empire: The Great Qing*, Cambridge, MA: Harvard University Press.

Rules for the Clothing Club at Stutton (1833), Ipswich.

Saïd, E. (1978), *Orientalism*, New York: Pantheon Books.

St. Jude's, S. Kensington Parish Magazine 11, (1894), no. 1.

Schaffer, T. (2000), "Fashioning Aestheticism by Aestheticizing Fashion: Wilde, Beerbohm, and The Male Aesthetes' Sartorial Codes," *Victorian Literature and Culture* 28, no. 1: 39–54.

Schantz, M. (2008), *Awaiting the Heavenly Country: The Civil War and America's Culture of Death*, Ithaca and London: Cornell University Press.

Schmidt, L. (1995), *Consumer Rites: The Buying & Selling of American Holidays*, Princeton: Princeton University Press.

Schoeser, M. (2007), *Silk*, New Haven: Yale University Press.

"Selected Patterns for Dress: Calico, Printed by Thomas Hoyle and Sons," (Nov 1849), *Journal of Design and Manufactures*, 2: 108.

Seligman, K. (1996), *Cutting for All: The Sartorial Arts, Related Crafts, and the Commercial Paper Pattern*, Carbondale: Southern Illinois University Press.

Severa, J. (1995), *Dressed for the Photographer: Ordinary Americans and Fashion, 1840–1900*, Kent, OH: Kent State University Press.

Shannon, B. (Summer 2004), "Refashioning Men: Fashion, Masculinity, and the Cultivation of the Male Consumer in Britain, 1860–1914," *Victorian Studies* 46, no. 4: 596–630.

—— (2006), *The Cut of His Coat: Men, Dress, and Consumer Culture in Britain, 1860–1914*, Athens: Ohio University Press.

da Silveira, P. (1992), "Les magasins de nouveautés," in *Au Paradis des dames: nouveautés, modes et confections, 1810–1870*, Paris: Paris Musées.

Silverman, K. (1986), "Fragments of a Fashionable Discourse," in T. Modleski (ed.), *Studies in Entertainment: Critical Approaches to Mass Culture*, Bloomington: Indiana University Press.

"Skeleton of the Greenland Whale in the Museum of the College of Surgeons," (February 24, 1866), *Illustrated London News*: 176.

Slade, T. (2009), *Japanese Fashion: A Cultural History*, Oxford: Berg.

Smiles, S. (1861), *Self-Help; With Illustrations of Character and Conduct*, Boston: Tickner & Fields.

Smith, C., and C. Greig (2003), *Women in Pants: Manly Maidens, Cowgirls, and Other Renegades*, New York: Harry N. Abrams, Inc.

Société Industrielle de Mulhouse (1902), *Histoire documentaire de l'Industrie de Mulhouse et de ses environs au XIXe siècle*, 1, Mulhouse: Veuve Bader and Cie.

Solomon-Godeau, A. (1996), "The Other Side of Venus: The Visual Economy of Feminine Display," in V. de Grazia (ed.), *The Sex of Things: Gender and Consumption in Historical Perspective*, Berkeley: University of California Press.

Sous l'empire des crinolines (2008), Paris: Paris Musées.

"Springfield Bloomer Celebration by a Patient of the Water-Cure," (October 1851), *The Water-Cure Journal*: 83–4.

Spurr, J. (2012), "The Kashmir Shawl: Style and Markets," in S. Cohen, R. Krill, M. Lévi-Strauss, and J. Spurr (eds), *Kashmir Shawls: The Tapi Collection*, Mumbai: The Shoestring Publisher.

Stallybrass, P. (1998), "Marx's Coat," in P. Spyer (ed.), *Border Fetishisms: Material Objects in Unstable Spaces*, London: Routledge.

Staniland, K., and S. Levey (1983), "Queen Victoria's Wedding Dress and Lace," *Costume: The Journal of the Costume Society* 17: 1–32.

Steele, F., and E. Adam (1892), *Beauty of Form and Grace of Vesture*, New York: Dodd, Mead & Co.

Steele, V. (1985), *Fashion and Eroticism: Ideals of Feminine Beauty from the Victorian Era to the Jazz Age*, New York: Oxford University Press.

—— (1996), *Fetish: Fashion, Sex, and Power*, Oxford: Oxford University Press.

—— (1998), *Paris Fashion: A Cultural History*, New York: Berg.

—— (2001), *The Corset: A Cultural History*, New Haven and London: Yale University Press.

Stemmler, J. (March 1993), "The Physiognomical Portraits of Johann Caspar Lavater," *The Art Bulletin* 75, no. 1: 151–68.

Stoller, R. (1968), *Sex and Gender: On the Development of Masculinity and Femininity*, London: Hogarth Press Institute of Psychoanalysis.

Stratton, J. (1996), *The Desirable Body*, Manchester: Manchester University Press.

Styles, J. (2007), *The Dress of the People: Everyday Fashion in Eighteenth-Century England*, New Haven and London: Yale University Press.

Sullivan, C. (2003), "Classification, Containment, Contamination, and the Courtesan: The Grisette, Lorette, and Demi-Mondaine in Nineteenth-Century French Fiction," Ph.D. diss.: University of Texas at Austin.

Summers, L. (2001), *Bound to Please: A History of the Victorian Corset*, Oxford: Berg

Svedenstierna, E. ([1804] 1973), *Svendenstierna's Tour: Great Britain 1802–3: The Travel Diary of an Industrial Spy*, trans. from the German edition of 1811 by E. Dellow, Newton Abbot: David & Charles.

Swanquill, S. (1833), "The First of September," *The New Monthly Magazine* 39: 52–63.

Sylvanus, N. (2007), "The Fabric of Africanity: Tracing the Global Threads of Authenticity," *Anthropological Theory* 7, no. 2: 201–16.

Tait, W. (1840), *Magdalenism: An Inquiry into its Extent, Causes, and Consequences of Prostitution in Edinburgh*. Edinburgh: P. Rickard.

Tarlo, E. (1996), *Clothing Matters: Dress and Identity in India*, London: Hurst.

Taylor, L. ([1983] 2010), *Mourning Dress: A Costume and Social History*, New York: Routledge.

Tétart-Vittu, F. (1992), "Couture et nouveautés confectionnées," in *Au Paradis des dames: nouveautés, modes et confections, 1810–1870*, Paris: Paris Musées.

Theis, F. (1903), *"Khaki" on Cotton and other textile material*, trans. E. Kayser, London: Heywood & Co.

Theophilus, L. (1998), *Peter Collingwood-Master Weaver*, Colchester: Firstsite.

"Topographical and Commercial History of Manchester," (August 1810), *The Tradesman; or, Commercial Magazine* 5, no. 26: 139–44.

Trilling, J. (2001), *The Language of Ornament*, London: Thames and Hudson.

Trusler, J. (1819), *Trusler's Domestic Management, or the Art of Conducting a Family, with Economy, Frugality & Method*, Bath: T. Smith.

Tseëlon, E. (1997), *The Masque of Femininity: The Presentation of Woman in Everyday Life*, London: Sage.

Tynan, J. (2013), *British Army Uniform and the First World War: Men in Khaki*, Basingstoke: Palgrave Macmillan.

Tytler, G. (1982), *Physiognomy in the European Novel: Faces and Fortunes*, Princeton: Princeton University Press.

Ugolini, L. (2007), *Men and Menswear: Sartorial Consumption in Britain 1880–1939*, Aldershot: Ashgate.

Unruh, A. (2008), "Aspiring to La Vie Galante: Reincarnations of Rococo in Second Empire France," Ph.D. diss.: Institute of Fine Arts at New York University.

Valverde, M. (1989), "The Love of Finery: Fashion and the Fallen Woman in Nineteenth-Century Social Discourse," *Victorian Studies* 32, no. 2: 168–88.

Veblen, T. ([1899] 1953), *The Theory of the Leisure Class: An Economic Study of Institutions*, New York: Macmillan.

Verdier, Y. (1979), *Façons de dire, façons de faire: la laveuse, la couturière, la cuisinière*, Paris: Gallimard.

Vincent, S. (2010), *The Anatomy of Fashion: Dressing the Body from the Renaissance to Today*, London: Bloomsbury Academic.

de Vries, J. (2008), *The Industrious Revolution: Consumer Behavior and the Household Economy, 1650 to the Present*, Cambridge: Cambridge University Press.

Waddell, G. (2004), *How Fashion Works: Couture, Ready-to-Wear, and Mass Production*. Oxford: Blackwell.

Wahl, K. (2013), *Dressed as in a Painting: Women and British Aestheticism in an Age of Reform*, Durham, NH: University of New Hampshire Press.

Wakefield, P. (1800), *Mental Improvement: or, the Beauties and Wonders of Nature and Art*, Dublin: P. Wogan.

Walkowitz, J. (1979), *Prostitution and Victorian Society: Women, Class, and the State*, Cambridge: Cambridge University Pres.

Walton, W. (1841), *A memoir addressed to proprietors of mountains and other waste lands, and agriculturalists of the United Kingdom, on the naturalization of the alpaca*, London: Smith, Elder & Co.

Warner, P. (1986), "Mourning and Memorial Jewelry of the Victorian Age," *Dress* 12: 55–60.

—— (2006), *When the Girls Came Out to Play*, Amherst: University of Massachusetts Press.

Watson, J. (1866), *Textile Manufactures and the Costumes of the People of India*, London: George Edward Eyre & William Spottiswoode for the India Office.

Watson, J., and J. Kaye (1868–75), *The People of India: A Series of Photographic Illustrations with Descriptive Letterpress, of the Races and Tribes of Hindustan*, London: C. Whiting.

Watson, W. (1925), *Advanced Textile Design*, London: Longmans, Green & Co.

White, S. (2012), *Wild Frenchmen and Frenchified Indians: Material Culture and Race in Colonial Louisiana*, Philadelphia: University of Pennsylvania Press.

White, S., and G. White (1998), *Stylin': African American Expressive Culture from Its Beginnings to the Zoot Suit*, Ithaca, NY: Cornell University Press.

Whorton, J. (1982), *Crusaders for Fitness: The History of American Health Reformers*, Princeton: Princeton University Press.

Wilde, O. (February 21, 1882), *Freeman's Journal and Daily Commercial Advertiser*: 7.

Williams, M. (August 1851), "The Bloomer and Weber Dresses: A Glance at their Respective Merits and Advantage," *The Water-Cure Journal*: 33.

Williams, R. (1982), *Dream Worlds: Mass Consumption in Late Nineteenth-Century France*, Berkeley: University of California Press.

Wilson, E. (1987), *Adorned in Dreams: Fashion and Modernity*, Berkeley: University of California Press.

Wilson, K. (2004), *A New Imperial History: Culture, Identity, and Modernity in Britain and the Empire, 1660–1840*, Cambridge: Cambridge University Press.

Wilson, V. (1986), *Chinese Dress*, London: V&A Museum.

Woods, R. (1995), *The Population of Britain in the Nineteenth Century*, Cambridge: Cambridge University Press.

"A Word for the Servant Girl," (November 1, 1883), *The Cornishman*: 6.

Wright, W. (September 1914), "Dame Fashion and the Movies," *Motion Picture Magazine*: 107–8.

Wrigley, P. (2002), *The Politics of Appearances: Representations of Dress in Revolutionary France*, New York: Berg.

de Young, J. (2012), "Fashion and Intimate Portraits," in G. Groom (ed.), *Impressionism, Fashion, and Modernity*, New Haven: Yale University Press.

Zamperini, P. (2001), "Clothes that Matter: Fashioning Modernity in Late Qing Novels," *Fashion Theory* 5, no. 2: 195–214.

Zola, E. ([1883] 1886), *The Ladies' Paradise: A Realistic Novel*, London: Vizetelly & Co.

Zutshi, C. (April 2009), " 'Designed for Eternity': Kashmiri Shawls, Empire, and Cultures of Production and Consumption in Mid-Victorian Britain," *Journal of British Studies* 48, no. 2: 420–40.

NOTES ON CONTRIBUTORS

Denise Amy Baxter is Associate Professor of Art History and Associate Dean in the College of Visual Arts and Design at University of North Texas. Co-editor with Meredith Martin of *Architectural Space in Eighteenth-Century Europe: Constructing Identities and Interiors*, her research focuses on the relationships between material culture and the constitution of the modern self.

Ariel Beaujot is Associate Professor of History at the University of Wisconsin, La Crosse. Her first book is titled *Victorian Fashion Accessories* (2012) and she is currently working on a volume about men's fashion in Victorian England.

Annette Becker is an independent scholar and museum professional who has worked at the Spencer Museum of Art, the Dallas Museum of Art, Historic Deerfield, and the Texas Fashion Collection. She studied at the University of Kansas in Lawrence and the University of North Texas in Denton. Her current research focuses on museum collecting practices and American fashion designers.

Heidi Brevik-Zender, Associate Professor of French and Comparative Literature at University of California, Riverside, is author of *Fashioning Spaces: Mode and Modernity in Late-Nineteenth-Century Paris* and other publications on fashion in French literature and art, including a catalog essay for the 2012–13 exhibition *Impressionism, Fashion, and Modernity*. Recent publications include a piece on Mallarmé's *La Dernière Mode* and the article "Interstitial Narratives: Rethinking the Feminine Spaces of Modernity in Nineteenth-Century French Fashion Plates."

Sarah Cheang is Senior Tutor in the History of Design at the Royal College of Art, London. Her research centers on transnational fashion, material culture, and the body from the nineteenth century to the present day, on which she has published widely. Her next book, *Sinophilia*, explores the role of Chinese material culture within Western fashion cultures, from "Chinese" hairstyles to wallpapers to Pekingese dogs.

Justine De Young is Assistant Professor of Art History at the Fashion Institute of Technology and editor of the forthcoming *Fashion in European Art: Dress and Identity, Politics and the Body, 1775–1925* (I.B. Tauris). She has contributed essays to *Visualizing the Nineteenth-Century Home* (2016), *Getting the Picture: The Visual Culture of the News* (2015), *Women, Femininity, and Public Space in European Visual Culture, 1789–1914* (2014), the catalog of the 2012–13 *Impressionism, Fashion, and Modernity* exhibition, and *Cultures of Femininity in Modern Fashion* (2011).

Susan Hiner is Professor of French and Francophone Studies at Vassar College on the John Guy Vassar Chair in Modern Languages. Her first book, *Accessories to Modernity: Fashion and the Feminine in Nineteenth-Century France* was published in 2010 and won the Millia Davenport publication award of the Costume Society of America in 2011. The author of articles on nineteenth-century French literary and visual culture, she is currently at work on a new book manuscript, entitled "Behind the Seams: Women, Fashion, and Work," focusing on women fashion producers in nineteenth-century France.

Vivienne Richmond is a senior lecturer and head of History at Goldsmiths, University of London. She works on the material culture of poverty, especially dress and needlework, and is the author of *Clothing the Poor in Nineteenth-Century England* (2013). She is currently researching the colonial transmission of needlework instruction, the history of disability and craftwork, and the cultural history of the apron.

Philip A. Sykas is a research associate at Manchester Metropolitan University. He is author of *The Secret Life of Textiles: Six Pattern Book Archives in North West England* (2005), and *The Beauty of Experiment: Shadow Tissues at Turnbull & Stockdale* (2013). He continues to explore the archives of textile manufacturers and finishers, working toward a new history of calico printing in Britain. But a broader underpinning interest is the human relationship to cloth, and how to read the evidence of historical artifacts.

INDEX